. . . a breathless Hunt arrived in Baldwin's room. He took one look at the scene below and fled to the bathroom. In the half-darkness of a summer night the street seemed to be filled with motorcycles, squad cars, paddy wagons, and men running in all directions. In the middle of the melee were his men being led away from the Watergate in handcuffs. When Hunt emerged from the bathroom he made straight for the white phone by the bedside. "I've got to call a lawyer," he explained, and dialed a local number. "They've had it," he said.

WATERGATE

THE FULL INSIDE STORY

**LEWIS CHESTER,
CAL McCRYSTAL,
STEPHEN ARIS AND
WILLIAM SHAWCROSS**

BALLANTINE BOOKS • NEW YORK

Cover illustration by Robert Grossman

Photo credits:
Wide World: pp 1, 11, 12, 13, 14, 16 *top*, 18, 19 *top*, 23 *bottom l*, 26 *top*, 28 *first row r, third row r, fourth row c*, 29 *second row l*, 30, 31 *top*.
United Press International: pp 2, 3, 4, 5, 10, 19 *bottom*, 21, 24, 25, 26 *middle row r, bottom row l*, 26–27, 28 *first row l & c, second row l, c, & r, fourth row l*, 29 *first row l & c, second row c & r, third row c & r, fourth row l, c, & r*, 31 *inset & bottom*, 32.
NBC News: pp 6 & 7.
David King: pp 8 & 9.
Wally McNamee, Newsweek: pp 15 *top*, 16 *bottom*, 26 *middle row l*.
Steve Northup: p 23.
Camera Press: pp 28 *third row l & c, fourth row r*, 29 *first row r*.

SBN 345-23530-4-150
First Printing: September, 1973
Printed in the United States of America
Ballantine Books, Inc.
201 East 50th Street, New York, N.Y. 10022

Contents

Acknowledgments

We would like to thank the many people who helped to bring this book to completion. In particular we are grateful to our chief researcher Laurie Zimmerman, to David King, who researched and layed-out the photo pages, and to Philip Jacobson, who took over many of our normal duties for the *London Sunday Times* and still found time to help on this project. We are also indebted to Walter Robinson, who pursued some very murky trails on our behalf; Rosemarie Wittman and Alistair Buchan also helped on the investigation. Bob Grossman not only designed the cover but kindly allowed us to set up camp in his apartment.

Harold Evans, the Editor of the *London Sunday Times*, provided us with encouragement throughout, as did Henry Brandon, the newspaper's Washington correspondent. Camilla Knapp, Susie Bidel, and Penny Chen all did valuable research and typed up the finished manuscript as well as the numerous drafts that preceded it. Georgetta Moliterno insured, in the nicest possible way, that we did not run over budget. Robert Ducas, the exotic manager of the *London Sunday Times'* New York office, both had the idea for the book in the first place and goaded us till it was done. Joe Petta is the best wireman we know in the business and Fred Crawford the coolest of assistants. We received enormous help from Fred Emery, who wrote so many distinguished dispatches on Watergate for our sibling newspaper, the *London Times*.

We also thank our many friends in the American press and are particularly indebted to those on the *Washington Post* whose work originally opened up the whole Watergate investigation. We must thank also the Harkness Foundation which allowed William Shawcross time off his fellowship to complete this project. At our publishers', George Young and David Frederikson were the most long-suffering but gently compelling of editors. George Davidson and Pat Coppinger calmly did the production under conditions which can only be described as hectic. The manuscript could never have been printed so quickly without the extraordinary patience and skill of everyone at Brown Bros. Linotypers, New York.

LEWIS CHESTER
CAL MACCRYSTAL
STEPHEN ARIS
WILLIAM SHAWCROSS

Washington, September 8, 1973

CHAPTER 1

The New Elite

THE POISON entered America's electoral bloodstream with the opening of an office. In April, 1971, three young presidential aides established themselves in new quarters on the second floor of an office building at 1701 Pennsylvania Avenue, Washington, D.C., just one block west of the White House. They were the advance guard of what over the next year would constitute a small army of White House personnel "on loan" to the enterprise. They put a sign up on the door—Citizens Committee for the Re-Election of the President—and quietly began a long crusade.

The birth of CREEP (as it became known to friends and enemies alike) had few public celebrants. It was some weeks, for example, before it received even a glancing reference in America's most comprehensive newspaper of record, the *New York Times*. *Newsweek* magazine acknowledged CREEP's existence but again only marginally; the weight of its editorial mind was directed at what appeared to be more urgent contemporary problems—"Europe: Another Step Towards Unity" and "The GI's Other Enemy: Heroin." Indeed, given the pressure of other news events, CREEP was perhaps fortunate to be favoured with a mention at all. This was to be the pattern for well over a year until the summer of 1972, when the American public was informed about the burgling and bugging of the headquarters of the Democratic National Committee in Washington's Watergate complex on the night of June 17. One of the five men caught red-handed on this mission was the security director of CREEP, James W. McCord. It was the first public hint that the Committee to

Re-Elect the President might have functions beyond that of the politician's orthodox public-relations machine.

It was to be fully another year before CREEP was finally revealed as the crucial mechanism used to distort democracy in the United States and contrive Richard Nixon's second term as President. In terms of polling, Nixon's campaign achievement was the most extraordinary success in American political history. In terms of its effect on the country's confidence in its own democratic institutions, it was unquestionably the most disastrous.

Behind the President's "statesmanlike" public campaign there was a CREEP- and White House–inspired matrix of wiretaps, burglaries, lies, forgery, strong-arm tactics, and black propaganda to make the election result come right. They are summed up by the word "Watergate": but the folly of the Watergate break-in was no more than a tiny fraction of the year's clandestine activity. Its discovery attracted most publicity but tended to divert attention from the pervasive corruption of the whole campaign and the fact that many of the highest figures in government felt free to deploy methods against their own citizens that the Central Intelligence Agency might hesitate to use in the most obscure banana republic. For 1972 was the year in which "the dirty tricks business" came home, and in a way that appalled the professionals in the CIA.

None of this could be predicted at the nativity of CREEP but, in retrospect, it is possible to see that most of the elements that made 1972 the most corrupt election in American history were gathered round the cradle. In the spring of 1971 the men around Nixon were obsessed by two linked problems— the President's low standing in the polls and the quest for a conclusion in Vietnam. Although most, like Nixon himself, were considered anti-Communists, they saw the war as the biggest single obstacle to his re-election. Peace had to be achieved but it had to be "with honour," and this implied the most delicate of secret diplomatic minuets behind the veil of national security policy. At that time the careful construction of Nixon as the strategic "peace" candidate— in China and the Soviet Union as well as Vietnam—was set in motion. There was, therefore, from the outset what appeared to be an identity of interest between the cause of national security and their own political well-being. The interests were, in fact, different but the confusion between the two is the clue to most of the domestic crimes they committed.

Nixon's men had one collective impediment that in the rough-and-ready tradition of American democracy was unusual—it was remarkably self-righteous, a complaint that makes men unusually prone to the erroneous assumption that what is good for them is good for everybody. The two men who surfaced at the top of the White House, Bob Haldeman, Nixon's chief of staff, and John Ehrlichman, his chief adviser on domestic affairs, were both Christian Scientists. In Washington a Christian Scientist came to be defined by the irreverent as "opposite of a hypochondriac—a man who has a chronic complaint but remains convinced that he is healthy." Neither Haldeman nor Ehrlichman showed much talent for self-criticism. In times of adversity, Haldeman's favourite remark was "let's hard-nose this one out."

By 1971 Haldeman, who was to play a central role in the development of CREEP, had become the most powerful figure in the White House. Humourless and rigid, he took pride in his role as his master's keeper, happily forgoing an easy popularity. "Every President needs his son of a bitch," he once said, "and I'm Nixon's." But he was more than the hatchet man. He knew, from personal experience, that Nixon could come apart under pressure. Haldeman was present at the awful end of the California campaign trail in 1962 when Nixon, in a rage of resentment at his defeat, announced his retirement from politics and told reporters: "You won't have Nixon to kick around anymore." Such outbursts might be forgivable in a losing candidate, but would handicap a President.

The organisation Haldeman put together as chief of staff was specifically designed to take pressure off the President and free his mind for strategic considerations. Haldeman monitored both the paperwork and the personnel ushered into the Oval Room of the White House. No detail was too small for his attention. The story is told of how, after routine low-level staff work, a memo was sent to the President urging him to place a sympathy call to a desperately ill Republican Senator. Haldeman intercepted it and decided that the exercise was not necessary at that stage, though the Senator's potential widow might need solace. The memo was sent back down the chain of White House command with Haldeman's crisp notation: "Wait until he dies."

Inside the Oval Room Haldeman would sit in a corner quietly taking notes during all Nixon's most important audiences. As the key expediter of the presidential will, he had every right to be there, but his unsmiling watchfulness naturally inhibited the blither spirits who made it as far as the innermost sanctum. Haldeman literally saw his function as that of a loyal servant, and was never apparently aware that he exercised real power. The servant, nonetheless, created a mood that deeply influenced the range of presidential decision-making. In an unconsciously revealing interview, Haldeman described the process of policy discussion in the White House as follows: "We started out trying to keep political coloration as much as possible out of policy and hiring matters. However, we realise that these things make for variety in decision-making, and so within reasonable limits we have tried to keep a spread of opinion on the staff, so that no one is to the left of the President at his most liberal or to the right of the President at his most conservative. . . . Ehrlichman, Kissinger [Nixon's National Security Affairs Adviser] and I do our best to make sure that all points of view are placed before the President. We do act as a screen, because there is a real danger of some advocate of an idea rushing in to the President . . . if that person is allowed to do so, and actually managing to convince [him] in a burst of emotion or argument. . . ."

It was a process that made Haldeman's judgment of the range of "reasonable limits" of political discussion a crucial determinant of its content, and, by the accounts of liberals who were squeezed out of Nixon's counsels, this range was not wide. This was scarcely Haldeman's fault but arose naturally from his own background.

Haldeman, like Nixon himself, was from Southern California, where he grew up in the privileged suburban enclave of Beverly Hills. His upbringing was both pious and dominated by a narrow world view. His grandfather had been a founder of the Better America Foundation, an early anti-Communist organisation, and Haldeman came to share his perceptions. After graduating in business administration at the University of California, Los Angeles, he joined the

J. Walter Thompson advertising agency and stayed with them until 1969 when, aged forty-two, he was wafted up to the giddy height of White House chief of staff. At JWT's Los Angeles office, Haldeman had been a highly regarded executive (Seven-Up, Sani-Flush, and Black Flag insecticide were among the accounts in his charge), but apart from occasional leaves of absence to help Nixon on the campaign trail—in 1960, 1962, and 1968—his administrative experience was confined to monitoring the output of a hundred-strong advertising staff. It was a demanding job but not the best training for piloting the complex currents of political Washington.

The White House staff he created was very much in his own image and its members were frequently from his own state. Dedicated and hard-working, they came from the ad agencies and the marketing departments to the centre of executive power. They thought of themselves as pragmatists and "can-do" guys, impatient with ideology but effective, a feeling that was epitomised by one of the staff's favourite catchphrases: "We believe in what works." The earnestness and near-fanatical loyalty of Haldeman's men earned them the nickname of "the beaver patrol." Two of the most eager beavers, Ron Ziegler, the President's press secretary, and Dwight L. Chapin, the President's appointments secretary, came from Haldeman's old office in Los Angeles. John Ehrlichman had a somewhat different background but his rise to the number-two position on the White House staff was specifically the result of Haldeman's patronage.

Ehrlichman had practiced law in Seattle—specialising in insurance and real estate work—but the most important thing about him was his long friendship with Haldeman. In their youth they had been fellow Eagle Scouts and classmates at UCLA where they made their first forays into right-wing student politics together. Ehrlichman joined Nixon's 1960 presidential campaign against John Kennedy as an "advance man" at Haldeman's behest, and it was the old friend who brought him in as "tour director" of the 1968 campaign, a job that earned him an awesome reputation for efficiency. He once ordered the campaign plane to take off, leaving two highly paid speechwriters stranded in a Lansing, Michigan, telephone booth. The schedule came first. Ehrlichman had a little more worldliness than most members of the beaver patrol, but he shared with them a nearly total ignorance of high-level politics before his arrival in the White House. For them all, government was a new and, as it turned out, dangerous toy.

By late 1970 the collective image of Nixon's White House entourage was set in most people's minds: unexciting, a bit bland and humourless, but diligent and respectable. They were, despite the "Tricky Dick" echoes of Nixon's past, precisely the kind of men from whom anyone would be happy to buy a used car. As an image it was not false, but the evident piety of Nixon's entourage concealed from most observers its most dangerous feature. Aside from Henry Kissinger, Nixon's flamboyant National Security Adviser, there was nobody within close range of the President who could be remotely classed as an intellectual and, perhaps more important, even those with experience of elective office were at a premium. All the charts, polls, and computer printouts of Nixon's men could not supplement this basic deficiency. Lacking any experience in the exercise of political power or even the intellectual's capacity to speculate about it, their limited understanding of politics derived from the salesmanship of the campaign trail. They were, for all their buttoned-down appearance and churchly habits, essentially apparatchiks—men whose destiny and identity depended on advancing the interests of a particular politician, President Richard Nixon. These were not necessarily the interests of the institution of the Presidency.

The apparatchik is in the deepest sense irresponsible, for everything he does is not to preserve himself but his patron, and his satisfaction derives from the patron's pleasure. Thus, he can be led into doing things that may be personally reprehensible to him as an individual but which, if they serve the larger vision of his master, are ethically acceptable. Elected politicians as a breed are quite different. Though not necessarily more noble, they are inclined to greater caution: nobody running for office wants his sins "exposed" suddenly, and dramatically, just before election day. They are used to the idea of being scrutinised. Intellectuals, who are by nature advocates, actually demand attention. Nixon's White House, in contrast, was staffed by watchers. They may have seemed docile enough but they were instinctively conspiratorial.

The first observers to perceive the inherent dangers in

Nixon's mix of advisers were not his political opponents, but his erstwhile supporters. Long before the Watergate case broke, Richard J. Whalen, a conservative intellectual who had worked for Nixon in the preconvention stage of the 1968 campaign, was putting up alarm signals about the White House. In a book entitled *Catch the Falling Flag,* published before CREEP's first detected peccadillo, Whalen savaged the White House mentality that gave it life. Whalen wrote: "The once-prestigious title of 'Special Assistant to the President' was bestowed wholesale on ex-advance men who had proved their fitness to govern by releasing the balloons precisely at the moment the candidate's arms shot skyward in a V. They were sober, industrious, efficient and almost completely unaware of a wider world and a larger politics than they had known. . . . We were under the heel of men basically unsure of themselves, second-raters playing over their heads and fiercely resentful of anyone who dared approach them at eye level. Nixon's own insecurity caused him to need the protection of men willing to do whatever he wished."

What Whalen accurately detected was a problem much larger than incompetence in high places. Nixon's staffers were not simply men who, on the Peter Principle, had been promoted above their level of competence. They were, in their previous roles, all competent men, but they found themselves having to operate in the very highest league of government with only the sketchiest knowledge of the ground rules; they were required, in effect, to run before they could even walk. In this situation, it is not surprising that they should react with the obstinacy of children of whom too much is asked: instead of acknowledging that they did not know enough, they adamantly implied that they knew it all. The fault was not so much theirs as that of their proud but insecure father, Richard Nixon.

The other centre of power in Nixon's Administration exaggerated the family problem. John Mitchell, Nixon's former law partner and his all-powerful Attorney General, was similarly inexperienced in the ways of government and openly contemptuous of "politicians." Though Bob Haldeman and John Mitchell came, in some ways, to be rivals for Nixon's ear, they respected each other and were united in the idea of a pragmatic, nonideological approach to government (Mitchell had been Nixon's campaign manager in 1968 when Haldeman was the chief of campaign staff). One of Mitchell's first remarks on becoming Attorney General was a few pragmatic words about the usefulness of wiretapping. Experience on the job had buttressed this view, and in April, 1971, he told a group of lawyers that government had an absolute right to use wiretaps without court orders because its right to defend itself against violent attack must prevail against some individuals' right of privacy.

Mitchell, who had risen in the world in the difficult business of municipal-bond financing, was not anybody's protégé. He was tough, independent and resourceful. In a sense, Nixon was Mitchell's protégé, as his mid-sixties political comeback was fashioned while working closely with Mitchell as a partner in the New York law firm, Nixon, Mudge, Rose, Guthrie, Alexander and Mitchell. It was said of Mitchell that he had an uncanny talent for seeing into the back room of men's minds. He could be charming and witty, but there was a hint of the bully-boy in his makeup. Once when trying to avoid an importunate lady reporter, he advised his chauffeur to mind her head when slamming the door and "be sure to catch her hand."

As Attorney General, Mitchell emerged as the most dominating adviser in Nixon's Cabinet, giving law and order a new priority in high-level policy discussions, but his role was much more crucial than that of the administration's wire-tapper-in-chief. He was essentially the custodian of Nixon's political majority, a task that led him into constant conflict with the administration's liberal figures. "This country," he once told a reporter, "is going so far right you won't recognise it." The perception was based partly on his experience in 1968 and partly on his shallow understanding of national trends. Nixon squeaked home in 1968 after predictions of landslide in his favour. The final figures gave Nixon victory with a minority vote of 43.4 percent against 42.7 percent for the Democratic candidate, Hubert Humphrey, while 13.5 percent went to the renegade Democrat and segregationist Governor George Wallace of Alabama. In Mitchell's, and many other people's, judgment, Wallace—who took five states in the Deep South—hurt Nixon more than he hurt Humphrey (i.e., in a straight fight between Nixon and Humphrey, Nixon's margin of victory would have been greater).

After the election Mitchell's advice on issues was dictated by a simple proposition: the people who voted for Nixon *and Wallace* in 1968 were Nixon's potential majority in 1972, and that meant that government policies should avoid anything that might alienate "the Wallace vote," particularly in the South. As the Wallace vote, in Mitchell's mind, was strong on law and order, antipathetic to liberalism, and hostile to integrationist policies, this naturally reduced the liberals' room for manoeuvre. Behind the fraternal message of Nixon's original slogan in 1969—"Bring Us Together"—there was a policy dynamic that was specifically divisive. For Mitchell's strategy was not to seek national unity but to capitalise on the things that disunited people in the interests of Nixon's, and hopefully the Republican Party's, electoral security. In pursuit of this objective Mitchell became the administration's all-purpose heavy: he pushed the nomination of reactionary figures for the Supreme Court; he blocked moves that would cut the protection of Southern oil interests (Big Oil had always been a generous contributor to Nixon's campaigns); and he was deeply involved in the moves to slow down desegregation in the South. Although Nixon kept his head above the bureaucratic battles, nobody within the administration doubted the fact that Mitchell was doing the President's bidding.

In December, 1969, Nixon increased the sense of isolation of liberals within government by becoming the first President to publicly "disagree" with a Supreme Court ruling on desegregation. In their excellent book *Nixon in the White House*, Rowland Evans and Robert Novak commented sourly: "As a way of conducting the U.S. government, it left much to be desired. But as a way of ingratiating himself with the South—of taking one step toward the ultimate goal of joining the 1968 Wallace votes and the Nixon votes—it was not bad politics."

For this strategy there was an intellectual justification of sorts. In 1969 a young lawyer named Kevin Phillips, who worked as Mitchell's special assistant in the Nixon campaign, produced a book entitled *The Emerging Republican Majority*. In his preface Phillips acknowledged the intellectual sustenance provided by Mitchell's "keen strategic sense." The Nixon White House was never noted for its bookish quality, but Phillips's work was an instant success there—becoming, like Nixon's own book *Six Crises*, almost required reading for aspiring staffers. It told them, in effect, that they had come to stay. Phillips's book unquestionably contained some interesting insights and much useful data, but for all its charts and tables it was no more than a promising first work by a very young man. Intellectually, it was less than half-baked. Yet it contained the seeds of most of the miscalculations of the Nixon years and was central to the philosophy that came to inform CREEP. Phillips's thesis underlay Mitchell's, and as it turned out Nixon's, brutalist approach to domestic politics.

The book heralded the emergence of "the new Populist Party," and one of its key elements was a brusque dismissal of the "privileged elite of the Northeast," which had for so long provided the nation with a political Establishment, under both Democratic and Republican administrations. This group, in Phillips's view, had become "blind to the needs and interests of a large national majority." His vision was of "a new American revolution coming out of the South and the West," and the party that became its political catalyst would reap huge majorities. The problems of catering for this newly emergent middle and lower-middle class would inevitably affect the party's attitude to other national groups. Some would have to be, in political terms, written off—among them the liberals in the Northeast, on the West Coast, and in parts of the Midwest; the off-white ethnic groups; and the blacks. Phillips saw the new majority as a coalition of conservatives revolving around the burgeoning suburbs and the newly affluent residents of what he called the Sunbelt, running from Southern California through to Florida. Their natural allies would be the white blue-collar workers in the North and working-class whites in the South.

As an analysis it was a neat summary of the complex ethnic resentments that are always a part of American politics, and part of its drift seemed to be corroborated by the population data which, in the words of Richard M. Scammon, the election analyst and Census Bureau Director under President Kennedy, indicated that the majority of Americans were "unblack, unyoung, and unpoor." The combined impact of Scammon's phrase and Phillips's analysis indicated a happy future for the politics of the right; and of the two parties, the Republicans seemed best equipped for such an inheritance (most blacks, after all, had long since ceased to vote for Richard Nixon). A new political constituency had been defined and it was not long before it gained and maintained a media title—"The Silent Majority."

In the 1970 midterm elections for Congress and state governorships, Nixon and Vice-President Spiro Agnew went out forcefully to claim the Republicans' new constituency. Both had been irked by the difficulties of working with Democratic majorities in the House of Representatives and the Senate. Their pitch was calculated to rouse all the resentments so carefully defined in *The Emerging Republican Majority.* It was an ugly episode in which the country's two highest officeholders thickened the air with rhetoric about "radiclibs," "impudent snobs," and "rotten apples." Nixon campaigned vigorously in twenty-two states and habitually responded to hecklers by warning them of the impending weight of the silent majority at the polls. In his election-eve telecast, on November 2, he tore into "the superhypocrites"— "those who carry a 'Peace' sign in one hand and who throw a bomb or a brick with the other." In the event, the voters reacted more forcibly against the hypocrisy of a campaign appealing to the basest emotions. Across the board the new majority not only failed to emerge, Republicans ended up worse off than they started.

The Republicans lost eleven governorships, reversing a six-year-long trend in favour of Republicans in state houses up and down the country. Democratic governors now outnumbered Republicans, 29 to 21. In the House of Representatives they lost nine seats, giving the Democrats a majority of 256 to 179, their best position since the 1964 high-water mark which had been reached with help from the tidal wave of support for Lyndon Johnson. Only in the Senate did the Republicans improve their situation—with a net gain of two seats—but not enough to shake Democratic control of the upper chamber. Democratic Senators outnumbered Republicans by 54 to 44.

The flaw both in Nixon's vituperative campaign and in the "new majority" analysis was the fact voters are not simply the sum of their prejudices expressed in opinion polls. Politics is infinitely more complex than a balancing of ethnic propositions about who does not like whom. And one ingredient

is the fact that voters like their national leaders to appear as
leaders and not as scaremongers.

The most bitter proof of this was not in the election results
but in the opinion poll findings. Ever since mid-1969, the
Lou Harris poll had, as a matter of routine, tested the
President's popularity against that of the Democrat who was,
at that time, thought most likely to oppose him in a presidential election, Senator Edmund Muskie from Maine. Up
to the midterm elections Muskie had never eclipsed Nixon in
any of those head-to-head polls, but on the night before the
election Muskie made a strong impression on television
viewers with a cool address asking them to repudiate "the
politics of fear." The November poll, taken shortly after this
telecast, showed Muskie moving into a clear six-point lead
over the President.

By 1971 most of the "issue-oriented" Republicans had left
the administration, and those who survived became increasingly desperate. One who lasted longer than most was Steve
Hess, an able liberal who had written Nixon's campaign
biography back in 1968. Hess, who had been a close student
of Nixon for many years, entered the White House on the
domestic-affairs staff as an aide to Professor Daniel Patrick
Moynihan. He started out with high hopes. "I was not," Hess
recollects, "one of those who naively believed in all that New
Nixon, Old Nixon stuff. I'd always thought of Dick as two
people—the good and the bad Nixon—the one I liked was the
one who was open to ideas and persuasion. The one that
made me nervous was the one who isolated himself and
retreated into formulas. As it happened the White House that
evolved brought out the bad Nixon." Pat Moynihan left the
White House in 1970 to return to Harvard, leaving Hess to
soldier on a little longer, but eventually even he gave up the
unequal struggle—"as a Republican liberal, I naturally work
on the proposition that you win some and you lose some. I
found I was losing them all."

Moynihan and Hess slipped away from the administration
almost unnoticed, in sharp contrast with the messy departure
of Walter Hickel, Nixon's redoubtable Secretary of the
Interior. Hickel had come into office classed as a hard-nosed
businessman but had shown an unsuspected radicalism on the
war, on the environment, and on youth policies. He was fired
on November 25, 1970. Within hours one of Haldeman's

aides had descended on Hickel's department with a purge list. He summoned six of the department's highest officials and addressed each of them as follows: "We want your resignation, and we want you out of the building by five o'clock." Even in a town inured to overnight reversals of fortune this struck people as unusually insensitive.

With the exodus of the liberals, the bland instinct to survive, personified by Haldeman and Mitchell, made its final takeover. In Washington they were virtually friendless outside the White House. Relations between Congress and the Presidency were at their nadir and were scarcely improved by the pathetic attempts at public relations of the President's congressional liaison staff. At one point they were issued buttons reading "I CARE ABOUT CONGRESS." Haldeman and Ehrlichman were openly described by pressmen and politicians, of both parties alike, as "the two Germans." The isolation of the President himself was attributed to the construction of a "Berlin Wall" round him by his two closest aides. Mitchell, the once-vaunted architect of Nixon's "Southern strategy," had been discredited in the eyes of Republican regulars by the dismal consequences of that strategy in the midterm elections. Many of the Republican Congressmen who survived were bitterly critical of the divisive, and unprofitable, national campaign.

Meantime, the economy seemed to be lurching dangerously out of control. In February, 1971, wholesale prices registered the sharpest one-month rise in seventeen years, setting off concern about a new inflationary boost in consumer prices. Its consequences further soured relations between the White House and organized labour, which had become progressively worse after a brief honeymoon during Nixon's first year in office. In the same month George Meany, the cantankerous boss of the AFL–CIO, was asked how he would vote if forced to choose between Nixon and the Democratic "dove," Senator George McGovern. Meany, who detested McGovern's stand on the war, gave the appalling choice considerable thought before replying: "George McGovern is a louse, but Nixon is a double louse."

In March, 1971, one month before the establishment of CREEP, *Newsweek* magazine speculated on the possibility that Nixon might be a one-term President. Muskie was still five points ahead in the polls and there had been no evidence of

White House fence-mending with a deeply divided and confused Republican Party. On this showing Nixon looked like becoming the first incumbent President to run for re-election and be defeated since Herbert Hoover in 1932.

Behind this grim public reality a secret strategy had already begun to emerge. The bitter lesson of the midterm election reverses were not entirely lost on the President's advisers. They were in fact the subject of two lengthy sessions, under Nixon's chairmanship, in the Key Biscayne White House shortly after the results came in. Out of these bull sessions—in which John Mitchell, once again, played a dominant role—two main lines of thought emerged. The first was a unanimous recommendation that the President curb his naturally combative campaign instincts and place himself above the battle. He would present himself to the nation as a statesman unconcerned with the wooing of sectional votes. The second, less clearly defined, thought was that some mechanism should be found, at a suitable distance from the President himself, to do the necessary fund-raising and aggressive wooing of the voters.

Mitchell and Haldeman were allotted the task of finding the machinery for a new, sanitised Southern strategy. The machinery to hand was the Republican National Committee in Washington, but as a vehicle for Nixon's re-election drive it had certain disadvantages. The RNC is primarily concerned about the vitality of the party as a whole. Though Haldeman was curtly dismissive of its role (he once told fellow presidential aides that the National Committee was never going to amount to anything, ever, and would they please take note of that fact), it does have a key function as a clearing house for the problems of Republican candidates around the country, be they liberal or conservative. As such, it has to cope with many apparently conflicting interests and be well versed in the arts of political compromise. Haldeman, who had no talent for such manoeuvring, and Mitchell, who had no taste for it, decided to look elsewhere. They came up with the idea of CREEP.

CREEP successfully divorced the problems of reselling Nixon for President from all the little local difficulties that mean so much to Congressional candidates around the country, and incidentally provided a mechanism that prevented Republican regulars, who were subsequently among those most aghast at the Watergate and associated revelations, from finding out exactly how the leader of their party was being marketed. Although nobody was aware of it at the time, Nixon, once considered the party loyalist par excellence, mounted his drive for a second term by instituting a policy of benign neglect for the electoral interests of his own party.

The task of levering CREEP off the ground was entrusted to three fresh-faced White House aides—Hugh Sloan, formerly on the President's appointments staff; Harry Flemming, formerly on the White House patronage staff; and Jeb Stuart Magruder, formerly deputy director of communications. Of the three, Jeb Magruder, just thirty-six, was the oldest and most important, responsible for planning and administration of the fledgling organisation. Magruder was born in Staten Island but considered himself a Californian. His business background, mainly on the West Coast, had been in advertising and merchandising. He had sold cosmetics and facial tissues and women's hosiery. Involvement in Republican politics had brought him into Nixon's 1968 campaign operation in Los Angeles, where he had impressed Haldeman, and in 1969 he was brought into the White House to work as a project manager under Haldeman. He was later transferred to beef up the Communications department run by the old Nixon retainer, Herb Klein. By the time Magruder moved to CREEP he had earned his spurs as a faithful Nixon knight but was not without assistance in tilting against the Democratic windmill.

Although CREEP was, for public consumption at least, supposed to be no more than a gathering of faithful citizens interested in re-electing Nixon (the chairman, who took little part in CREEP's day-to-day affairs, was Francis L. Dale, publisher of the Cincinnati *Enquirer* and president of the baseball Reds), in reality it was being steered by some of the most authoritative hands in government. From the outset, Magruder was instructed to privately clear all decisions about the committee's activities with Attorney General John Mitchell. Another influential godfather closely connected with CREEP's infancy was Herbert Kalmbach, President Nixon's personal lawyer.

Kalmbach, who was a key Republican fund-raiser in 1968, had already performed some odd services in the cause of the Southern strategy. After Nixon's election he took personal charge of nearly $2 million in unspent campaign funds. As far as the mass of the Republican Party was concerned, the existence of these funds was unknown. Indeed, fund-raising events had been held in 1969 and 1970 to raise money from Republican pockets "to pay off 1968 campaign debts." Kalmbach, however, was putting some of the money to strategic use—attempting to destroy the career of George Wallace.

In 1970 Wallace, then the former Governor of Alabama, was involved in a bitterly contested Democratic primary election with the then Governor Albert P. Brewer. Much to every observer's surprise, Brewer won the primary though he failed to gain a majority vote (in the subsequent runoff Wallace won by a narrow 3 percent margin). Had Wallace failed to win his own state, of course, there was little likelihood of his re-emerging in 1972 as a presidential candidate—a consummation devoutly wished by the presidential Southern strategists. One reason for Brewer's strong showing against Wallace, it emerged much later, was the fact that Kalmbach had funneled over $400,000 of unspent Republican funds into his campaign chest. With Kalmbach around, CREEP could be assured that its funds would be deployed in some weird yet wonderful ways.

A third godfather, who was to take a deep personal interest in the more exotic aspects of CREEP's activity, was Charles "Chuck" Colson, whose White House title was Special Counsel to the President. Colson, a very rugged character indeed, was once quoted as saying: "I would walk over my grandmother if necessary [for Richard Nixon]." He joined the White House, aged thirty-eight, in November, 1969, and rapidly achieved a close intimacy with the President. Over the bar in his den, he displayed an unofficial Green Beret motto: "If you've got 'em by the balls, their hearts and minds will follow." A former Marine officer, Colson, unlike others on the staff, had been around Washington for a long time working as a lawyer and political aide. His duties were never clearly defined, but he had a high opinion of his own abilities—only exceeded by his estimate of Nixon's. "I always considered myself something of a hotshot," Colson said in an interview with *Alumni,* the magazine of his old alma mater, Brown University, "but I've met my match in Mr. Nixon. He has a brilliant mind, is completely dedicated and possesses total recall."

When the CREEP revelations started to roll in the latter part of 1972, great public-relations efforts were made to distance the President from the mistakes of overzealous supporters. But CREEP had been Nixon's creature from the word go, and its quartet of remote controllers—Mitchell, Haldeman, Kalmbach, and Colson—shared one privilege in common: personal access to the President himself.

With hindsight, it is possible to see the midterm elections as the key turning point in Nixon's administration. After the reverses at the polls Nixon still could have gone back to mainstream politics and reunited the Republican Party on traditional lines. Instead, he chose to go after an adman's dream of the Silent Majority. For this objective he did not need old-style politicians and issues men but new-style manipulators. (One of the charms of the Silent Majority concept for the manipulator is the fact that as it is, by definition, "silent," words can be put into its mouth.) A key consequence of this decision was a new low not only in the morality, but also in the quality, of government.

As long ago as the sixteenth century, Niccolò Machiavelli observed, "The first impression that one gets of a ruler and his brains is from seeing the men about him." By this yardstick, Richard Nixon, despite the encomiums of the egotistical grandmother-stomper Chuck Colson, was not a very brainy President. There was no crime in this, but it is a fact that from 1971 Nixon chose to work with an entourage of a lower intellectual wattage than any White House staff since Calvin Coolidge. At a time of enormous complexity in national and international affairs, the President of the United States fashioned (or allowed to be created) an elite of mean-minded, middle-brow conformists: men who were simply not up to the job of government. There was bound to be trouble.

Some commentators predicted as much at the time, but most saw in the White House one shining exception to the prevailing philistinism, and that man was the closest of all to the President. By early 1971, Dr. Henry Kissinger, the President's adviser on National Security Affairs, had become the second most powerful man in the government. Most liberals thought this was a good thing and that Kissinger's presence somehow guaranteed that the potential excesses of the administration would be kept within pardonable limits. This, as it turned out, was a serious mistake.

CHAPTER 2

Presidential Pardner

HENRY KISSINGER was not like the others: he had charm. In a dour administration that had little time for such frippery, Kissinger's quality shone, for those who appreciated it, with a rare effulgence. Most journalists were grateful for him. Washington hostesses adored having him. Haldeman and Ehrlichman were suspicious of him. John Mitchell could not stand him.

Nixon's blunt-spoken Attorney General once growled that in his opinion Kissinger was an "egotistical maniac." The remark was relayed to Kissinger at a White House press briefing, where he delighted most hands with the observation: "At Harvard, it took me ten years to develop a relationship of total hostility with my environment. I want you to know that here I have done it in eighteen months." The combination of apparent frankness and flattering intimacy was immensely engaging, especially for a press corps that found it hard to obtain the time of day from the likes of John Mitchell and Bob Haldeman. At the same time it was obscurely disturbing. It gave an excellent indication of where Henry Kissinger did not stand but no very definable idea of where he did. He was, after all, at that time the man closest to the President and, according to informed observers, spent more time with Nixon than all the members of the Cabinet put together. Moreover, according to academic friends who had been interested Kissinger-watchers over the years, Henry had never looked or sounded happier. Despite his wry reflections on the White House environment, there was something about it that agreed with him. He certainly was pleased with the public attention. When asked by the journalist Oriana Fallaci how he explained his popular success, Kissinger had an interesting explanation. "The main point," said Kissinger, "stems from the fact that I have always acted alone. Americans admire that enormously. Americans admire the cowboy leading the caravan alone astride his horse, the cowboy entering a village or city alone on his horse. Without even a pistol, maybe, because he doesn't go in for shooting. He acts, that's all: aiming at the right spot at the right time. A Wild West tale, if you like."

Kissinger is one of those attractive but elusive characters who are able to appear many things to many men. He thrived on ambiguity and the apparent contradictions of his situation. But his complexity was not a pose; his rise to the position of presidential alter ego in foreign affairs defied all the conventional categories of American politics. For a start, he was not American-born.

Heinz Alfred Kissinger was born on May 27, 1923, into a middle-class Jewish family in the German town of Fürth. As a young child he lived in the ominous environment created by the collapse of the Weimar Republic and the rise of Nazism. His father lost his teaching job at a local girls' school, and young Heinz was expelled from the gymnasium where he was a student and forced to enter an all-Jewish school. In 1938, when Kissinger was fifteen years old, the family succeeded in getting out of Germany and made their way to London and from there to New York. As soon as he was of military age Kissinger joined the U.S. Infantry as a private and served in Europe. He achieved the rank of sergeant and was attached to the staff of the European Command Intelligence School, where, after the war, he gave instruction in legal procedures against former Nazis.

His services were so valued that on demobilisation he was offered a handsome $10,000-a-year job to stay on the school staff. Kissinger turned it down in order to pursue his education at Harvard, where he became a distinguished scholar and, after graduation, a teacher at the School of International Studies. He gradually established his name as a foreign-policy expert and military strategist, operating within the accepted ethos of the Cold War. His key area of interest was in the interplay of power politics between nation-states and the use or threat of force in the international pattern. He drew on his expertise in this area to write an impressive book about Metternich, the Austrian statesman who dominated the European diplomatic scene after the Congress of Vienna. For students of nineteenth-century balance-of-power politics, Kissinger's *A World Restored* is indispensable reading. In 1957 he completed a better-known but much less worthwhile book called *Nuclear Weapons and Foreign Policy,* in which he argued the practical uses of tactical nuclear weapons. It became a best-seller and attracted the attention of policy-makers in Washington; it also revealed some of Kissinger's intellectual blind spots.

Boiled down to its essentials, *Nuclear Weapons and Foreign Policy* presupposed that nation-states would act in a rational way while using on each other weapons that, in human terms, defied rationality. Kissinger saw the limits of war as being contained by shrewd, neo-Metternich-style diplomacy. He notes that "an energetic diplomacy addressed to the problem of war limitation can serve as a substitute for lack of imagination on the part of the Soviet General Staff." However, it was Kissinger whose imagination was at fault. He envisaged a situation in which America, as the possessor of the bulk of the world's nuclear arsenal, could by judicious application of nuclear force get its way militarily while its seasoned diplomats could persuade the other side when to call it quits, presumably by some elaborate "face-saving" formula. Removed from the context of academic war-game plans, the dangerous flaws in the argument became apparent.

One of them was a failure to appreciate the complex interaction between domestic and foreign policy, particularly in an era of ideology which cuts across the loyalties created by nation-states. The reality it ignored was the domestic consequences of nuclear policy in a world shrunk by advances in communications; what McLuhan later called "the global village" was already coming into existence. It is difficult, for example, to imagine that there would have been Nagasaki if the human cost of Hiroshima had been the subject of an action-replay on network television on the day after the first A-bomb was dropped. Technology, fortunately perhaps, not only increased man's military firepower, but also heightened awareness of its consequences.

But there was another, perhaps more important, level of unreality about Kissinger's book. It failed to recognize how the raised technology of war had destroyed most of the old assumptions about the limits of war. The misconception stemmed from Kissinger's exaggerated faith in diplomacy. In his mind the terrifying prospect of all-out war would oblige the participants in a limited nuclear exchange to act rationally through their diplomatic representatives. But would they? Twentieth-century war, almost by definition, is the signal for the unleashing of irrational hatreds, and one started by the use of nuclear force—no matter how "surgically" applied—might be expected to exaggerate that condition. Even the most skilled diplomats must operate within a framework of shared assumptions; they can only do their job—which Kissinger once described as "the manipulation of reality"—within bounds prescribed by the mood of the countries they represent. When one, or perhaps both, of the countries involved has been driven into intransigence or even madness by the fact of war, diplomats tend to take a back seat until the time comes to pick up the pieces later.

Kissinger was to admit later that some of his basic assumptions in *Nuclear Weapons* had been overtaken by events, but it was revelatory of a cast of mind—particularly in its low appreciation of domestic concerns—that guided his actions when he achieved political power. Like many other "action-academics" at Harvard, he sought political influence and became through the sixties a regular traveler on the Establishment triangle—Boston, New York, Washington. His first experience of high-level policy-making in the John Kennedy administration, as a consultant to the National Security Council, was not an entirely happy period. In the wisecracking councils of Camelot, Kissinger seemed a ponderous figure. And Kissinger felt a natural aversion to the grandiloquent sweep of Kennedy's "Free World" pronouncements, which seemed large on promise but uncertain of delivery. Foreign affairs, he felt, were not being properly conceptualised.

He was more closely drawn to Nelson Rockefeller, the New York Governor and perennial aspirant for the Republican presidential nomination. In Kissinger's estimation, Rockefeller was the kind of man who could afford to take the large view; his foreign policy would be above the eddies of public opinion. In 1964 and 1968 Kissinger worked as Rockefeller's foreign-affairs adviser on his presidential campaigns, a job that obliged him to think seriously about America's most serious problem—Vietnam.

Rockefeller's campaign speeches reflected Kissinger's analysis. In 1964 Rockefeller outlined a course between Goldwater's rhetoric of virtually unlimited escalation and Johnson's advocacy of restraint. He called for defeat of the Communists in South Vietnam; "hot pursuit" by South Vietnamese troops of Vietcong guerrillas in Cambodia, Laos, or North Vietnam; and air strikes against Vietcong supply lines in Laos and North Vietnam by South Vietnamese planes and pilots. It was, in fact, an early version of Vietnamisation. In 1968 Rockefeller was the nearest approximation to a Republican "dove" candidate; he wanted out, with the barest minimum of safeguards for South Vietnam.

By 1968, Kissinger's knowledge of the Vietnam scene had been supplemented by two delicate exploratory missions on behalf of the U.S. government. They confirmed his pessimism about the situation, and he came to be virtually indistinguishable from other academic critics of the war. But his dissent was not so much founded on liberal revulsion at the conflict but on a gloomy analysis of Vietnam's effect on America's credibility as a great power; it came to be an important distinction.

Even so, Kissinger's appointment came as a complete surprise both to him and his academic friends. While on the Rockefeller campaign staff he had incautiously let slip his view that Nixon was "not fit to be President." It was not the remark of a man who expected to receive a favour from Richard Nixon. However, Kissinger's skepticism about Nixon's "fitness" had been based on his belief that Nixon might be too set in his old anti-Communist reflexes to appreciate that new international alignments were possible. Kissinger, from his academic vantage, had seen the opportunity to break the ice of the Cold War and make a start on some positive measures of arms control. As it happened, Nixon himself was making precisely the same judgments. The one-time Cold Warriors of the academic and political worlds found they had a lot in common. There were great feats of statecraft that they could do, together. In the meantime, there was Vietnam.

Nixon's inheritance in Southeast Asia was unenviable. From the outgoing administration he took over the sketchy beginnings of peace talks with the North Vietnamese in Paris and the brute fact of 540,000 American troops committed to defense of President Thieu's conspicuously undemocratic regime in South Vietnam. At home he took over a country divided as it had never been before in time of war. Two candidates for the Presidency, Robert Kennedy and Eugene McCarthy, had run and come close to nomination on specific withdrawal policies before being cut down, Kennedy by assassination and McCarthy by the Democratic Party's nervousness about the "new politics" of his youthful supporters. But they had left a potent legacy—a liberal establishment almost entirely converted to the notion that prosecution of the war was a mistake and an immoral one at that. A corollary of this mood was a virtual disappearance of the political species "hawk." Politicians now were either "doves," still a somewhat radical connotation, or "pragmatists," a much-favored label. Between the two there was no dispute about the fact that the war had increased and ought to be diminished, but the argument was about how to go about it with, if possible, "honour." One powerful thought in the electorate's mind in 1968 was that Nixon might be more capable of achieving this miracle than his opponent Hubert Humphrey who, as Vice-President, had been closely tied to Johnson's politics of escalation in Vietnam.

Nixon had no problem of loyalty to what had come to be seen by Republicans as a Democrats' war, and he had, in the course of the campaign, given a pledge that his administration would get American troops out of Vietnam. It was a pledge that he took very seriously.

At the outset Nixon's Vietnam team had an intriguingly balanced appearance. Its two key members were Melvin Laird, a tough politician from Wisconsin and reputed "hawk," as Defense Secretary, and Kissinger, who if not a "dove" was known throughout the academic community as a trenchant critic of the previous policy. The apex of the policy-making trio was the President himself. Long before his election Nixon had confided to the journalist-historian Theodore H. White his view of the key function of the President in foreign affairs. "I've always thought," said Nixon, "this country could run itself domestically without a President. All you need is a competent Cabinet to run the country at home. You need a President for foreign policy; no Secretary of State is really important; the President makes foreign policy."

On his election, Nixon made it clear that ending the war was to be his prime foreign-policy objective. In pursuing this policy, it emerged that he and Kissinger shared a common suspicion of bureaucracy, which they both felt militated against bold initiatives, and a common passion for secrecy. The story is told of how, shortly after beginning his term, Nixon gathered the National Security Council staff around him to impress on them the ethos of the new regime. After abusing the Department of State as an inflexible instrument of policy, he told the group that their responsibilities would be upgraded. "Watch the world," he told them, and then, turning to Henry Kissinger: "You and I are going to end this war."

The policy that Nixon and Kissinger made in Vietnam was called Vietnamisation. It implied, in short, that the Americans should only stick around for as long as it took for the South Vietnamese to take over the war against the Communist North themselves. As war policies go it was not dishonourable in intention and it was, in many respects, a great advance on that pursued by President Johnson, which had had only two logical conclusions: complete overkill through total Americanisation of the war or complete withdrawal, in deference to the public outcry at home, followed by prompt collapse of a South Vietnamese population grown accustomed to dependency. For the new policy Laird provided the hardware and Kissinger the advice and, in times of crisis, the therapy. None of them told the American public the precise implications of this policy when dealing with a war in a country capable of easy military infiltration across the frontiers of those neighbouring nations, Laos, Cambodia, and North Vietnam.

In order to Vietnamise the war it became necessary to widen it. There was, at least in the view of the policy-makers, no way of getting the South Vietnamese into shape to run their own war unless the steady infiltration of men and supplies from North Vietnam could be stopped, or at least abated, before they reached the country. To do this there were only two options. The first was stopping the infiltration at its source, in North Vietnam itself. But this option had already been foreclosed: in order to get the Paris peace talks going, Johnson had halted the bombing of the North. Resumption would inevitably torpedo the peace talks and with them even the public-relations appearance of progress towards peace. Politically, this option was nonviable. The fall-back option was to bomb the infiltration routes which passed through what were, in theory at least, two independent, sovereign nations—Laos and Cambodia. This option was taken and concealed not only from the American public but also from the United States Congress, who unwittingly voted the money for the raids on the basis of falsified estimates from the Pentagon. Under Johnson the stress of Vietnam policy had produced the famous "credibility gap" between administration rhetoric and combat realities. Under Nixon, however, the war policy was from the very beginning based on the presumption that lying to America was an essential ingredient.

Over a period of fourteen months in 1969 and 1970, the United States conducted a total of 3,630 secret B-52 bombing sorties against Cambodia—a country whose neutrality Washington then professed to respect. The code name for the bombing was "Operation Menu." In the same period many more B-52 missions were flown over Laos, where heavy concentration bombing was directed at the Ho Chi Minh supply network winding down into South Vietnam. The cloak of secrecy was preserved at the Pentagon by a new type of double-entry bookkeeping. One book, for select internal consumption, logged where the raids had actually taken place. Another, for consumption by officials who did not "need to know" and the watchdogs on the Senate Armed Services Committee, reported the Cambodian raids as bombing missions in South Vietnam.

It was all part of the Nixon-Kissinger game plan for ending the war, but it also created a highly developed official interest in suppression of the truth. On May 9, 1969, shortly after there had been newspaper speculation about the President thinking of launching a retaliatory strike against North Korea for shooting down the EC-121 American spy plane (a proposition which, intriguingly, Kissinger favoured and Laird opposed), the *New York Times* published a story that created panic reactions in the White House. William Beecher, the paper's Pentagon correspondent, wrote a front-page story which began: "American B-52 bombers in recent weeks have raided several Vietcong and North Vietnamese supply dumps in Cambodia for the first time, according to Nixon administration sources, but Cambodia has not made any protest." The story was routinely denied by the administration, but within the government itself a miniature witch-hunt was conducted to try and find the "leak" merchant who had told the American public something that only the recipients of the B-52 bomb-loads were supposed to know. A central feature of this hunt was the use of wiretaps, and a central figure in it was Henry Kissinger, who sanctioned taps on some of his best friends and acquaintances, both within and outside the government.

In May, 1969, the FBI, at the request of the White House, placed taps on thirteen government officials, among them five of Kissinger's closest aides on the National Security Council staff, Morton B. Halperin, Winston Lord, Helmut Sonnenfeldt, Daniel I. Davidson, and Anthony Lake. A parallel set of taps was placed on four newsmen suspected of receiving leaked information: Marvin Kalb of CBS; Henry Brandon, Washington correspondent of the *(London) Sunday Times;* Hedrick Smith, diplomatic correspondent of the *New York Times;* and Beecher. The taps were maintained for periods ranging from a month to twenty-one months. As a result of the taps three "blabbermouths" were apparently eased out of the administration, but the source of the Cambodian leak was never discovered.

The legality of the taps is still a matter of dispute. Although the President's right to authorise telephone taps to protect "national security" had long been recognised, no real attempt had ever been made to define exactly what national security was. The first taps for this purpose were made in 1940, when President Roosevelt instructed the FBI to use them against "Fifth Columnists" but to limit the targets as far as possible to alien groups. Under President Truman this category was broadened to encompass domestic subversives. In the mid-sixties, as a result of pressure from civil libertarians, some efforts were made to refine this power. In 1967 the Supreme Court held that wiretapping without a court order violated the Fourth Amendment's provision against unreasonable search and seizure. Even so nothing was done to limit the President's constitutional power "to protect national-security information against foreign intelligence activities." Subsequently, John Mitchell became an aggressive proponent of the President's inalienable right to tap any domestic group "which seeks to attack and subvert the government by unlawful means." On June 19, 1972, two days after the Watergate break-in, the Supreme Court in a unanimous 8–0 decision gave the Mitchell doctrine a final thumbs-down: no domestic group or individual could be tapped without a warrant. (The Government's case for unauthorised wiretapping was so weak that the Solicitor General, Erwin Griswold, refused to argue it despite strong pressure from John Mitchell. Griswold subsequently lost his job.)

But the limits of the President's right to tap without a warrant in cases involving foreign intelligence was left unresolved. Did the National Security Council and newsmen's taps fall in this category? Was the newspaper "leak" about the Cambodian bombing important foreign intelligence? It is probably true that Prince Sihanouk, then the ruler of Cambodia, was prepared to wink at the campaign so long as it were secret, and that he would have had to protest had it been officially acknowledged by Nixon. But, at least as important, was the need to keep the American public in ignorance, and that, in a democracy, seems a somewhat insecure basis on which to found an argument of "national security."

When the details of government prying began to surface in the explosion of Watergate revelations in early 1973, Kissinger, it was assumed, would be the last person to be associated with ungentlemanly procedures like wiretaps. It turned out that he was among the first: both in approaching J. Edgar Hoover, the FBI's then director, about concern over "national security" leaks, and in having his office prepare a list of potential culprits. He subsequently read summaries of some of the taps. For some of those who experienced the wiretaps, the image of Kissinger as eavesdropper was difficult to deal with. Both Marvin Kalb and Henry Brandon, for example, considered themselves close friends of Kissinger. On receiving the news that he had been subjected to an electronic loyalty test, Brandon wryly observed: "Henry used to tell me that I was the one correspondent in this town that he doesn't try to manipulate."

The issues involved in the wiretapping episode were more than a question of what constituted good manners between friends. For they illustrated how soon the Nixon administration had, under pressure of its Vietnam policy, embarked on a policy of corruption. As early as mid-1969 this corruption operated at three levels. The first was in the decision not to entrust the American people with the true nature of the war policy. The second was in the readiness to deceive the people's elected representatives, even in secret session, about that policy. The third, and ultimately most destructive, was a logical outcome of the first two: they could not trust even themselves. In the aftermath of Watergate this distrust became almost a galloping disease with "friend" tapping "friend" without any hint of conscience. Paranoia reigned. For the inception of this disease Kissinger, once considered the liberals' friend at court in the Nixon administration, bears a heavy responsibility.

Kissinger, of course, genuinely wanted to liquidate the war in Vietnam, but like his predecessors in the White House he found it easier to see what was wrong than to know what to do about it. Furthermore, he was the prisoner of his own arguments about the importance of America's diplomatic "credibility": he maintained that he and Nixon could engage the Russians and Chinese in exciting new relationships only if America were seen not to "lose" in Vietnam. But nothing suggested that the North Vietnamese and Vietcong could be induced to abandon their historic objective even for just long enough to enable America to claim "honour" in its withdrawal. The pressure on the Communists just had to be maintained, even intensified. But Nixon had also to meet his domestic commitment to reduce troop levels. This meant, from 1969 on, an ever-increasing reliance on air power which, in troop terms, provided the cheapest way of continuing the war. But the administration calculated that until American combat forces had all been withdrawn, this would arouse furious protest at home as another escalation—bombing had always been the most unpopular aspect of Vietnam policy in the eyes of antiwar activists. Lying about it seemed the easiest thing to do.

In early journalistic analyses of Vietnam decision-making, Kissinger was almost invariably cast as the "soft" man in Nixon's counsels while Mel Laird's role was said to be that of the "heavy." In fact, as those alert reporters Evans and Novak subsequently discovered, the situation was almost exactly the reverse. Laird, of course, had the problem of securing appropriations from Congress, a process that put him in intimate touch with the increasing war-weariness of both the Senate and the House. Kissinger, who was cut off from such pressures, saw Vietnam as the intractable element in his plans for international peace-making. In an effort to make the war "winnable" he was led to the adoption of more hawkish positions. Once again the logic of escalation was taking over.

On April 30, 1970, President Nixon informed the nation in a telecast of the decision to invade Cambodia with U.S. troops; the objective was to clean out the Vietcong "sanctuaries" above the Parrot's Beak area northwest of Saigon. It was a warlike speech, but the President laid emphasis on the restraint shown by the military in the past in the face of continued provocation. "For five years," the President said, "neither the United States nor South Vietnam has moved against these enemy sanctuaries [inside Cambodia] because we did not want to violate the territory of a neutral nation." (At the time this assurance was given, the U.S. Air Force on Nixon's instructions had been secretly bombing Cambodia for fourteen months.)

News of the Cambodian invasion—coming, as it did, shortly after revelations about the My Lai massacre and cover-up in South Vietnam—drove the students and a fair proportion of the faculty staff practically berserk. There were student riots and strikes all over the country. Over four hundred colleges closed down or suspended their academic schedules. On many campuses the offices of the Reserve Officers' Training Corps (ROTC) were ransacked or the object of arson attacks. Disturbances took place on campuses with no history of radicalism in Colorado, South Carolina, and New Mexico. The National Student Association called for Nixon's impeachment, as did sixty-eight members of the Cornell faculty. The climax came quickly. Students at Kent State University in Ohio went on a mass rampage which ended with the ROTC building being burned to the ground. The Governor of Ohio, James Rhodes, declared martial law and ordered units of the 145th Infantry of the National Guard into the campus. On Monday, May 4, men of the 145th turned on the protesting students and fired their M-1 rifles, killing four, among them a ROTC cadet, and wounding eleven.

At a public level Nixon put out an extraordinary olive branch. He had, before the Kent State shooting, been quoted as describing the demonstrating students in an off-the-record meeting as "bums." On the night of May 8 he wandered down to the Lincoln Memorial, accompanied by his valet and Secret Service guards, to chat with a handful of students who were sleeping rough, waiting for a great rally scheduled for the following morning. "I feel just as deeply as you do about this," he told them. It was difficult to determine who was the more embarrassed—the students or the President. After a few more generalities the talk moved into a hesitant discussion of football teams and whether one of the students, who came from California, liked surfing. The two Americas met and drifted apart in a state of mutual incomprehension.

Kissinger also had an embarrassing experience. In the same month a dozen of his most eminent Harvard colleagues came to see him and express their outrage at the President's Cambodian decision. They included men like Edwin Reischauer, Adam Yarmolinsky, and Francis Bator, all of whom had advised on earlier phases of Vietnam decision-making. After the meeting, the organiser of the group, Thomas Schelling, described what had been a frosty occasion: "We made it clear to Henry that we weren't here lunching with him as old friends, but were talking to him solely in his capacity to communicate to the President that we regard this latest act as a disastrously bad foreign-policy decision even in its own terms." Kissinger, finding himself face-to-face with a reality that could not be manipulated, chose to take the meeting as a personal affront. Without breaching his own by now highly circumscribed ideas of security, he was in no position to offer a step-by-step justification of the policy. Instead, he asked for an act of faith. "When you come back a year from now," said Kissinger, "you will find your concerns are unwarranted."

One year later, almost to the day, the domestic reflection of the Nixon-Kissinger war policy had produced a situation in which Washington itself was under siege.

CHAPTER 3

The Enemy Within

In May, 1971, two ideas of America met violently in the nation's capital. There had been antiwar protests in Washington many times before, but the May Day disturbances had a specially unnerving quality—both in the intensity of the demonstrators and in the ruthlessness of the official response.

During the early months of 1971 the battle-hardened domestic legions of the peace movement had reached a new level of desperation in response to another, apparently futile, escalation of the war in Southeast Asia. On February 8, 1971, the rhetoric of Vietnamisation was put to a dramatic test as troops of the South Vietnamese army (the ARVN) drove across the Laotian border to interdict the Ho Chi Minh Trail, Hanoi's legendary infiltration and supply route for troops headed South. The accompanying drumbeat of publicity suggested that this was it—President Thieu's regime in South Vietnam had moved to a new level of military capability. Its army was about to confirm the success of Vietnamisation by taking the offensive.

The operation was a near-total disaster. After penetrating eleven miles into enemy territory the ARVN was hurled back, and only the rapid succour of the American army prevented a military defeat turning into a massacre. Back in the United States, images of panic-stricken ARVN soldiers evacuating on the skids of U.S. helicopters filled the nation's television screens. It was not the complete picture—many of the ARVN troops had fought bravely and retreated under discipline—but it underlined a potent message. If the United States was obliged to stay in Vietnam until the ARVN was capable of taking on the North Vietnamese Army (NVA)

without assistance, then it looked like staying there a long
time. Within the peace movement, it was a message that demanded a response. But in early April, Nixon told the
nation on national television: "Tonight I can report that
Vietnamisation has succeeded." After the Laotian fiasco it
seemed like an insult to their intelligence. The only response
available was an escalation of the level of domestic protest.

Invoking "Mayday," the international distress call, as their
slogan, they descended on Washington with the grandiose objective of "stopping the government." Initially, they succeeded in doing no more than stopping a lot of traffic, and
for several days it seemed as if this would measure the extent
of the disorders. The Washington police department's worst
problem was the task of discouraging choleric commuters
from driving over prone demonstrators. As the police seemed
to be firmly attached to a policy of killing the Mayday
Tribe with kindness, some of the earlier confrontations had
an almost prankish quality. Quite suddenly, the official reflex
changed.

On instructions from President Nixon, then working out
of the "Western White House" in San Clemente, Attorney
General John Mitchell moved more aggressively into the role
of "coordinating" the official strategy. As the nation's top law-
man, with an excellent view of the protestors' antics from his
balcony at the Justice Department, Mitchell had fine official
credentials for the role. At the same time he had a certain
impatience with the fuzzy policies of defusing confrontations
by kid-glove police tactics. Demonstrators got under his skin.
Back in November, 1969, when the antiwar movement was
trying to impress with its orderliness and discipline, a quarter
of a million protestors had marched with solemn decorum
through the streets of Washington. After witnessing this
spectacle Mitchell confided to his wife, Martha, that it
reminded him of the Russian revolution. Mrs. Mitchell, with
characteristic respect for her husband's confidences, told
everybody. In May, 1971, Mitchell took on the task of ending
the Mayday Tribe's impertinence with the zeal of a Cheka
chief hurling back the Bolsheviks.

Reinforced by National Guardsmen and the Army, the
police conducted a gigantic dragnet operation, scooping up
the orderly demonstrators and even innocent bystanders with

the most defiant practitioners of civil disobedience. The result was the most massive bust in American history: 7,200 arrests in a single day and a total of 13,400 over a period of four days. The forces of law and order routed the opposition, filling the jails to the bursting point and accommodating the overflow in an open-air stockade, a fenced-in practice football field near the Robert F. Kennedy Memorial Stadium. As an example of official power it was impressive, but it left a peculiar aftertaste. The action was effected in almost complete neglect of normal arresting procedures which require police to fill in a form giving the name of the person arrested, the arresting officer, and the time and place of the incident. No such niceties had inhibited the "Mayday" bust and, as an inevitable consequence, there were scarcely any convictions. The demonstrators had been swept off the streets like so much garbage.

The human detritus in the open-air stockade, promptly renamed Insurrection City by its inmates, provided an interesting study. Most were young with a length of hair that suggested a desire to identify with America's counterculture. They sang to keep their spirits up and express their alienation "God Bless America" (ironically) and "We all live in a con-cen-tra-tion camp" to the pop cadences of the Beatles' number "Yellow Submarine." But there were older figures behind the wire, among them Doctor Spock, the child-rearing expert, who had nailed his colours to Senator Eugene McCarthy's antiwar candidacy for the Presidency in 1968. Spock, looking chilly and out of place in a light raincoat, had followed his principles to a somewhat embarrassing but logical conclusion. There was Abbie Hoffman too, stouter and less fun-loving than in his days as a Yippie leader in 1968 when he thought that America could be laughed out of its repressive tendencies. His nose was broken and taped, a consequence of the day's skirmishing. "Like, man," explained Hoffman, "that's defacing a national monument."

It could have been classed as the old peacenik crowd but for one thing, the conspicuous number of young men wearing their army combat jackets—Vietnam Veterans Against the War. It was the key difference between demonstrations before Nixon became President and those that came after, and it was a difference that greatly infuriated Nixon's men. Charles Colson, Nixon's political jack-of-all-trades, had

sought to reduce their impact by setting up a counter group
of Veterans for a Just Peace, but it could not efface the
disturbing image of young men demonstrating against a war
in which they themselves had fought; there was no more
potent symbol of rejection.

Yet it was a symbol that cut both ways. On the one hand,
it crystallised disgust with the war but, on the other, it
roused the more atavistic forms of patriotism in those who
felt the American uniform was being dishonoured. In their
different ways, Congressional doves, who by 1971 were
edging towards a majority, were as horrified by "Mayday"
as were the men around Nixon. Democratic Senator John
Tunney complained that the "foolish and useless" acts of the
demonstrators "well might have ruined several months of
hard work by the real advocates of peace." It was a harsh
judgment—particularly in view of the fact that a recent Harris
poll had indicated that 51 percent of Americans felt their
country was "morally wrong" to be fighting in Vietnam—but
it pointed up the basic dilemma of the peace movement.

Ever since Chicago in 1968, when the Democratic convention had been reduced to a shambles by demonstrators,
politicians had been acutely aware of the counterproductive
impression given to the electorate by violent protest. Most
Democratic regulars, even opponents of the war, felt that
Nixon's victory had been won as a result of their own
internal disorders, which had given a new potency to Nixonian
rhetoric about the need for law and order. At the same time
it was difficult—indeed impossible—to persuade those who
had demonstrated against the war in the sixties to pursue a
wait-and-see policy when the war was still raging in 1971 in
Vietnam and Cambodia and Laos. Elected politicians appreciated that however limp the electorate's support for the
President's policy in Southeast Asia, it would always be more
concerned about the security of its own streets. A determined
executive could always, in the short term at least, turn the
argument about a distant foreign war into a popular appeal
for order at home, and this was precisely what happened
after "Mayday."

While the legal journals were preparing learned articles
about the issues raised by indiscriminate arrest and unlogged
detentions, President Nixon put his seal of approval on the
mass bust in a talk with Republican leaders on his return to

Washington: "I think Jerry Wilson [the Washington Police Chief] and the police did a magnificent job. John Mitchell and the Department of Justice did a fine job, too. I hope you will all agree to make that point when you leave here." John Mitchell did not think that elaborate justifications were necessary though he did change a metaphor. The demonstrators no longer reminded him of Russian revolutionaries. This time they merited comparison with Hitler's Brownshirts.

The events of May 1971 seemed to demonstrate that whatever the monthly fluctuations of Nixon's popularity in the polls, his government was one with an unusually firm grip on the levers of authority. No appearance could have been more delusive. For in the areas that were central to the nation's security, both in domestic and foreign affairs, the competence of Nixon's administration had become a key question of debate. It had started at the highest levels of the Federal Bureau of Investigation and the Central Intelligence Agency, and had by degrees poisoned the relations of both agencies with the White House. In both agencies there were men who shared John Mitchell's ostensible concern about a Fascist threat to the state, but it came, in their view, from a different source. They were less worried about the long-haired wierdos in the streets than they were about the buttoned-down apparatchiks in the White House.

CHAPTER 4

"Recommendations: Top Secret"

THE PARADOX of the whole Watergate story is that the real
threat to American democracy was first perceived by those
whose calling suggested, to radicals at least, that they were
no great friends of civil liberties—the professionals in the
FBI and the CIA. Of all the miles of testimony produced by
the Senate committee of inquiry into Watergate, no passage
was more important than that uttered by James W. McCord,
Jr., the former CIA man turned Watergate burglar. Speaking
on the intelligence situation as it struck him during the first
Nixon administration, McCord said: "It appeared to me that
the White House had for some time been trying to get
political control over the CIA assessments and estimates in
order to make them conform to 'White House policy.' . . .
Among other things, this also smacked of the situation which
Hitler's intelligence chiefs found themselves in, in the 1930s
and 1940s, when they were put in the position of having to
tell him what they thought he wanted to hear about foreign
military capabilities and intentions, instead of what they really
believed, which ultimately was one of the things that led to
Nazi Germany's downfall. When linked with what I saw
happening to the FBI under Pat Gray [L. Patrick Gray III,
Nixon's appointee as FBI chief after the death of J. Edgar
Hoover in May, 1972]—political control by the White House
—it appeared then that the two government agencies which
should be able to prepare their reports, and to conduct their
business, with complete integrity and honesty, in the national
interest, were no longer going to be able to do so."

McCord dated his frightening perception to mid-1972, but
within the intelligence service it was obtainable much earlier,

as early, in fact, as 1969, the first year of the Nixon administration. At the time no hint of the struggle between the security services and the White House surfaced in public. It was conducted behind closed doors, on memoranda couched in the euphemistic language of officialdom and marked "Top Secret," and when, late in 1971, some indications of the struggle "leaked," it was perceived as a problem of personalities. But much more than personalities was involved: the first, and ultimately most crucial, battle for American liberties was being fought out not in Congress nor even the courts but within the murky bureaucracies of the secret world.

It was an astonishing situation but not, as McCord later indicated, without historical precedent. In the late 1930s a group in the Abwehr led by Colonel Hans Oster, Chief of the Central Division of Intelligence, played a central role in the attempt to mobilise military and civilian opposition to the Nazi regime which it thought was leading Germany to disaster. The plotting of the Oster group continued right down to April, 1943, when most of its members were arrested and the Abwehr came under the direct and hostile surveillance of the rival SS and Gestapo. Oster and his associates were subsequently executed at Flossenburg concentration camp. Historical analogies, of course, are only helpful up to a point. The American system of government in 1969 was not remotely comparable to that of Germany in 1938, but the fact remains that the perversion of a government's secret intelligence sources is the most ominous of political developments, turning the apparatus of security into extralegal gangsterism. The United States was fortunate in having a security establishment that recognised the danger; its misfortune was in having an administration that did not.

The story of how relations deteriorated between the White House and its two top security agencies is the hidden key to the Watergate drama. For it was this experience that provided the White House with a reason, or excuse, to reach outside the conventional agencies to satisfy its lust for information and come up with the answers that it wanted on "national security" questions. In doing so it found itself up against two of Washington's most sophisticated political in-fighters—J. Edgar Hoover, the curmudgeonly G-man who had served as director of the FBI under seven previous administrations, and Richard

Helms, the elegant mandarin who had headed the CIA since
1966. No two men could be more dissimilar and on occasion
both they and their agencies were barely on speaking terms.
But at the same time they shared some interesting similarities
inside Washington's bureaucratic power structure. Both were
career professionals who, for that reason, enjoyed a rather
higher loyalty quotient within their bailiwicks than is customary
in most government departments. Both headed organisations
that were necessarily secretive. Both had an intensely personal idea of the historical functions of their agencies—White
House administrations may come and go but the FBI and CIA
go on, perhaps forever. Both were imbued with the idea of the
importance of maintaining their agency's independence from
political pressure. And both, in their different ways, were enormously skilled in the art of bureaucratic manoeuvre.

Hoover first began to get unhappy about his new political
masters during the Cambodia "leak" wiretaps episode, in the
summer of 1969. While being no objector to phone-tapping on
principle, he was less than enthusiastic about the blanket tap
policy, and found those on the newsmen particularly alarming.
One reason appears to have been the somewhat equivocal state
of the law on "national security" taps and the fact that none
of the newsmen concerned could, even by the remotest stretch
of the imagination, be considered hostile to the government
(Beecher, the original author of the Cambodian bombing
story, subsequently obtained employment in the Pentagon).
Hoover, in consequence, took elaborate pains to obtain Attorney General Mitchell's written authorisation for the taps.
But beyond the legal point there was a smell of lousy publicity
if news of the taps ever got out. And Hoover, like any good
cop, appreciated the importance of public relations. As a loyal
servant of the administration, he operated the taps but insisted
that the original transcripts be kept within the FBI—only
copies were sent to the White House. Hoover, a past master at
protecting his bureaucratic flanks, felt that one day they might
come in handy. He referred to the transcripts as his "insurance."

The CIA's road to disillusionment came from a different
direction. One of Nixon's first initiatives as President was an
affront to the agency's pride: he downgraded Helms's function
on the National Security Council, the bureaucratic summit of
secret foreign policy-making. Whereas, under previous Presi-

dents, the head of the CIA was always present for Council meetings, Helms found that at the start of the Nixon era he was expected to present his report and then leave the room. The exclusion was subsequently revoked—but its very occurrence made clear that under the Nixon administration the CIA could not expect the direct Presidential access that had once been taken for granted. Helms never did manage to establish any degree of intimacy with the President, and the relationship was not helped by the CIA's failure to vindicate one of Nixon's pet theories.

Shortly after his election, Nixon became convinced that the continuing unrest on the university campuses and the intransigence of radical black leaders in the cities was inspired by foreign enemies of the state. Cases of bombing and arson were on the increase, while the rhetoric of many radicals had shifted from being antiwar to being anti the American system. It was an ominous development. Specifically, he suspected that East European, Egyptian, and Cuban money might be funding student revolutionary leaders. The source of the Black Panthers' money he assumed to be the Caribbean and Algeria. In the fall of 1969 President Nixon instructed the CIA to find the external culprits. Both wings of the agency, the eggheads (or evaluators) and the spooks (or clandestine operators), were put to work. It is very rare for both departments to work together, and even rarer for them to come up with the same conclusion. The clandestine branch tends to be more hard-line than the liberal evaluators. In this instance, however, both wings came back with the same answer: the origins of the unrest were not foreign-inspired but specifically domestic.

The White House then instructed the FBI to continue the same quest for subversive foreign gold. To help them in this mission, the FBI was empowered to expand its activities in twenty foreign countries—a dispensation that did not exactly thrill the CIA, which felt that its own sphere was being impinged on. Predictably, the FBI also drew a blank. Nonetheless, the White House fantasy that opposition to Nixon was being seriously funded from abroad persisted throughout his first term. (The search for evidence of such funding was offered by the Watergate burglars as one of the reasons for the break-in. No "evidence" was found.)

Back in 1970, however, the negative results from the CIA

and FBI led the White House to the conclusion that neither
was doing an effective job. It was a view, of course, that prevented serious thought being given to a more uncongenial explanation of domestic unrest—that it was the policies of the
administration, particularly on the war, which were driving
loyal Americans into dangerous forms of opposition. After the
campus riots that greeted news of the invasion of Cambodia,
Nixon was determined to do something about what he perceived
as a deteriorating situation. He wanted the FBI and CIA to be
both more aggressive in their approach to the problem and
more amenable to White House direction. In its desperate
search for domestic security, the White House produced a
working document that, on its public discovery three years
later, struck Senator Sam Ervin, chairman of the committee
of inquiry into Watergate, as suggesting "evidence of a Gestapo mentality."

In fact, the techniques which the White House tried to foist
on its security services—including expanded use of wiretaps
and burglary—were not completely alien to the American tradition. The FBI, in carrying out its counterespionage function,
had used them with the tacit approval of every previous administration since the war. As one veteran FBI man put it:
"The boys would do what they had to do. And if they got
caught, Hoover would disavow them." But in response to
growing demands for accountability during the sixties, some of
the FBI's more unorthodox procedures had been tapered off.
In 1966 the FBI, on orders from the then Attorney General,
Ramsey Clark, quietly discontinued its "special programs"
group, which specialized in burglary of suspects' premises.
Nixon wanted the "special programs" back on a grand scale.
What was novel about the plan was not so much the methods
involved but the idea of how widely, and usefully, they could
be applied.

The architect of the plan was Tom Charles Huston, a
twenty-nine-year-old White House speechwriter turned security expert. Huston was a rather unconventional but very eager
young man. He kept a red scrambler telephone in his White
House desk drawer, collected presidential campaign biogra-
phies—he had them going back to 1824—and speculated enthusiastically, if somewhat incoherently, on the true nature of
conservatism. Within the White House he was regarded as a

bit of an egghead and ideas man. With the full backing of the President, Huston began the task of converting to his vision of the new domestic security order the nation's top intelligence chieftains: Hoover for the FBI, Helms for the CIA, Lieut. Gen. Donald V. Bennett, director of the Pentagon's Defense Intelligence Agency, and Admiral Noel Gayler, director of the National Security Agency, which makes and breaks codes and monitors foreign communications.

On June 5, 1970, this formidable quartet were called to a meeting in the Oval Office, where President Nixon told them of his hopes for strengthened domestic intelligence. They were told to form a committee with Hoover as chairman and report with their recommendations as soon as possible. An official photograph was taken. Almost immediately a working group was set up with Tom Huston sitting in, with his draft plan. Given the perennial hostilities and rivalries in the security field, business appeared to proceed with amazing dispatch. The proposals in the draft plan were accepted by all hands with one exception—J. Edgar Hoover. Huston thought that he would be no problem. In the discussions Huston sometimes felt it necessary to tell Hoover, his senior by forty-seven years, his business. At one point, when Hoover struggled to explain the need for a "historical view" of objective intelligence, Huston remarked with what he evidently thought was keen insight: "We're not talking about the dead past; we're talking about the living present."

By June 25, Huston's views were substantially enshrined in a forty-three-page document which called for the following improvements in domestic intelligence-gathering: 1. Lifting of the ban on "surreptitious entry"; 2. Increased wiretapping of domestic security suspects and foreign diplomats; 3. Relaxation of restrictions on illegal "mail coverage" (i.e., steaming open and reading people's letters); 4. Increasing the corps of FBI informers on university campuses; 5. Monitoring of American citizens using international communications facilities; 6. New budgetary arrangements to cover the increased cost of domestic security; 7. Increased CIA coverage of students (and others) living abroad; 8. A new Interagency Group on Internal Security, with representatives from the White House, the FBI, the CIA, the NSA, the DIA and the three military counterintelligence agencies, to be set up with effect from August 1, 1970, the director of the FBI to serve as chairman. The document, in short, envisaged the most comprehensive attempt ever made by an American government, in peace or war, to spy on its own citizens.

There was one snag. Hoover, far from being beguiled by the possibility of crowning his career as chairman of the secret police, was not going along with the idea. Not only did he not want the chairmanship, he did not want any part of the plan. He appended his objections as a footnote.

For a student of the Washington bureaucracy, that should have indicated game, set, and match to Hoover. But Huston and, curiously enough, Nixon himself were both novices in this league. In early July Huston wrote "Recommendations: Top Secret" for Bob Haldeman which, were it not for the gravity of the subject matter, might constitute history's most touchingly innocent political memorandum. As far as Huston could tell, the recommendations were sound and "Everyone knowledgeable in the field, with the exception of Mr. Hoover, concurs that existing coverage is grossly inadequate. CIA and NSA note that this is particularly true of diplomatic establishments, and we have learned at the White House that it is also true of New Left groups."

He noted the total unreasonableness of Mr. Hoover: "His objections are generally inconsistent and frivolous—most express concern about possible embarrassment to the intelligence community (i.e., Hoover) from public disclosure," and the total reasonableness of the other parties involved. For example: "I went into this exercise fearful that the CIA would not cooperate. In fact, Dick Helms was most cooperative and helpful." Huston's rapport with the other two principals was even more extraordinary: "Admiral Gayler (NSA) and General Bennett (DIA) were greatly displeased by Mr. Hoover's attitude and his insistence on footnoting objections. They wished to raise a formal protest and sign the report only with the understanding that they opposed the footnotes. I prevailed on them not to do so since it would aggravate Mr. Hoover and further complicate our efforts. They graciously agreed to go along with my suggestion in order to avoid a nasty scene and jeopardize the possibility of positive action resulting from the report. I assured them that their opinion would be brought to the attention of the President."

Any intelligent bureaucrat reading between the lines of this memorandum would make a number of somewhat cynical, but sensible, deductions. Domestic security is, no matter how you look at it, essentially an FBI problem. The FBI is run by J. Edgar Hoover, an obsessive collector of "secret files" on his political masters. He is against the proposals, ergo they will not be accepted. No man in America, after all, had a greater capacity for getting his own way. The ostensible enthusiasm of the other intelligence chiefs might have been genuine. On the other hand, it might not. They could have been adopting the well-established bureaucratic ploy of showing enthusiasm for an idea that pleased their political masters in the certain knowledge that it would come to naught. There was no harm, after all, in earning free good marks from the President.

The Huston memorandum was engagingly frank about the illegality of some of the techniques recommended. Opening mail was a clear violation of the law but Huston considered that the advantages to be derived from this practice "outweigh the risks." Of "surreptitious entry" he said: "Use of this technique is clearly illegal; it amounts to burglary. It is also highly risky and could result in great embarrassment if exposed. However, it is also the most fruitful tool and can produce the type of intelligence which cannot be obtained in any other fashion." In an aside Huston comments, "The deployment of the executive protector force has increased the risk of surreptitious entry in diplomatic cases." The Executive Protective Service was a uniformed branch of the Secret Service whose normal duties were confined to acting as bodyguards for the President and, in election years, presidential candidates. Nixon had set up the EPS in March, 1970, four months earlier, and given it the specific job of guarding foreign embassies in the Washington area. Now, he had the intriguing problem of how to circumvent his own generously bestowed protective apparatus.

But the outstanding problem was how to persuade Mr. Hoover of the illogic of his objections. Huston saw it as a two-tier process involving the President's manipulative skill. First: "Mr. Hoover should be called in privately for a stroking session at which the President explains the decision he has made, thanks Mr. Hoover for his candid advice and past cooperation, and indicates he is counting on Edgar's cooperation in implementing the new report. . . ." Stage two would involve calling all four intelligence chiefs back to the Oval Room where "the President should thank them for the report, announce his decisions, indicate his desires for future activity, and present each with an autographed copy of the photo of the first meeting which Ollie took."

Huston concludes with some thoughts on the character of the FBI chief. "I might add," writes Huston, "that it is my personal opinion that Mr. Hoover will not hesitate to accede to any decision which the President makes, and the President should not, therefore, be reluctant to overrule Mr. Hoover's objections. Mr. Hoover is set in his ways and can be bull-headed as hell, but he is a loyal trooper. Twenty years ago he would never have raised the type of objections he has here, but he's getting old and worried about his legend. He makes life tough in this area, but not impossible—for he'll respond to direction by the President, and that is all we need to set the domestic intelligence house in order."

On July 15, having persuaded the President to overrule Hoover's objections, Huston wrote up a "decision memo" which effectively rubber-stamped his own plan, complete to almost the last detail. On July 23 the memorandum was sent out to the chiefs of the four agencies with the President's approval. It remained "operational" for precisely five days, the time it took for Hoover, as one of his aides put to, "to hit the roof," storm round to Attorney General John Mitchell with his objections, and through Mitchell persuade the President to back off from the plan. The "decision memorandum" was recalled on July 28. The thought of what Hoover if crossed might do about those potentially embarrassing "national security" wiretaps may not have been far from the administration's mind.

Huston bravely soldiered on, firing off furious memos about Hoover's intransigence. On August 5 he bitterly observed in another "Top Secret" to Haldeman: "All of us are going to look damn silly in the eyes of Helms, Gayler, Bennett, and the military chiefs if Hoover can unilaterally reverse a presidential decision. . . ." But it was a lonely struggle and one in which, unsurprisingly, the intelligence chiefs who had been so "helpful" and "gracious" in originally discussing the plan showed little interest. All Huston achieved was his own political eclipse. His intelligence assignment was subsequently transferred to a rising young man called John Wesley Dean III. The following autumn Huston quietly packed his bags and returned to his books and his law practice in Indianapolis. Later he ruefully complained, "The administration's domestic programs were never rooted in any philosophical view of what the government ought to be doing."

The demise of the Huston plan made it clear to Nixon's men that as long as Hoover remained in charge of the FBI, it was going to concentrate on its traditional targets—card-carrying Communists and Mafia gangsters. The so-called "student revolution," which obsessed the White House, was not being taken seriously enough. Hoover has, since his death, been criticised for his apparently callous disregard for the threat posed by the youthful New Left. His motivation, it has been suggested, had nothing to do with civil liberties but was based on a cautious concern for his own reputation. But there were sensible professional reasons for his attitude. It scarcely required investigative sophistication to "penetrate" the student movement; excellent intelligence could be obtained by reading the mimeographed handbills that were thrust into the hands of all and sundry. As the student movement essentially depended on mass action, its leaders made little secret of their intentions. Moreover, the intensity of student outrages almost exactly mirrored the degree of disgust caused by some new turning-point in, or revelation about, the war in Vietnam, and that was something that the FBI was in no position to predict. Indeed, the experience of the Kent State riots indicated that suspicion of FBI informers on campus made the situation worse. (At the time of writing, the Justice Department is investigating an allegation that the Kent State killings were prompted by random shots fired by an inexperienced, trigger-happy, FBI informer.)

Within the secret world Hoover's power play against the White House had masked, but not obscured, another more delicate bureaucratic struggle. Henry Kissinger in his role as chairman of the National Security Council was one of the main customers of CIA intelligence. But he was not a happy one. On several occasions he had been heard to complain loudly that the CIA reports arriving on his desk were long on undigested facts but distinctly short on analysis. He went so far as to scrawl "piece of crap" on a CIA Vietnam report. The problem was later personalised as a dispute between Kissinger and Helms, but it was more complicated than that.

The CIA had long been ambivalent about the war in Vietnam, an attitude that stemmed from the split function of the agency between Plans and Intelligence. Shortly after the CIA was established by statute in 1947, it set up a Directorate of Plans (recently renamed "Operations") charged with responsibility for clandestine espionage and the conduct of secret political operations overseas on behalf of the U.S. government. This was the side of the CIA that lived and operated under the wraps of maximum security and which figured in Communist demonology as the "dirty tricks" extension of "U.S. imperialism." The tricks ranged from organising coups d'état to bankrolling foreign political parties and organisations favourable to the American cause. The record of its "blown" operations over the years constitute a litany for all left-wing critics of the CIA—Iran 1952 (Pro-Communist Premier Mossadegh deposed); Guatemala 1953 (Marxist President Arbenz overthrown); Indonesia 1958 (abortive coup directed against left-wing President Sukarno); the U-2 spy flights, 1960 (pilot Francis Gary Powers captured in Russia); Cuba, 1961 (the Bay of Pigs attempt to overthrow Castro); Vietnam, 1963 (the Diem brothers deposed); Chile, 1964 (Marxist presidential candidate Allende thwarted); United States, 1967 (long-time secret funding of student groups and foundations exposed).

This side of the CIA had always been deeply involved in the Southeast Asian conflict and was, during the Nixon years, as industrious as ever. In Laos it maintained, as it had done under Kennedy and Johnson, a "secret army" of Laotians at a cost—revealed in 1971—of $300 million a year. In Cambodia it established some imaginative programs after Prince Sihanouk's overthrow in 1970 and his retirement to the sanctuary of Peking. (Although there is no evidence that the CIA organised the coup, the American military machine did feel more comfortable with the government of Sihanouk's successor, General Lon Nol.) The CIA assisted the cause by establishing a phony radio station on which a giggly "Prince Sihanouk" advised Cambodian women to sleep with Vietcong "liberators." In Vietnam it was operationally responsible for a joint U.S.–South Vietnamese program designed to "neutralise the Vietcong infrastructure." The program—called Operation Phoenix—was widely criticised as one that involved systematic assassination. This was strenuously denied by government officials. It was, however, an extremely ruthless enterprise, even on the evidence of official figures. The enemy was "neutralised" by being killed, jailed, or "rallied"—i.e., being persuaded to defect. According to figures submitted to a House subcommittee in 1971 by William Egan Colby, the CIA head of the program, in the period between 1968 and 1971 almost 70,000 people were "neutralised"—28,978 were captured or jailed, 17,717 were "rallied," and 20,587 were killed.

The White House had few complaints about the contribution of the CIA's Directorate of Plans to the total war effort. And William Colby, after his exertions on the Phoenix program, rose steadily in the estimation of the President. (In the spring of 1973, shortly after Helms's premature retirement to become Ambassador of Iran, Nixon nominated Colby as the new CIA chief.)

The branch of the CIA that irritated Kissinger and finally the President was the Directorate of Intelligence. Staffed by highly educated analysts, the Directorate of Intelligence was charged with the task of sifting intelligence, from both open and covert sources, and providing objective estimates of developments in other countries. In outlook they were perhaps closer to the academic community than they were to their cloak-and-dagger brethren in Plans. A third of them had PhDs, and they provided the substance for one of Helms's few public boasts. "Our people," he once said, "have academic degrees in 298 major fields of specialisation." Most of them worked and sharpened their wits on each other at the CIA headquarters in Langley, Virginia. On Vietnam, the CIA's analyst-evaluators had for many years provided the Government's most pessimistic stream of advice, a process that brought them into regular collision with the policies advanced by the Joint Chiefs of Staff.

As far back as 1965, before President Johnson's massive military build-up, the CIA recommended against deeper involvement in Vietnam. Later it opposed the bombing of strategic targets in North Vietnam on the grounds that this would be counterproductive and redouble the Communists' will to fight. Lyndon Johnson graphically expressed his exasperation with the CIA's attitude in his book *The Vantage Point:* "Policy-making is like milking a fat cow. You see the milk coming out, you press more, and the milk bubbles and flows. And just as the bucket is full, the cow whips its tail around the bucket and everything is spilled. That's what the CIA does to policy-making."

When Nixon came to power, the CIA's analyst-evaluators

were still mired in a gloomy complexity about Vietnam. In the service of a White House that prized the value of positive thinking, this was not an attitude calculated to win friends or even influence official policy which, under pressure of the Nixon-Kissinger grand design, began seeking ways of making the war "winnable." In 1970 exasperation with CIA's analyses was compounded by two specific current intelligence failures. During the Cambodian invasion of 1970 it was discovered that the port of Sihanoukville had been used as a Vietcong base to resupply their forces in the Mekong Delta. The CIA, in contradiction with the military, had previously said that Sihanoukville had no strategic importance. Then, in November, 1970, the CIA was held directly responsible for the embarrassing Son Tay prison raid. Acting on CIA intelligence which indicated that the camp, situated twenty-three miles west of Hanoi, contained a large number of American POWs, the Army staged a daring and dangerous rescue attempt. When the rescuers arrived they found an empty camp.

Although neither "failure" was crucial to the overall development of the war strategy, each gave an increasingly impatient White House grounds for doubting the validity of the CIA's advice. Nixon, in any case, had no curiosity about the minutiae of the foreign intelligence-gathering process. In contrast with his two predecessors, Kennedy and Johnson, he rarely asked for tidbits of raw intelligence (though the news that Hanoi had sent out a team of mobile barbers to shear the city's long-haired youth was passed on as being something that might interest the President). Nixon wanted his analysis uncluttered by "irrelevant" detail. As time went by this need was met by the researchers on Kissinger's rapidly expanding NSC staff in the form of "National Security Study Memoranda." Over a hundred of these papers were produced during Nixon's first term and they came to supplant the CIA's estimates as the analytical basis for presidential decision-making.

Although Richard Helms had served for most of his career in Plans, as Director of the CIA he became increasingly associated with the pessimism of the Intelligence department. He could see the influence of his agency slipping away in all but the more pugnacious areas of its activity. His personal access to the President had been curtailed, and now the work of his best men was being virtually ignored. He was too old and sophisticated an operator to make an issue of the situation.

He did not, unlike Hoover, have any "insurance" in the form of secret files that might embarrass the White House, and confrontation tactics were not his style. "To succeed in this town," he once told a Washington friend, "you have to walk with a very quiet tread." In Nixon's Washington he had to tread more quietly than ever. His background before assuming the mask of CIA "objectivity" was that of a wealthy, East Coast, cosmopolitan liberal. Such men had to watch what they said if they wanted to stay in government; they were not, after all, part of the new majority. All that Helms could do was hang in, and if he could not have influence at least try, in the nicest possible way, to preserve the integrity of his agency. That alone, as we shall see, was going to be a man-sized job.

By the time of the May Day demonstrations in 1971, the White House found itself in an odd relationship with its two top security agencies. Both the FBI and the CIA had, in its view, somehow failed them in their pursuit of identifiable "enemies" at home and abroad. To counterbalance this deficiency on the home front the Justice Department had beefed up the Internal Security Division, a bureaucratic relic that had lain dormant since the Cold War witch-hunting days of the mid-1950s. The man put in charge of this operation was John Mitchell's golfing partner, Robert Mardian, a second-generation American of Armenian descent with an intensely patriotic disposition. A Justice Department colleague once observed of him: "You talk about wearing flags in lapels—this guy would have sewn a flag on his back if they'd let him." It was said that he could tell a man's political affiliation from the length of his hair (Mardian was balding). With Mardian around, the White House could be assured that "subversives" would be found and pursued. Under his leadership, the ISD put together a whole string of conspiracy cases against antiwar radicals, many of which were ultimately thrown out by the courts on the basis of unsound prosecution evidence.

Mardian's Internal Security Department also acted as host for yet another White House–inspired attempt to bring the security agencies together, under the umbrella title of the Intelligence Evaluation Committee. The President later described this committee—composed of representatives from the White House, FBI, CIA, NSC, Secret Service, and the Departments of Justice, Treasury, and Defense—as a vehicle "to improve

coordination among the intelligence community and to prepare evaluations and estimates of domestic intelligence."
Among its working documents were copies of the Huston plan;
rumours of its death had been much exaggerated.

While these high-level domestic security discussions were
going on, Mardian engineered an unusual exercise in coordination between the security agencies. In the summer of 1971, he
found out that the President was worried about J. Edgar
Hoover's custody of those embarrassing logs of telephone taps
on newsmen and NSC staff. The thought had crossed the presidential mind that Hoover might be churlish enough to use
them as a form of blackmail to maintain his position as director. Mardian solved the problem by persuading one of
Hoover's deputies, William Sullivan, to remove the logs from
the FBI safe without Hoover's knowledge. They finally wound
up in the comparative security of John Ehrlichman's safe at
the White House. Hoover's rage when, in July 1971, he found
out that someone had "done a bag job" on (i.e., burgled) his
precious files, was apparently something worth seeing.

Thus far, all the White House efforts to bring the security
agencies together had been spectacularly successful in driving
them further apart both from the White House and one
another. There is no contemporary evidence about what Nixon
himself thought of this shambles though, presumably, posterity
will know. From the spring of 1971, in what was literally the
White House's best-kept secret, Nixon had the establishment
wired for sound.

Acting on Bob Haldeman's instructions, the Technical Services Division of the Secret Service began routinely taping all
the President's conversations in the Oval Office, his office
in the Executive Office Building, and on four of his personal telephones. The recording system was linked to an electronic "locator" device run by security personnel, that showed
President Nixon's whereabouts in the White House by lights
for each of seven locations. When the President was in the
Oval Office or his Executive Office Building office and the light
flashed for that location, it automatically turned on the tape
recorders. The telephone tapes were automatically activated
by lifting the receiver. There was also a recording system in
the Cabinet Room: this was operated manually—it was not
perfect. All the other devices were superb—even the quietest
of conversations could be picked up in the President's offices.

The recordings were maintained by date and stored in the basement of the Executive Office Building where there were, ultimately, acute storage problems. Future historians will doubtless find them a boon. The contemporary fact, however, was that the Nixon White House was becoming a very surreal place indeed.

CHAPTER 5

The Room 16 Project

THE PENTAGON Papers tipped the Nixon administration over the edge. Until the summer of 1971 White House manoeuvres in the security field could be characterised as a combination of clumsiness and incompetence, but their effect, domestically at least, was kept within reasonable limits by the shrewdness of the traditional agencies. From June 13, 1971, the day on which the *New York Times* started its serialisation of a Pentagon archive detailing the secret history of America's involvement in Vietnam, it moved actively into the clumsy and dangerous phase. The White House began to go into security on its own account.

Nixon was horrified by the massive "leak" in the *New York Times*. Publication of the once "Top Secret" documents confirmed all his worst suspicions about the recklessness of the Liberal Establishment; and the fact that the papers revealed that the American public had—under both Kennedy and Johnson—been comprehensively misled about the war only made matters worse. At a time when he was trying to defuse Vietnam, the Pentagon Papers stoked up all the old hyperthyroid divisions over "hawks" and "doves" and "credibility gaps." If his own carefully constructed scenario for peace, operated through Henry Kissinger, was to work at all, he could not afford any further leaks of this kind in the run-up to the election. The next set of revelations, after all, might open up his own credibility gap: it would by this time at least equal that of his Democratic predecessor. Although the source of the Papers, Daniel Ellsberg, a former administration official and Rand Corporation think-tank expert, was rapidly discovered and under FBI investigation, Nixon instructed Ehrlich-

man both to plug the leaks and to supplement the FBI's enquiries. The White House Special Investigations Unit was born.

It was all very formal, with lines of authority going down
from the President through Ehrlichman, to the unit's administrative section located in Room 16, a basement office in the
Executice Office Building next door to the White House. The
head of the unit was Egil Krogh, Jr., a young Ehrlichman protégé and a Christian Scientist of unusual piety. He was jokingly called "Evil Krogh" on account of his presumed incapac-
ity for wrong-doing. Krogh was assisted by David Young,
another young man in his early thirties, who had been loaned
to the project from Kissinger's NSC staff. Young, who had a
slightly more irreverent turn of mind, approached the leak-
plugging project with panache. He stuck up a sign on the door
of Room 16: "David Young—Plumber." By early July the
new enterprise was almost ready to take off; all it required was
the men ready to go out and get their hands dirty—the actual
"plumbers."

There were already two accomplished in-house candidates
for the job. Both were skilled and resourceful operators with
strong stomachs for the seamier side of political life. Jack
Caulfield and his friend Tony Ulasewicz were hired by John
Ehrlichman back in 1969 for the purpose of providing "investigative support for the White House." They were former
New York cops and veteran undercover investigators; both
had worked for the city's Bureau of Special Services and Investigations (BOSSY) monitoring the activities of extreme left-
wing groups. Caulfield's official task at the White House was
to "liaise" with the various law-enforcement agencies. Ulasewicz, the more rugged of the two, was kept at a greater distance. He had come on the team after a clandestine meeting
with Ehrlichman at LaGuardia Airport, and never set foot in
the White House. To ensure maximum security Ehrlichman
arranged with Haldeman that Ulasewicz's salary of $22,000 a
year be paid from funds supplied by Herbert Kalmbach, the
President's personal lawyer. Ulasewicz received his assignments from Caulfield who, in turn, received them from Ehrlichman and subsequently from Ehrlichman's successor as the
President's legal counsel, John Dean III. The assignments
ranged from investigating rumours that the brother of a leading Democrat was involved in a homosexual incident, through

research into the drinking habits of unhelpful Senators, to
placing a wiretap on the phone of Joseph Kraft, a distinguished Washington columnist who was, as it happens, an
overall supporter of Nixon at the time. Ulasewicz also spent
some time, before it was realised the attempt was futile, on
trying to prove the My Lai massacre story was untrue or
capable of being discredited. But their key target, especially
after the death in July, 1969, of Mary Jo Kopechne in a motor
accident involving Edward Kennedy at Chappaquiddick, was
the life-style of the Senator from Massachusetts. Senator
Kennedy had always been considered the main Democratic
threat to Nixon's hopes of re-election.

Caulfield and Ulasewicz dug and dug into the mud of Chappaquiddick but never, it appears, came up with anything more
than that exposed in the public prints. Part of the equipment
acquired for this enterprise was an "office" on 46th Street in
New York furnished with a king-sized bed, velvet walls, and
deep fur rugs where, it was apparently thought, indiscreet girl
friends of Mary Jo Kopechne might be encouraged to talk. In
the event, no business was transacted in these exotic surround-
ings. After two years of such imaginative muckraking on behalf of the White House, Caulfield and Ulasewicz had established credentials for the work that was in hand for the President's new Special Investigations Unit. They then proceeded
to blot their copybooks.

In the fallout of paranoia created by publication of the
Pentagon Papers, Morton Halperin, a former administration
official, fell under deep suspicion. Halperin had been in overall
charge of the Pentagon Papers project within the government
and had worked as one of Kissinger's closest aides on the NSC
(he was among those on the Kissinger wiretap list). Halperin
was also a friend of Daniel Ellsberg. On leaving the administration, he had gone to the Brookings Institution, an academic,
political-research organisation in Washington. In June, 1971,
Caulfield was instructed by Chuck Colson, the presidential
hard man, to find a way of getting into the Institution and
bring back some "leaked documents" thought to be in Halperin's possession. The resourceful Ulasewicz inspected the
premises and brought back the regrettable news that security
at Brookings was exceptionally tight. Colson then, according
to a chronology later provided by John Dean, told Caulfield
that "if necessary he should plant a firebomb in the building

and retrieve the documents during the commotion that would ensue." The former New York cops felt that enough was enough. Caulfield complained to John Dean, who emplaned to California and complained to John Ehrlichman, then in attendance at the San Clemente White House, who rang Washington and put the kibosh on the idea. Colson was later afflicted with acute amnesia about the whole event, although a friend of his suggested that he may have put up the bombing idea as a joke. Colson's sense of humour was to become a key element in the election year, but back in the summer of 1971 it badly distorted the career structures of Messrs. Caulfield and Ulasewicz; after the Brookings episode they found the White House demand for their services tapering off sharply.

New men were required for the new demands of the Special Investigations Unit and, as is often the case at a key turning point in history, the time produced the men. For the final vault into dangerous absurdity, Nixon's White House security advisers came up with two of the most absurdly dangerous operators on the Washington scene—E. Howard Hunt and G. Gordon Liddy. Hunt was a Colson discovery; the uncertain credit for hiring Liddy belonged to Egil Krogh. Both came into their inheritance as the first White House plumbers with a sense of manifest destiny. Their careers, though constructed along different lines, had prepared them for what was to come.

Hunt, a fascinating but deeply flawed individual, was fifty-two years old when he was taken on Colson's staff as a White House "consultant" for a useful $100 a day. He was a slight, sandy-haired man of medium height with a lifetime's experience in the spy business. Like most of the early recruits to what became after the war a major growth industry, he came from a respectable middle-class background. Hunt's father was a judge in Hamburg, New York. After graduating from Brown University he joined the Navy, only to be invalided out in 1942. He spent nearly two years working as a writer, for newspapers and the movies, before he found his real métier. In 1943 he joined the Office of Strategic Services (OSS), the fledgling precursor of the CIA, and was trained as a "black" (clandestine) intelligence operative. The end of the war saw him in China working with the guerrillas behind Japanese lines, a mission that brought him to the attention of

Tracy S. Barnes, one of the early intelligence barons, who later headed the CIA's clandestine operations.

Hunt inevitably graduated to the CIA and spent the late forties working in Paris, where he developed a profound affection for all things French and served, in his cover role, as the liaison officer between the American Embassy and the Economic Cooperation Administration, the organisational underpinning of the Marshall Plan. At the ECA Hunt worked with Richard M. Bissell, an economist who later became the CIA's Deputy Director for Plans. These were the high and heady days of the agency when the sense of saving the "Free World" from the encroachments of Communism was intensely strong. As long as this mood prevailed, Hunt's career prospered. He went on to do a variety of more responsible jobs in Europe and Central and South America. In 1957 he became the CIA station chief in Montevideo. Early in 1960 his career reached its apogee when, working directly under Bissell, he began to organise secret preparations for the invasion of Cuba. To improve his cover he "resigned" from the agency and traveled first to Mexico and then to Miami, posing as a writer who had suddenly come into a windfall inheritance. For the next year and a half he acted as liaison between the CIA and the Cuban Revolutionary Council, the group of exiles who were going, with CIA assistance, to overthrow Castro's government. Hunt's code-name in his contacts with the Cubans was "Eduardo."

According to his own account of the Bay of Pigs operation, to be published this fall under the title *Give Us This Day*, Hunt made a secret trip to Cuba in the spring of 1960 and recommended to Bissell that the CIA assassinate Castro as part of the uprising. *Give Us This Day* is a curious book, intensely moving in parts, but informed by the most simplistic political philosophy. It is clear, for example, that Hunt felt that Cuba was the turning point; that the right application of force against Castro would have solved in advance all the tortured problems of U.S. power in the sixties both in the Americas and Asia.

The book explains a great deal about Howard Hunt's own political beliefs and aspirations, and goes some way towards explaining why he eventually felt it so easy to slip from dirty tricks against foreign countries into dirty tricks against the Democratic Party. Apart from "Eduardo" himself, there is no hero of the book (though Vice-President Richard Nixon, who promoted the idea of an anti-Castro invasion force within the administration despite President Eisenhower's indifference, is treated very sympathetically), but there are very clear villains —President Kennedy and the New Frontiersmen who took over Nixon's going concern in the Caribbean. Howard Hunt blames their "ambivalence towards Communism" and their hesitation at crucial moments of the invasion for its failure.

He obviously loved the Cuban operation, at least in its early stages. At the beginning of the book he describes how good it was to see and greet warmly friends and spying colleagues whom he had not seen for years—"the old crowd was rallying to the new cause." He sits on a mountainside training camp in Guatemala with Colonel Luke, "my World War II comrade who was training the paratroopers." Luke does virtuoso parachute displays, tells Howard of the problems of VD because "these Indian girls come here at night and stick their butts through the fence for a quetzal. You know Cubans. They don't believe in condoms even if I had them to pass out," and asks him,

"Remember the first B-26 we ever saw?"

"Kumning Airport, 1945."

He laughed. "I can still see that poor bastard landing with his wheels up, spinning down the strip. . . . That plane was going to win the war for us in China," said Luke nostalgically. "What good times they were."

Later things began to turn sour, particularly when, on instructions from John Kennedy's White House, the CIA was asked to include the more left-wing exiles in the invasion strategy. Hunt eventually resigned over this issue. "I turned in," he writes revealingly, "reflecting that it was becoming increasingly hard to identify the enemy."

Hunt blames the fiasco of the invasion on Kennedy's failure to provide air support and becomes even more bitter in his analysis of Administration moves in the official post mortems. He saw these as a deliberate attempt "to whitewash the New Frontier by heaping guilt on the CIA." From then on, nothing that the Kennedy Administration did in foreign affairs lessened Hunt's disgust for its "soft on Communism" approach. Even the Cuban missile crisis was a climb-down, for Khrushchev "gained a great deal for very little—the supposed removal of Soviet missiles in exchange for a promise by JFK that he

would never invade Cuba." Hunt ends his book with the hope
that his "analysis of needless failure" will be a lesson to America's leaders.

But in the more complex political currents of the sixties, it
was Hunt himself who was the failure. The world had moved
on, leaving him stranded with an increasingly redundant set of
skills—espionage was moving into the technological era of
U-2s and space satellites—and an increasingly irrelevant political attitude. After the Bay of Pigs, Hunt's career at the CIA
was a dying fall though he lingered on, after numerous humili-
ations, until April, 1970. In 1963 the American Ambassador
in Madrid refused to accept him as deputy chief of the local
CIA station because of his reputation as an intriguer. For the
most part, Hunt appears to have been deployed on projects
that used his literary skill; he was no longer entrusted with
"sensitive" assignments.

As compensation for the lack of romance in his agency
work, Hunt wrote more furiously than ever. In his ample
spare time he reeled off spy and adventure stories, under a
variety of pseudonyms, at a rate of two or three a year (forty-
six have been published). The recurring heroes of his later
novels are Steve Bently, a hard-nosed Certified Public Accountant, and Peter Ward, an elegant CIA agent, fastidious
in his appreciation of the best cuisine, wines, and women and
implacable in pursuit of the Communist foe. In *Hazardous
Duty* Peter Ward sums up the "black" operative's personal
philosophy: "We became lawless in a struggle for the rule of
law—semi-outlaws who risk their lives to put down the sav-
agery of others." In *The Berlin Ending,* Hunt has an old CIA
hand glooming about the new ethos of an Agency "grown
old and cautious. Prim. Reliant on technology far more than
human beings."

The novels, while evoking admiration for the men who do
the dirty work, also show an instinctive distrust for those
whose money and position place them above the struggle.
One of his most recent books, *The Coven,* characterised a
Senator who, according to Hunt's friends, represented the dis-
tilled essence of what Hunt felt about the Kennedys. The
Senator, Newbold Vane, repelled the tough, pipe-smoking
lawyer hero, Jake Gault. Jake felt that "the Vanes were non-
serious people who demanded to be taken seriously. His trans-
parent ambition, their whole imperious lifestyle was prepos-

terous. Vane was about as qualified to be President as I was
to practice open-heart surgery." But Jake fully appreciates
the Senator's wife, with whom he has an affair. "Mind-blowing
hot pants concealed her delta as she flexed the knee of one
long and lovely leg. . . . stretching back her arms, she re-
sembled Athena in full flight. And just as braless. I gobbled
some of my drink." Later the Senator's wife gasps: "Oh Jake,
oh you bastard. You brutal God-damn woman-killer."

In the real world, Hunt, a married man with four children,
was not having much fun at all. The state of the nation de-
pressed him. In the late sixties he wrote several letters to the
Brown University *Alumni Monthly*, complaining about the
lack of patriotism among the young. He was outraged by the
refusal of some students to listen respectfully to a speech on
campus by Henry Kissinger in 1969, and wrote that Brown
was designed to produce men of "usefulness and reputation,
not hirsute know-nothings as seems increasingly the case."
And after his retirement from the CIA he found little in the
way of job satisfaction working with Robert R. Mullen and
Co., a Washington public-relations firm with very strong Republican ties. "In a sense he never left the CIA," said a friend.
"His heart was always there."

Hunt worked on contracts for the commanding heights of
capitalism—General Foods and the Hughes Tool Company
were among his accounts. And on one occasion he succeeded
in persuading Julie Nixon, the President's daughter, to appear
in a television commercial endorsing an educational venture
represented by his firm. He received a Christmas card from
the President and his first lady which he framed and gave
pride of place on the wall of his windowless office. But such
symbols were no substitute for the glamour of the life he had
once led. The secretaries at the Mullen agency thought that
Hunt was a rather sad man.

Then, in the early months of 1971, Hunt renewed acquaintance with another Brown alumnus whom he had first met in
the mid-sixties, Charles Colson, now elevated to the dizzying
heights of Special Counsel to the President. The two men
found they had a lot in common, particularly their resentment of the Liberal Establishment and their detestation for
the very name of Kennedy. Early in July, Colson called Hunt's
superior at the firm and asked him to let Howard "moonlight"
for the White House. Given the political sympathies of the

Mullen agency, that was no problem at all. Their employee was taken off salary and paid on a $125-per-diem basis for the time he could fit in between White House assignments. E. Howard Hunt was operational again.

G. Gordon Liddy, who came on the White House "plumbers" team two weeks later, was something else. Liddy's past was less exotic than that of Howard Hunt, but his character was much more flamboyant and aggressive, and he was altogether better dressed. With his trim moustache and upright military bearing, Liddy was much harder to lose in a crowd than the rumpled Hunt in his sagging suit and cheap straw hat. Like Hunt, he came from a family with experience in the law. Liddy's father was a lawyer in Manhattan, and after military service—as an Army officer in Korea—Liddy finished his education at Fordham Law School. He then went on to become an FBI agent and, in the mid-sixties, an Assistant District Attorney in Poughkeepsie, New York. "We always regarded him as someone who would ultimately receive either national fame or notoriety," said Albert Rosenblatt, an attorney who worked alongside Liddy in the DA's department. "He was a man of extraordinary ambition." There was no doubt that Liddy was an exceptional man, but for someone asked to operate at the highest levels of clandestine activity, he had one remarkable deficiency: he loved publicity.

The taste for the limelight was first developed at Poughkeepsie where Liddy and Rosenblatt became serious rivals—each wanted the DA's job, which had just fallen vacant. They seized on the issue of drugs, posed by the presence of Dr. Timothy Leary, the acid trippers' guru, in nearby Milbrook. Recalling this wacky era, Noel Tepper, a Poughkeepsie lawyer, said, "It got to be real Keystone Cops stuff with both of them trying to cash in on Leary's notoriety." In 1966 Liddy upstaged his rival by taking public credit for the arrest of Leary, an enterprise in which, according to an associate, his role was "almost nonexistent."

Liddy's courtroom style was a unique echo of the era before the West was won. On his crime-busting rounds he would invariably wear a pistol either under his shoulder or tucked into his belt, and he once fired a gun during an impassioned plea in the courtroom of county judge Raymon Barratta. It went off accidentally as he seized it, in a dramatic gesture, from the evidence table in front of him. "The jurors were terribly startled," said the judge. On another occasion, while prosecuting a man accused of assault with a wooden board, Liddy grasped the key exhibit, the wooden board, and emphasised a legal point by smashing it down on the rail in front of the jury. Liddy was sent a bill for damage to the courtroom.

In 1968 Liddy contested the Republican nomination in New York's 28th Congressional District. Poughkeepsie had never seen anything quite like it. On the stump, Liddy gave the impression that only he stood between Poughkeepsie and Gomorrah, afflicted as it was with a rising tide of drug freaks and crypto-Communists. He used to climax his public appearances by stripping off his jacket and revealing the answer to it all— a shoulder holster complete with firearm. "He knows the answer is law and order, not weak-kneed sociology," read his campaign literature. "Gordon Liddy doesn't bail them out—he puts them in." Poughkeepsie Republicans awarded their nomination to a somewhat less ferocious figure named Hamilton Fish, but Liddy was not beaten yet; he popped up again before the Congressional elections as the candidate of the Conservative Party. It was time to make a deal. Liddy withdrew from the race, helping Fish to win by five thousand votes, and for this uncharacteristic exercise in self-effacement he received the enthusiastic sponsorship of the local Republican establishment for a job in Washington. Mr. Liddy came to town, carrying his gun collection, to work in the Bureau of Narcotics and Firearms Control in the Treasury Department.

His first work was on Operation Intercept, a drug-control program designed to try and stop the flow of heroin and marijuana across the border from Mexico. His task was to travel down into Arizona and New Mexico and brief the local undercover agents on their work and on the program as a whole. He is said to have done this quite well: he is a very forceful speaker, and back home in Poughkeepsie the local paper ran the admiring headline, "Liddy Helps in U.S. Effort to Slow Drugs from Mexico."

Operation Intercept was in fact more ballyhoo than anything else; it involved stepped-up watches on the border which aggrieved the tourists, irritated the local customs agents, and made little difference to the drug traffic—it went by sea. Still, those press photographs of sweaty queues at the Mexican border seemed to be evidence that the government was doing something about the drug menace. Egil Krogh, the young, impressionable aide who was coordinating the White House-staff end of Operation Intercept, was impressed.

Within the Treasury Department, however, Liddy's colleagues were finding him a pain. They could stand the self-glorification and even admire some of his more imaginative ideas, but he did not seem to understand the need for bureaucratic restraint. An associate remembers him as that somewhat irksome figure—"a staff man who kept trying to set policy." While at the Bureau, one of his duties brought him into close contact with the National Rifle Association. In theory, he was supposed to induce its members to accept modest legislation for further control of firearms, but in practice he found it more congenial to speak for rather than against the NRA. When his superior in the Treasury Department, Eugene T. Rossides, objected to the closeness of this relationship, Liddy went behind his back to his new-found friend in the White House, Egil Krogh. Krogh advised Rossides to be patient: Liddy had ability; all he needed was a little guidance.

In April, 1971, Liddy went too far. At the hundredth-anniversary celebration of the NRA, Liddy made an unauthorised speech in lyrical praise of gun ownership ("This Administration" said Liddy, "does not confuse the forty million law-abiding, responsible Americans who rightly own firearms with criminals"). Rossides, brushing aside pleas for further clemency from Krogh, fired Liddy. "This was the last straw," said a colleague. "We just couldn't control him." Krogh, nonetheless, was anxious to retain Liddy's talents in the administration. On July 19, Liddy, the uncontrollable law-enforcement officer, joined Hunt, the superannuated spy, to form the operational nucleus of President Nixon's super-secret Special Investigation Unit.

Anything that the Liddy-Hunt duo might do was bound to be imaginative, but, on the basis of their track records, it was not likely to be overdelicate, especially when it involved a man they regarded as an arch traitor to everything they held dear—Daniel Ellsberg, the latest hero of the antiwar radicals.

CHAPTER 6

Mission Improbable

THE NEW undercover men needed new identities. This was more of a problem than it sounds. Outside the more rarefied echelons of the criminal establishment, there were only two specialised sources for phony documentation—the FBI and the CIA—and both presented difficulties. At the FBI, J. Edgar Hoover, still fuming over "the bag job" done on his files, was in no mood to do any extracurricular favours for the White House; while the CIA, under the terms of its founding statute, was specifically precluded from any involvement in domestic-intelligence operations.

It was a time for re-activating old friendships with elaborate caution. One of Nixon's older friends in Washington was Gen. Robert Everton Cushman, Jr., the man he had appointed as Dick Helms's deputy at the CIA. Back in the late fifties, Cushman, a Marine combat veteran, had served for four years as Nixon's chief adviser on national security and acted as the Vice-President's liaison officer with the CIA and NSC during the early planning stages of the Bay of Pigs operation. His diligence in this role was said to be one of the reasons for his appointment as the CIA's Deputy Director. Cushman also knew Hunt quite well, and John Ehrlichman very well. Early in July, 1971, Ehrlichman called Cushman with a studiously vague request.

Ehrlichman informed the general that the White House wanted Howard Hunt ("a bona fide employee, a consultant on security matters") to be given some assistance by the agency. Mr. Hunt would be around to see him in the near future. Cushman said that he would see what he could do to oblige the President.

Cushman, however, now owed career loyalties to the CIA, and was not entirely comfortable with the request. Nor was Director Helms. But as no mention of anything illegal had been made, they decided to assist the White House, as far as they could, and in the process try to find out exactly what was going on. Hunt came round to see Cushman at the CIA headquarters in Langley, Virginia, on July 22 and, as a precautionary measure, Cushman did something he rarely did for routine interviews: he flicked on his hidden tape recorder without telling his visitor. Two years later in the rich effluent produced by the Senate Watergate hearings, the transcript of the conversation was put in evidence. It is a tantalising document, flawed at certain sensitive parts by the convenient frequency of airplane noise, but as a record of how two mistrustful spymen go about their business while trying to pump one another for more information, it is a minor classic. Cushman opens the proceedings with: "Hey, good to see you. Come on in, have a seat."

HUNT: Could we make this just the two of us?
GENERAL CUSHMAN: All right, sure. We certainly can.
HUNT: Thank you very much. I've been charged with quite a highly sensitive mission by the White House to visit and elicit information from an individual whose ideology we aren't entirely sure of, and for that purpose they asked me to come over here and see if you could get me two things: flash alias documentation, which wouldn't have to [it's ——— to be backstopped ———] and some degree of physical disguise, for a onetime op—in and out.
GENERAL CUSHMAN: I don't see why we can't.
HUNT: We'll keep it as closely held as possible. I don't know how you or your cover people want to work it, but what I would like would be to meet somebody in a safe house [Note: plane comes over at this point, and words are very indistinct.] physical disguise. We're planning on [traveling] either Saturday or Sunday. Tomorrow afternoon probably would be the earliest it could be accomplished, so if somebody could do it by tomorrow afternoon, it would be a great job.
Well, you're looking very well.
GENERAL CUSHMAN: Well, it's a nice job.

After they tell each other how they manage to keep fit (Hunt worked-out in a gym; Cushman jogged), Cushman asks:

Say, I can get in touch with you at the White House, can't I? [To tell you] what address to go to, and so forth.

HUNT: Right. So we can lay on—you think tomorrow afternoon is ample time?

GENERAL CUSHMAN: I'll give it a try, yes. I haven't talked to anybody yet. I suppose they can do it. I haven't been in this business before, haven't had to.

HUNT: Well, Ehrlichman said that you were the—

GENERAL CUSHMAN: Yes, he called me. I mean I haven't been in the cover business, so I don't know if they operate real fast, but I suppose they do.

HUNT: Well, I know they can.

GENERAL CUSHMAN: Yes, I suppose they [————]

HUNT: It's just a question of getting some—some physical disguise.

GENERAL CUSHMAN: What do you need? That will be the first thing they'll ask.

HUNT: Well, I'll need, let's see, what have I got here? I probably need just a driver's license and some pocket litter.

GENERAL CUSHMAN: Driver's license—

HUNT: Driver's license in any state at all, I don't care; some pocket litter of some sort, [————] pretty standard stuff.

GENERAL CUSHMAN: Pocket litter?

HUNT: Yes, that's what they call it.

They agree that Hunt should pick up the gear in an anonymous CIA apartment downtown, and Hunt assures Cushman:

I'm convinced that the reason we're doing all this is for a good purpose.

GENERAL CUSHMAN: Yes.

HUNT: An essential purpose.

GENERAL CUSHMAN: If you see John Ehrlichman, say hello for me.

HUNT: I will indeed. [I expect to see him tomorrow.]

GENERAL CUSHMAN: He's an old friend of mine from previous days. He's got a full platter too.

HUNT: Oh, that he does.

GENERAL CUSHMAN: How's that Domestic Council working out? You don't hear about it much in this business.

HUNT: It's working out pretty well. Of course, two things that have really electrified the White—and I don't know why I'm telling you this, because your contacts are undoubtedly much higher than mine over there—but, the Pentagon Papers, of course.

GENERAL CUSHMAN: Well, John—I think John is in charge of the security overhaul, isn't he?

HUNT: That's right.

GENERAL CUSHMAN: Well, I guess that's right. It's sort of a domestic problem rather than a Kissinger problem.

HUNT: [That it is indeed.] . . .

On the day after this conversation, a representative of the
CIA's Technical Services Division rang Hunt and told him to
go to a CIA "safe house" on Massachusetts Avenue, where he
would be provided with the necessary tools of the trade. These
included a driver's license, a Social Security card, several association membership cards—all in the name of "Edward Joseph
Warren"; a speech alteration device shaped like the upper
plate of a set of dentures; and a reddish-brown wig. After receiving these *objets d'espionage*, Hunt fixed up a second
meeting and obtained more false papers for Liddy—made out
in the name of George Leonard—and a miniature camera
concealed in a tobacco pouch. But tricking out Hunt and
Liddy was to be only the beginning of the new White House
demands on the CIA.

In pursuit of all they could find on Daniel Ellsberg's associates and motives, the White House unit came up with the
idea of running a fine-tooth comb through Ellsberg's medical
history. Around the end of July the Special Investigations Unit
discovered, through copies of FBI reports that were being
passed on to the White House, that Ellsberg had been under
psychoanalysis for two years. On July 20 two FBI agents
visited the psychiatrist, Dr. Lewis J. Fielding, in Beverly Hills,
Los Angeles, and raised the subject of his old patient. After
consulting his attorney, Dr. Fielding told the FBI that he did
not feel that he could violate the confidentiality of the doctor-
patient relationship. And as Ellsberg's treatment related to a
period well before the Pentagon Papers were leaked, neither
Dr. Fielding's memory nor his files could be much help in determining how they were filched from the government. The
FBI agents filed a routine report, and that ended the matter as
far as the Bureau was concerned. But for the "plumbers" it
was the real starting point.

The idea of doing "a bag job" on Ellsberg's psychiatric files
began to fascinate the men in Room 16 of the Executive Office
Building. In the meantime, there was still more that could be
dredged from the official agencies, if they could be persuaded
to cooperate. The CIA had for many years run a psychiatric
division which specialised in analysis of behavioral patterns;
its reports were designed to assist American policy-makers in
face-to-face confrontations with foreign leaders. John Kennedy, for example, had a CIA "psychological profile" done of

Nikita Khrushchev before meeting the Soviet leader in Vienna in 1961. But it was, under the terms of the CIA's charter, a service that was designed for export only. Only one such profile had been done on an American citizen, and that was on Captain Lloyd Bucher of the *Pueblo* spy-ship after he had been captured by the North Koreans. It was a rather exceptional case. In late July, David Young of the "plumber" unit asked the CIA to regard Daniel Ellsberg as another exception.

Richard Helms approved the project, even though the CIA's Dr. John R. Tietjen, chief of medical services, and Dr. Bernard Malloy, head of the psychiatric division, both had what they later described as "apprehensions" about it. Still, it was a request direct from the White House and, as Helms observed wryly before a Senate committee two years later, "until recently it was not a crime to deal with the President of the United States."

For their "profile" of Ellsberg the CIA collated material from the press and selected State Department and FBI memoranda. The report they produced, in early August, was not exactly what the White House Unit had hoped for. On balance, it was complimentary to the man they regarded as a traitor. The report stated that, given the fragmentary nature of the information on Ellsberg, it could not be considered "definitive," but its preliminary finding was: "There is nothing to suggest in the material reviewed that the subject suffers from a serious mental disorder in the sense of being psychotic or out of touch with reality." Ellsberg was described as an intense, brilliant man of great flair and zeal. But it noted that people who lived with an image of themselves as "bright young men" often experienced difficulties in the years between thirty-five and forty-five. "The evidence reviewed suggests that this was so for Ellsberg, a man whose career had taken off like a rocket but who found himself at midlife not nearly having achieved the prominence and success he expected and desired. Thus, it may well have been an intensified need to achieve significance that impelled him to release the Pentagon Papers."

But beyond the problems of an aging bright young man, there could have been a more idealistic motivation for his action. The report continued:

There is no suggestion that the subject thought anything treasonous in his act. Rather he seemed to be responding to what he deemed a higher order of patriotism. His exclusion [from the published portion of the Pentagon Papers] of the three volumes of the papers concerned with the secret negotiations would seem to support this.

Many of the subject's own words would confirm the impression that he saw himself as having a special mission, and indeed as bearing a special responsibility. On several occasions he castigated himself for not releasing the papers earlier, observing that since he first brought them to the attention of the Senate Foreign Relations Committee [back in 1969], there had been "two invasions," more than nine thousand American lives lost, and hundreds of thousands of Vietnamese deaths.

He also on several occasions had suggested quite strongly that his action will not only alter the shape of the Vietnam war, but will materially influence the conduct of our foreign policy and the relationship between the people and the Government.

The stuff about "higher order of patriotism" and "special missions" did not much please the CIA's customers in the White House. On August 11, Krogh and Young sent Ehrlichman a memorandum in which they described the profile as "very superficial" and outlined their determination to get a better service—"We will meet tomorrow with the head psychiatrist, Dr. Bernard Malloy, to impress upon him the detail and depth we expect." But Krogh and Young reckoned that the CIA and, more importantly, the White House could only do a proper job on Ellsberg if they had access to his psychiatrist's reports. "In this connection," they wrote, "*we would recommend* that a covert operation be undertaken to examine all the medical files still held by Ellsberg's psychiatrist covering the two-year period in which he was undergoing analysis." Underneath this recommendation was typed "Approve _____ Disapprove _____." Ehrlichman returned the memo with an "E" after "Approve" and the notation: "If done under your assurance that it is not traceable."

In order to assure their employers of that requirement, Hunt and Liddy, suitably disguised, flew out to Los Angeles on August 25. Their mission was to conduct, in Hunt's touchingly bureaucratic phraseology, "a preliminary vulnerability and feasibility study" of Dr. Fielding's premises. In the more recognisable language of the trade, they cased the joint. That evening Hunt opened his tobacco pouch and photographed the outside of 450 North Bedford Drive, with Liddy standing beside the doctor's brass nameplate. Hunt then calmly walked into Dr. Fielding's office in Room 212, reassured the cleaning lady with the words "I am a doctor," and took some more shots. A drive out to Dr. Fielding's home, carefully timed, completed the study. Before leaving Los Angeles, Hunt called the CIA and arranged that they should be met at Dulles Airport as they stepped off the "red-eye special" the following morning. There Hunt gave his CIA contact the rolls of film and asked that they be developed and printed as soon as possible.

Hunt was given the prints that afternoon and rapidly convinced his administrative masters that "surreptitious entry" would be no problem. On the same day, Young sent another memo to Ehrlichman outlining progress on the Ellsberg project and proposing that they try and set up a Congressional investigation on the Papers case. "We have already," Young affirmed, "started on a negative press image of Ellsberg. If the present Liddy/Hunt project is successful, it will be absolutely essential to have an overall game plan developed for its use in conjunction with the Congressional investigation." The subtle deterioration that seemed to overtake all White House enterprises in the security field was already far advanced; what had started out as a leak-plugging operation was being transmuted into a smear campaign based, or hopefully based, on stolen medical files. Hunt and Liddy received their marching orders for the burglary but were told to make sure that the actual entry was performed by people who could not in any way be connected with the White House. Hunt already had candidates for the job.

As history had, in a sense, stopped for Hunt at the time of the Bay of Pigs invasion, nothing was more natural than that he should turn to the comrades who served with him in the high and hopeful days before John Kennedy spoiled everything. He had already picked up on some of his old contacts. In April, 1971, Hunt and his wife had gone to Miami to renew acquaintance with fellow veterans who were meeting for a reunion on the tenth anniversary of the invasion. On the day before the dinner, Hunt dropped by the home of an old friend and left his address at a Miami Beach hotel with the note: "If you are the same Barker I once knew, contact me. Howard."

It was indeed the same Barker. The Barker who had been born in Cuba in 1917 and registered at the Embassy as an American citizen, child of American parents. The Barker who was educated half in America, half in Cuba, who loved Cuba with the same ferocity as he loved the United States, who signed up for the Army Air Corps the Monday after Pearl Harbour to become the first Cuban-American to volunteer during the Second World War. The Barker who, as a result, spent sixteen months in a German POW camp, who joined the Cuban police force after the war was over, and who was recruited, at the U.S. Embassy in Havana, to work for the CIA, after Castro seized power.

It was the same Barker who, using the code name "Macho," had acted as paymaster to the Cuban "freedom fighters" and as principal assistant to Hunt (then "Eduardo") during the invasion's planning period. Time had thickened both "Macho" and "Eduardo," but when they got together again to discuss the old days over lunch on April 16, 1971, the years slipped away; they still shared the same enthusiasms.

Four months later Hunt was back in Miami again with a proposition for his old friend: would he be willing to assist on a "national security" matter, working with an organization that was "above both the CIA and the FBI"? Although Barker was a busy man, running a real-estate agency with a sales staff of ten people, he was overjoyed at the opportunity for further service. He innocently believed that such work might one day help in obtaining White House aid for the liberation of Cuba. Barker also produced, from his own sales staff, two more Cuban-exile recruits for the new cause—Felipe DeDiego, a man who, according to Barker, had successfully stolen vital secret documents from Castro's government, and Eugenio R. Martinez, another Bay of Pigs veteran credited by Barker with "over 300 infiltrations into Castro's Cuba." (Martinez still picked up a $100-a-month retainer from the CIA for information on the Cuban scene.) The cast of burglars, for Watergate as well as for Dr. Fielding, was assembling.

The level of frankness between the various actors in the drama was never very high. In August Hunt told Barker only that the operation involved discovering information about a traitor who was passing information to the Soviet Embassy. (It was rumoured that a set of the Pentagon Papers had been delivered to the Soviet Embassy after publication had started in the *New York Times*. There was no evidence linking Ellsberg with such a delivery.) It was not until the three Cuban-

Americans had actually flown to Los Angeles and registered, under assumed names, at the Beverly Hilton Hotel, that Hunt told them what they were supposed to do and mentioned to them the name of Daniel Ellsberg.

At nine in the evening of September 3, they all went to work. Two of the Miami team, wearing delivery men's overalls and carrying a large green suitcase covered with "Air Express" stickers and marked "Rush to Dr. Fielding," went round to the psychiatrist's office. They were let in by the cleaning staff and allowed to deposit the suitcase. Before leaving they punched the unlocking button on the inside of his office door. Hunt, meantime, was staked outside Dr. Fielding's house with his walkie-talkie at the ready in case the psychiatrist decided to pay a surprise visit to his office. There was nothing to worry about; the doctor had an early night. "I more or less put him to bed," Hunt said later. Back in downtown Beverly Hills he linked up with Liddy, who was cruising around in a hired car, on the lookout for cops.

Around midnight the three Miami men went in, using a glass-cutter and masking tape on a ground-floor window, and forcing the lock on Fielding's office door (the cleaning staff had thoughtfully relocked it). Out of the green suitcase they lifted a 35-mm camera, a spotlight, and some film, but it turned out that there was not much to photograph. The only trace of Ellsberg they found was his name in an address book. This was photographed along with the ransacked file cabinets, as evidence for their superiors that they had tried hard.

By 4 A.M. the entry team and the lookouts were all back in the Beverly Hilton with their meager findings. Liddy called Krogh (it was then 7 A.M. Washington time) and told him that they had entered without being detected, nothing more. It was a "clean job." The task of breaking the dismal news that it was without tangible results was left to Hunt on his return to Washington. Ehrlichman told them not to do it again.

This was a bad patch in Hunt's new career. Not only had the burglary, for which he had vigorously lobbied, proved useless, but he had also overstrained the cooperation of the CIA. Although the CIA apparently knew nothing about the burglary itself, it was finding his requests for help increasingly unreasonable. In August he had asked the agency for a back-stopped address and a phone contact in New York, but had been told this was impossible as it might compromise the agency. When he also asked that the CIA transfer a particular secretary from Paris to work with him, he confirmed a growing impression among the agency's top executives that he was involved in more than the "one-time op" for which they had originally agreed to render assistance. Helms told his deputy, General Cushman, to make it clear to the White House that in future Hunt would be persona non grata with the CIA and would receive no further assistance. On August 27, Cushman broke the news to Ehrlichman; he seemed to take it like a man.

By this time, however, Hunt was proving himself indispensable to the White House for other reasons. By September he had not only taken over the old Caulfield-Ulasewicz function of dredging the Chappaquiddick mud, he was also working on a bright idea for the White House that had literally nothing to do with national security but had a lot to do with rewriting history in a manner that might suit President Nixon's renewed candidacy if a Kennedy was in opposition—he was forging, with helpful access to the State Department files, two cables that implicated President Kennedy in the assassination of Ngo Dinh Diem, the President of South Vietnam, in November, 1963.

Oddly enough, it was President Nixon who publicly called to mind the murky episode of the Diem coup. On September 16, he gave one of his press conferences—which, rare today, were then merely unusual. It was a period when some comment was being aroused, at least on the Op-Ed pages of the liberal press, by the one-man presidential election campaign that was then being waged by Nguyen Van Thieu in South Vietnam. Given that one of the main official rationalisations for the U.S. presence in Vietnam was the need to assist the development of "democracy," and given that democracy has often been thought to involve electoral choice, the editorial comment seemed reasonable. Even Senator Jackson, one of the more hawkish of the President's war supporters amongst the Democrats, had suggested that the United States might be in a position to exert discreet pressure upon President Thieu to observe at least some of the ground rules. Questioned by Peter Lisagor of the Chicago *Daily News* about Senator Jackson's statement and about what if anything Washington should do in this situation, President Nixon observed, "If what the Senator is suggesting is that the United States should use its leverage now to overthrow

Thieu, I would remind all concerned that the way we got into Vietnam was through overthrowing Diem, and the complicity in the murder of Diem; and the way to get out of Vietnam, in my opinion, is not to overthrow Thieu."

The remark drew little attention at the time, but it was fairly startling. The Pentagon Papers published that June had confirmed what many people already believed—that the U.S. had had a role in the overthrow of President Diem in 1963, but till now no responsible official had ever publicly suggested that the U.S. government was guilty of complicity in his murder.

Shortly after this press conference, Hunt—who, as part of his duties, had been comparing the "leaked" Pentagon Papers with the original official documentation—had a chat with his paymaster, Chuck Colson, about the direct evidence of President Kennedy's complicity in Diem's murder. According to Hunt, he told Colson that the complicity might be deduced "inferentially" from certain State Department cables which he then showed the President's Special Counsel. He recalls the following subsequent exchange, initiated by Colson.

"Do you think you could improve on them?"

"Yes, I probably could, but not without technical assistance."

"Well, we won't be able to give you any technical help. This is too hot. See what you can do on your own."

Using a razor blade and the Xerox machine in the Executive Office Building basement, Hunt managed to transpose the bottom line of an original cable which carried the signatures of the releasing reviewing officers and the originating officers on a State Department message to the U.S. Embassy in Saigon. Hunt then, from his own fertile imagination, composed two phony communications to go with the authenticating details. One, with the date October 29, 1963, three days before the assassination, started: "At highest-level meeting today, decision reluctantly made that neither you or Harkins [General Paul Harkins, the commander of U.S. forces in Vietnam] should intervene in behalf of Diem or Nhu [the President's brother] in event they seek asylum."

Hunt showed Colson the results of his work and, according to Hunt, Colson expressed satisfaction. Much later, when this grotesque enterprise surfaced publicly, Colson denied asking Hunt to commit forgery, though he felt it was "entirely possible that Hunt misunderstood something I said." What is certain is the fact that in October, Colson got in touch with

William Lambert, an experienced investigative reporter with *Time* magazine. Colson asked Lambert if he had noticed Nixon's comments about the Diem assassination and suggested: "There's a big story there." Colson steered Lambert in the direction of E. Howard Hunt for details.

Fortunately, Lambert was a shrewd enough reporter not to run a story on this evidence (Hunt made it clear that the "cables" could not be taken away and could only be copied by hand for publication purposes); though had Lambert been able to follow his enquiries through to an ultimate conclusion, it seems, with hindsight, that the late President Kennedy would have emerged with more credit from this episode than the incumbent President Nixon. After this vain attempt at a posthumous smear on the Kennedy administration, the forged cables were put in Hunt's safe at the White House, where they lay for another eight months, virtually forgotten and ticking away like a time bomb.

While Hunt and Liddy were establishing themselves as indispensable White House operators, various strategic changes were taking place in the foreign intelligence community. As part of his determination to improve the service of the traditional agencies, President Nixon commissioned a secret study of the problem by James R. Schlesinger, then assistant director of the Office of Management and Budget and a man with a reputation as an incisive executive. Schlesinger saw the problem as essentially one of leadership and communication—a view that was earnestly endorsed by the White House. The combined results of Schlesinger's study and White House thinking on this subject was a set of reforms which were publicly unveiled on November 4, 1971. Most people were impressed.

Richard Helms was given what President Nixon described as "an enhanced leadership role" in streamlining the various fiefdoms in the intelligence community. The move was widely construed as a response to public complaints about the rising cost of the nation's "invisible government." By 1971, the intelligence community numbered some 200,000 people, dotted around a dozen or so different departments and agencies—the Pentagon, for example, maintained large intelligence staffs for the three separate services as well as the DIA. Total expenditure on this massive information-gathering operation was around $6 billion a year, of which almost half was spent on high-cost technological projects like satellite reconnaissance. (The CIA's annual budget was in the region of $750 million.)

Although public emphasis was placed on the cost-cutting aspects of the scheme, experienced observers of the bureaucracy were more intrigued by some of the structural changes. As part of the new reform "package," the White House set up a National Security Intelligence Committee, chaired by Henry Kissinger, to sift Helms's new budgetary recommendations and advise him on what intelligence the President needed to make foreign-policy decisions. To help Kissinger in this job, a Net Assessment Group, comprising members of his NSC staff, was set up to review all intelligence and assess the relative strengths of various world powers, in particular the U.S. and the Soviet Union. Although most contemporary press accounts wrote up Dick Helms as the new "super spymaster," it was Kissinger who was assuming this role. In fact, Helms's position in the bureaucracy of the invisible government became more precarious than ever. His new job effectively removed him from day-to-day management of his secure base in the CIA and placed him in a role that was unlikely to win friends in the other agencies. Budget-cutters are not enormously popular at the best of times, and Dick Helms was about the last man the Pentagon wanted puddling around their intelligence operation. At that time the DIA was engaged in one of its running battles with the CIA's analysts over the capability of Soviet strategic missilery—the DIA thought the Russians were going for a "first strike" capability; the CIA saw the Soviet buildup as "defensive."

The reason for the structural changes was officially explained by the need to improve the "quality" of intelligence reporting and analysis. In background briefings for the press, the White House indicated that it was tired of what it felt were wordy, imprecise, and often contradictory reports emanating from the intelligence community. It had been particularly irritated by the conflicting estimates that had delayed starting the Strategic Arms Limitation Talks, the centrepiece of the Nixon-Kissinger policy of detente with the Soviet Union. Kissinger's NSC group had spent four months ironing out the discrepancies between the various agencies on how well the U.S. could detect possible Soviet violations of an arms-control agreement. These irritations, added to the presumed "failures" of the CIA's current intelligence in Southeast Asia, had dictated the White House drive for a better-coordinated and more responsive intelligence community.

In the general chorus of approval for the proposals, some anguished squeals from the Pentagon could be heard. Deputy Defense Secretary David Packard went sourly on the record about intelligence "coordination" by the White House. Packard acknowledged that there were valid criticisms of overspending and even inaccuracy by the intelligence agencies, but he did not like the solution to the problem: "There have been people that think if we just had someone over in the White House to ride herd on this overall intelligence, that things would be improved. . . . After having experience with a lot of people in the White House the last couple of years trying to coordinate all kinds of things, I think if anything, we need a little less coordination from that point than more." Packard's prophetic voice, however, was a minority one which, in some ways, assisted public acceptance of the reorganisation. Many liberal commentators assumed that if the new shoe was not a comfortable fit for the Pentagon, then it must be well designed. The Pentagon, after all, was no friend of liberalism; its apparent subordination to the new Kissinger-Helms axis was reckoned, on balance, to be "a good thing."

Congress was more cautious in its attitude. Two of the most sophisticated observers of the secret world, Senator Stuart Symington of Missouri and Senator William Fulbright of Arkansas, were perturbed on grounds of accountability. They saw in the structural changes the beginnings of a subtle attempt to wrest from Congress its oversight responsibilities in intelligence affairs. This was scarcely an issue that would ignite the nation, particularly as Congress had never shown itself very vigorous in its watchdog function, but it represented an important shift in constitutional power.

Helms, as director of the CIA, was accountable to Congress and, within the constrained limits imposed by his job, was reckoned one of the more candid department heads in testimony before the various Senate committees. Symington and Fulbright perceived that the real effect of the reforms was to erode Helms's authority and draw all the intelligence threads together into the hands of Henry Kissinger who, as a White House staff member, was protected from congressional questioning under the doctrine of executive privilege. Even so, the Senators' criticisms were restrained; it is, of course, difficult for a politician to come out strongly against a program that promises improved quality for less money.

The beguiling aspects of the reforms concealed from most eyes the fact that the whole enterprise was constructed on a fallacious premise—that there is such a thing as "objective" analysis of intelligence data on which all the agencies could agree. Indeed, in a large intelligence community, disputes over analysis are a sign of health rather than incompetence. Since most high-level intelligence analysis concerns predictions about the intentions of another country, raw facts, though crucially important, are helpful only up to a point. The skill of the analyst is in making hypothetical judgments of what the data mean; this involves assumptions which inevitably are influenced by the analyst's training and personal background—which is one of the main reasons why the CIA's civilian experts rarely agreed with the DIA's military staff. Sometimes the analyst's job requires him to tell his political masters things they would rather not know or, to borrow Lyndon Johnson's graphic image, to upset the policy-makers' pail of milk. This goes against the grain of a career bureaucrat's natural desire to please his superiors, but without the readiness to displease, he becomes positively dangerous. The risk inherent in any highly centralised intelligence community is that it will simply become a machine for buttressing the assumptions of its political masters.

This might be no great problem in the service of political masters who themselves entertain a wide divergence of views, but Nixon's White House in 1971 was not such an establishment. Its denizens were in the grip of an increasingly monolithic set of assumptions about both foreign and domestic policy, which, for those who valued preferment, were beyond question. Most of those who had entertained more heterodox opinions had either left or been eased out; and with them had gone much of the feel for the complexity of human affairs. The White House, in short, was fast insulating itself from aspects of reality that did not accord with Nixon's "goals" as President. In foreign affairs, one of the key symptoms of this condition was the attempt to "coordinate" the intelligence community. In domestic affairs, its most chilling manifestation was something that became known as the White House "Enemies List."

CHAPTER 7

The Retribution List

BEFORE THE mantle of sanctimony settled on the Nixon administration, Walter Hickel, the Secretary of the Interior, could be relied on to liven up the proceedings. Back in 1938 he won the welterweight division of the Kansas Golden Gloves boxing championships before going on to strong-arm his way to a fortune in the construction business and to political eminence as Governor of Alaska. Both as businessman and politician he was a throwback to a more rugged, pre-Organization Man era. Loud-mouthed and shrewd, if he believed strongly in something he made sure everyone knew it. In conference he would pound the table, laugh raucously, and lace his points with lurid profanities. Generally he was not very demure. Washington did not change him.

He found George C. Scott's performance in the movie biography of General George Patton profoundly moving. "My God," said Hickel, after seeing the celluloid *Patton*, "that's me." It was, as it turned out, the only gut reaction he shared with his employer in the White House. *Patton* was the top film on the President's private viewing list—he watched it seven times—but Nixon could not abide Walter Hickel, his hero's fleshly equivalent. After Hickel publicly criticised the administration's reaction to student protest over the Cambodian invasion, it was obvious that he would have to go. But the manner of his leaving in November, 1970, after an embarrassing interview in the Oval Office, was puzzling to both men. Hickel later described it as follows: "He repeatedly referred to me as an adversary. Initially I took this as a compliment, because to me an adversary within an organization is a valuable asset. It was only after the President had used the term many times and with a disapproving inflection that I realized he considered an adversary an enemy. I could not understand why he would consider me an enemy."

Given this attitude at the summit, it was perhaps unsurprising that around the summer of 1971, Nixon's upper-level operatives in the White House and on the Committee to Re-Elect the President should start shuffling furtive memoranda back and forth on the general subject of "political enemies." Over the latter part of 1971 a file, entitled "Political Enemies Project," in the office of the President's Special Counsel, Charles Colson, expanded to a thickness of four inches; it included, of course, the name of Walter J. Hickel. When news of the enemies list surfaced publicly two years later, Colson was ready with an emollient explanation. It was, explained Colson, the counterpart of the "friends" list which was terribly helpful to the White House social office when it came to dishing out invitations and making appointments. "Frankly," Colson observed, "I think it is quite appropriate for the presidential staff not to want at a White House dinner, for example, someone who had signed an advertisement calling for the impeachment of the President or someone who had made a large contribution to defeat the President in a political campaign."

Frankly, Colson was being disingenuous. The real purpose of the list had nothing to do with preventing embarrassment at White House social occasions. It was the basis of a quite deliberate attempt to use the Federal bureaucracy to victimise people of whom the President and his aides did not approve. The purpose emerged with some clarity from a memorandum written by the President's Legal Counsel, John Dean, in August, 1971. Dean, who was Colson's principal helpmate on list-making, was informing Haldeman and Ehrlichman of the problems involved in getting the enterprise off the ground. He began:

This memorandum addresses the matter of how we can maximize the fact of our incumbency in dealing with persons known to be active in their opposition to our Administration. Stated a bit more bluntly—how can we use the available federal machinery to screw our political enemies.

Dean went on to say that what the enterprise required was a good coordinator whose function should be advertised internally. After this, the following strategies could be developed:

    —Key members of the staff could be requested to inform us as to who they feel we should be giving a hard time.

    —The project coordinator should then determine what sorts of dealings these individuals have with the Federal Government and how we can best screw them (e.g., grant availability, Federal contracts, litigation, prosecution, etc.).

    —The project coordinator then should have access to the full support of the top officials of the agency or departments in proceeding to deal with the individual.

After outlining these specific proposals for providing specified American citizens with inequality before the Federal bureaucracy and the law, he concludes with the recommendation that they should start with a limited set of names as a pilot test for the project. This would be valuable for three reasons:

    (1) A low visibility of the project is imperative; (2) it will be easier to accomplish something real if we don't over-expand our efforts; and (3) we can learn more about how to operate such an activity if we start small and build.

As far as it is possible to distinguish any underlying logic in the selection of the names, they fell into the following broad categories: Democratic money men, Vietnam "doves," active Democrats in show-biz, and a general mixed assortment of liberal academics and journalists with a few prominent lawyers and doctors thrown in for good measure. Only a handful could realistically be regarded, other than in the White House, as hard-core left-wingers. Indeed, at first glance, it looks like the Social Register of the Liberal Establishment, radic-chic rather than radical. But then George Wallace, bracketed as an "enemy" with the politician-poet Eugene McCarthy—surely the oddest political couple in history—was not exactly a limousine liberal, nor was the balding technocrat Ralph Weller, President of the Otis Elevator Company (as far as can be determined Weller's inclusion was determined by a malfunctioning of one of the Otis elevators installed in the San Clemente White House). And Congressman Wright Patman, a crusty fiscal conservative from Texas, did not seem to fit any category except that of a man who asks awkward questions. In

1970 he spoiled a $200-million loan guarantee offered by the Nixon administration to the tottering Penn Central Railroad Company. The offer was withdrawn when Patman disclosed in the House that the railroad was being represented by Mudge Rose (the old law firm of John Mitchell and Richard Nixon) and that Nixon had been a director of Investors Diversified Services, a major Penn Central stockholder.

At its peak, the enemies list contained the names of over two hundred individuals and eighteen organisations, loosely divided into different categories—political, trade unions, media, show-biz, and so on. The people listed were among the most distinguished in America, including the President of Yale, the Dean of Harvard Law School, one Nobel and at least four Pulitzer Prize winners, four ex-Cabinet ministers, two ex-Ambassadors, the former chairman of the U.S. Council of Economic Advisors, the chairman of IBM, and America's most colorful football player. Several had actually been on the payroll of the Nixon administration, among them Hickel and two former members of Kissinger's NSC staff, Morton Halperin and William Watts, who had resigned rather than take over the role of White House "coordinator" of the Cambodian invasion.

Some of the names were predictable enough, given the White House's broad definition of what constituted an enemy. The leading Democratic politicians were all there: Ted Kennedy, Ed Muskie, George McGovern, William Fulbright, and the fire-eating Congresswoman from New York, Bella Abzug. The entire Black membership of the House was there, as was John Lindsay, the immaculately WASP Mayor of New York City. Among the organisations to which the White House gave "enemy" status were "high profile" groups like the Black Panthers, Common Cause (a citizens' pressure group for social and political reform), and the National Student Association. The Brookings Institution made the list, as did the Farmers Union and the National Education Association. The media section was the most crowded of all; it accommodated a total of fifty-seven reporters, columnists, editors, television commentators, and occasional pundits who had publicly expressed something less than total enthusiasm for Richard Nixon and his administration. The big names were: Jack Anderson, James Reston, Daniel Schorr, Mary

McGrory. The *Washington Post,* the *New York Times* and
the St. Louis *Post-Dispatch* received special individual men-
tions.

The show-biz section embraced those glamorous figures
who would not follow the example of Bob Hope, Frank
Sinatra, Sammy Davis, Jr., and John Wayne by backing
Nixon. Jane Fonda and Paul Newman were naturals, both
vocal and active antiwar campaigners. Gregory Peck, Steve
McQueen, Barbra Streisand, and Carol Channing joined them
on the list.

Every section had its eccentricities, and sometimes absurd
mistakes. Joe Namath, the notoriously apolitical football
star, was listed as playing for the New York Giants; his team
is the Jets. Samuel Lambert, the National Education Association's president, voted for Nixon in 1968 and 1972; so did
many of his colleagues. The eminent scholar Professor Hans
Morgenthau was listed in mistake for Robert Morgenthau, a
former crime-busting U.S. Attorney. One of the reporters
named was dead.

The very diversity of those on the list indicates the random-
ness of White House political philosophy at that time. Put
in the same room, the "enemies" would probably end up by
shaking each other warmly by the throat, an indication of
perhaps the only basic characteristic they appear to have in
common: an ability to think for themselves. But as citizens of
a government that came to view political ideas as something
to be "packaged" and "sold," they were clearly dangerous.
What the list provides is a remarkable printout of the Nixon
administration's instinctive aggressiveness; those who were
not 100 percent for it were, by definition, against. The White
House had been cleansed of "adversaries"; now it was the
turn of the country.

On September 9, 1971, Colson's office, having delved in
the master list, came up with a list of twenty names for
special "go status." In view of Colson's later attempt to
dismiss the "enemies list" as a social convenience, it is an
interesting reflection on how the mind of the President's
Special Counsel worked. The names were listed "in priority
order" as:

1. Picker, Arnold M., United Artists Corporation, 929 Seventh
Avenue, New York, N.Y.: Top Muskie fund-raiser. Success here
could be both debilitating and very embarrassing to the Muskie

machine. If effort looks promising both Ruth and David Picker should be programed and then a follow-through with United Artists.

2. Barkan, Alexander E., national director of AFL-CIO's Committee on Political Education, Washington, D.C.: Without a doubt the most powerful political force programed against us in 1968 ($10 million, 4.6 million votes, 115 million pamphlets, 176,000 workers—all programed by Barkan's COPE—so says Teddy White in The Making of the President '68). We can expect the same effort this time.

3. Guthman, Ed, managing editor, L.A. *Times* [In fact, Guthman was national editor]: Guthman, former Kennedy aide, was a highly sophisticated hatchetman against us in '68. It is obvious he is the prime mover behind the current Key Biscayne effort. It is time to give him the message. [When asked, after the list became public, about the Key Biscayne effort behind which he was supposed to be the prime mover, Guthman said that he had "no idea" what it could be.]

4. Dane, Maxwell, Doyle, Dane and Bernbach, New York: The top Democratic advertising firm—they destroyed Goldwater in '64. They should be hit hard starting with Dane.

5. Charles Dyson, Dyson-Kissner Corporation, New York: Dyson and Larry O'Brien [chairman of the Democratic National Committee] were close business associates after '68. Dyson has huge business holdings and is presently deeply involved in the Businessman's Educational Fund which bankrolls a national radio network of 5-minute programs—anti-Nixon in character.

6. Stein, Howard, Dreyfus Corporation, New York: Heaviest contributor to [Eugene] McCarthy in '68 [when McCarthy was the leading antiwar presidential candidate]. If McCarthy goes, will do the same in '72. If not, Lindsay or McGovern will receive the funds.

7. Lowenstein, Allard, Long Island, New York: Guiding force behind the 18-year-old "Dump Nixon" vote drive. [Lowenstein also organised the successful "Dump Johnson" drive in 1968.]

8. Halperin, Morton [formerly one of Kissinger's senior NSC staff], leading executive at Common Cause; a scandal would be most helpful here.

9. Woodcock, Leonard, UAW, Detroit, Michigan: No comments necessary. [Woodcock was one of the leading antiwar advocates in the labor movement.]

10. S. Sterling Munro Jr., Senator [Henry M.] Jackson's aide, 711 Lamberton Drive, Silver Spring, Md.: We should give him a try. Positive results would stick a pin in Jackson's white hat. [Jackson was then shaping up as a potential candidate for the Democratic Party's presidential nomination.]

11. Feld, Bernard T., President, Council for a Livable World:

Heavy far-left funding. They will program an "all court press" against us in '72.

12. Davidoff, Sidney, New York City [Mayor John] Lindsay's top personal aide: a first-class SOB, wheeler-dealer, and suspected bagman. Positive results would really shake the Lindsay camp and Lindsay's plan to capture the youth vote [Lindsay was making presidential-candidate noises at that time]. Davidoff in charge.

13. Conyers, John, Congressman, Detroit: Coming on fast. Emerging as leading black anti-Nixon spokesman. Has known weakness for white females.

14. Lambert, Samuel M., President, National Educational Association: Has taken us on vis-à-vis Federal aid to parochial schools [a policy favoured by the President]—a '72 issue.

15. Mott, Stewart Rawlings, Mott Associates, New York: Nothing but big money for radic-lib candidates.

16. Dellums, Ronald, Congressman, California: Had extensive EMK-Tunney [Edward Kennedy and Senator John Tunney] support in his election bid. Success might help in California next year.

17. Schorr, Daniel, Columbia Broadcasting System, Washington: a real media enemy.

18. S. Harrison Dogole, 2011 Walnut Street, Philadelphia, Pa.: President of Globe Security Systems—fourth largest private detective agency in U.S. Heavy [Senator Hubert] Humphrey contributor. Could program his agency against us.

19. Paul Newman, California: Radic-lib causes. Heavy McCarthy involvement in '68. Used effectively in nationwide TV commercials. '72 involvement certain.

20. McCrory [a misspelling of McGrory], Mary, 2710 Macomb Street, Washington columnist: Daily hate-Nixon articles.

Several days after Colson's office had produced its top twenty, John Dean's office was hard at work on its short list. Most of the names overlapped with those on the Colson list, but there were some intriguing additions, among them Thomas Watson, the head of IBM, listed as a "Muskie backer"; Leonard Bernstein, the conductor and composer; Clark Gifford, a misspelling for Clark Clifford, Johnson's former Secretary of Defense; and Eugene Carson Blake, General Secretary of the World Council of Churches.

All were listed by Dean as persons "who have both the desire and the capability of harming us." All, by any reasonable estimate, were loyal, indeed patriotic, citizens of the Republic. Watson, the dangerous "Muskie backer," ended up by donating $300,000 to Nixon's re-election chest.

The problem of how to "screw" their "enemies" was never effectively solved by the White House staff—though it was not for want of trying. The story of Daniel Schorr, the top CBS correspondent in Washington, illustrates one aspect of the problem. On the Colson list, Schorr figured as "a real media enemy," and insofar as he is one of the most honest and incorruptible members of the permanent Washington press corps (James Reston described him as "a tough-minded and nosey old pro"), the term was probably justified. In August, 1971, according to John Dean, Haldeman's assistant Larry Higby "received a request from Mr. Haldeman when he was traveling on the President's plane, to direct the FBI to do an investigation of Schorr." Hoover agreed to this, but with private reservations about the wisdom of unnecessarily offending the media: he ordered what Dean later described as "a sort of full-field, wide-open investigation," which was discovered with the help of judicious leaks. The White House hurriedly put about the story that Schorr was being considered for a government job and that the investigation was designed to insure that there were no embarrassing skeletons in his cupboard before his appointment.

At a White House press conference on November 12, Ronald Ziegler earnestly assured the press corps that Nixon had felt that the Schorr affair had been handled in a "clumsy way." The President, he said, had decided that in future, people considered for government posts would be informed the FBI check was being carried out so that they could have the opportunity of declining the honor, should they so wish. In the meantime, Schorr stayed on the secret "enemies list." The Schorr episode, coming on top of so many other frustrations with the FBI, apparently reinforced the President's desire to do something about J. Edgar Hoover. Shortly before Christmas, 1971, Nixon invited Hoover over to the White House for a private chat about the FBI chief's retirement plans. Hoover, refusing to take the hint, said that he had none. After the meeting Hoover informed a friend that he had told the President that he was staying on "to protect him from those people around him."

Although the White House was keen to use all the Federal agencies against its enemies, the one most easily adaptable to political purposes was the Internal Revenue Service, with which almost all Americans—and certainly all the "enemies"

—came into contact. But again there were problems of recalcitrance in the bureaucracy. Even before the enemies list was composed, the White House had been trying to turn the IRS into an instrument of political attack. Back in 1969, acting on instructions from the President, the IRS had set up a secret Special Services Group—or, as it was later described, "a central intelligence-gathering facility"—whose purpose was "to receive and analyse all available information on organisations and individuals promoting 'extremist' views and philosophies." As far as the White House was concerned, the IRS's efforts in this direction were never very satisfactory. In September, 1970, the ineffable Tom Huston, fresh from his abortive effort to outwit Hoover and establish a secret police, addressed an irritated memorandum to Bob Haldeman about the slackness of the tax authority. "Nearly eighteen months ago," he reminded Haldeman, "the President indicated a desire for IRS to move against leftist organizations taking advantage of tax shelters. I have been pressing the IRS since that time to no avail."

Huston continued: "What we cannot do in a courtroom via criminal prosecutions to curtail the activities of some of these groups, IRS can do by administrative action. . . . Moreover, valuable intelligence-type information could be turned up by IRS as a result of their field audits." The attempt to use the IRS as an instrument of political repression foundered on a simple problem: left-wing tax avoidance was no different than the right-wing variety, except that, in most cases, smaller amounts of money were involved. If it was within the regulations, there was nothing the IRS career bureaucrats could do about it; their job was to administer the regulations, not make up new ones for different categories of citizenry.

As was often the case when the White House staff encountered difficulties, it was immediately assumed that the problem was one of faulty leadership. With the construction of the enemies list, the problem of "leadership" in the IRS became more pressing than ever. Once again, John Dean summed things up in a way that seemed persuasive to his political masters. The objective, he wrote, was to make the IRS "'politically responsive": it had become a "monstrous bureaucracy," dominated by Democrats, who persisted in frustrating every effort to proceed "in sensitive areas." More jobs for our boys was Dean's urgent recommendation.

The first step was getting rid of the Commissioner, a Georgia lawyer called Randolph Thrower. Back in 1970 Thrower had irritated the White House by refusing to give a job to John Caulfield, who as part of his investigative duties was exploring methods of involving the IRS in the enemy-screwing enterprise. In January, 1971, Thrower resigned for reasons that he described as "between me and the President." He later was replaced by Johnnie M. Walters, an Assistant Attorney General, hand-picked for his presumed loyalty to Nixonian ideals. The White House sat back and waited for results.

They did not arrive. Soon after his appointment, Dean was complaining bitterly to Haldeman that Walters was no better than Thrower. His memorandum noted that Walters "has not yet exercised leadership" and, worse, seemed strongly disinclined to do so. Dean advised: "Walters must be made to know that discreet political actions and investigations on behalf of the Administration are a firm requirement."

Jack Caulfield was even more severe. In a memorandum written for John Dean, he described the problem with the IRS as one involving "lack of guts and effort." This, he said, prevented crackdowns on the tax exemptions of left-wing organisations, access to information "about our political enemies," and the "stimulation" of special audits for chosen victims. "Walters should understand that when a request comes it is his responsibility to accomplish it—without the White House having to tell him how to do it."

The White House never did manage to bend the IRS commissioners to its will, but it made some use of a fallback tactic that Caulfield had discovered in his burrowings. It was possible to "stimulate" special audits without the Commissioner's knowing that they were being used. All it required was an anonymous letter to the "enemy's" local tax office, skillfully worded to convey exactly the amount of information which would compel the IRS, under its statute, to authorise an investigation. Several of the enemies found themselves subject of surprise tax audits in 1972. It is impossible to determine how many were the consequence of Jack Caulfield's ingenious idea, though it was certainly Caulfield who

advised the IRS to drop an audit on one of Nixon's friends—
the film star John Wayne.

What had started out as a grand strategy for "screwing"
political opponents tailed off into ad-hoc instances of vin-
dictiveness. In October, 1971, *Newsday*, the Long Island
newspaper, published a special issue devoted to the laby-
rinthine financial affairs of Nixon's best friend, Charles Bebe
Rebozo, the Cuban-born real-estate operator. "I got instructions," Dean said later, "that one of the authors of the
article should have some tax problems." Robert Greene, a
Newsday editor who had worked on the issue, found himself
the subject of a surprise audit. It cost him $100 in ac-
countancy fees, he says, "but I did not owe them a nickel."
In June, 1972, Colson sent Dean a memorandum suggesting
an audit of Harold J. Gibbons, the vice-president of the
Teamsters Union, whom he described as "an all-out enemy, a
McGovernite, ardently anti-Nixon. . . . one of three labor
leaders who were recently invited to Hanoi." Colson asked
if there was an "informer's fee," as he knew "a good cause
to which it can be donated." Gibbons was audited, and had
to pay a little more tax on travel-expense items.

Of all the Watergate ironies, perhaps the most curious is
the fact that the country owes a large debt to the taxman.
For the petty and pathetic end of the "enemies" enterprise
was due not to any outraged public debate but to the subtle
obstructions of career civil servants. It is still an almost
standard refrain of radical rhetoric, from both the left and
the right, that the bureaucracy is bad news: a monstrous
regiment of grey men armed with infinite lengths of red
tape which they use to throttle any hint of change. But that
part of the able bureaucrat's equipment that makes him
suspicious of novel ideas, however praiseworthy, has more
than a negative function: he can spot a really lousy idea
almost immediately. Fortunately for the radicals, as well as
everyone else, the IRS bureaucracy had such men during
Nixon's first term as President.

When the enemies list finally became public in June, 1973,
as part of John Dean's marathon testimony before the Senate
committee enquiring into Watergate, there were a lot of
jokes made. Mary McGrory, the Washington columnist, said
her telephone had not stopped ringing with calls from "jealous
friends who did not make it." Paul Newman said: "I am

sending Gordon Liddy to collect my award and I would like to thank John Mitchell, Maurice Stans, Jeb Magruder, and John Dean for making it all possible." Some hilarity at the revelation was of course in order. But it was Clark Clifford, the seasoned lawyer-politician, who made the real point. He said: "One of the first acts of a police state in gaining control of a government is to list the names of persons for liquidation. We have not got to that point yet. But here were people listed for retribution."

CHAPTER 8

Money, Money, Money

At his Senate confirmation hearings in 1969, Nixon's nominee for Attorney General assured Sam Ervin, the Democratic Senator for North Carolina, that he would be only a legal adviser and not a political adviser to the President. Even a man as trusting as Sam Ervin cannot have imagined that it was a promise that John Mitchell was going to keep. They were simply preserving, for the record, one of the necessary hypocrisies of politics.

The practice of appointing hard-nosed campaign supremos, rather than legal luminaries, as head of the Justice Department was strictly bipartisan. Harry Truman's Attorney General had been chairman of the Democratic National Committee. Dwight Eisenhower and John Kennedy both appointed their campaign managers. Since the Second World War only Lyndon Johnson had departed from the tradition (the cynics' explanation of this was that the Bobby Baker scandal, an embarrassing overhang from Johnson's former days as a senatorial wheeler-dealer, had scared him into an uncharacteristic concern for public propriety). When Nixon promoted his own campaign manager to the position of Attorney General, he was simply reestablishing a time-honoured practice. There was no mystery about the reason for this, though it was not one that politicians liked to shout about. While every department in Washington is in a position to grant favours, Justice is acknowledged to be the best vantage for overseeing the really big ones; and favours in politics mean a lot when campaign time comes around, not least in terms of money.

Money is not everything in American politics, but without it nobody gets very close to the starting line. According to a recent study by Herbert L. Alexander of the Citizens' Research Foundation in Princeton, the cost of the various political campaigns in 1968—presidential, senatorial, gubernatorial, and congressional—was a monumental $300 million, 50 percent more than in 1964. Although nobody has yet been able to compute the total sum for 1972, those studies that do exist indicate that the rate of political inflation maintained its momentum. Sample surveys, conducted by Common Cause, show that it took an average of $600,000 in contributions to finance campaigns for each Senate seat in 1972; the figure for Congressional elections was well over $80,000.

But these figures pale beside the investment required to elect a President. Of the $300 million spent in 1968, a third was spent by the various contenders for the presidency; the largest single sum—over $33 million—was spent on the campaign of the eventual winner, Richard Nixon. For his re-election attempt Nixon, of course, had the vast free personal publicity machine provided by the office of the Presidency itself. But, as his popularity sagged in the polls through the spring and summer of 1971, it seemed that this would not be enough. He would need money again—big money. To Attorney General John Mitchell, as he manipulated the growing cast of characters at the Committee to Re-Elect the President from his office in the Justice Department, this was a pressing concern.

In politics, as in everything else, attracting money for a potentially lost cause is a thankless task, but Mitchell was fortunate in one basic respect: big business liked Richard Nixon. Although Nixon himself has never exhibited any inordinate desire for personal wealth, he had always attracted the enthusiastic support of the rich and would-be-rich; in 1952 it was his fund from wealthy California backers that occasioned the famous "Checkers" crisis. Most businessmen considered that Nixon was a politician who understood their problems.

Mitchell was fortunate, too, in being able to draw on the talents of Herbert W. Kalmbach and Maurice H. Stans, both masters at the near-painless extraction of large wads of money. All they needed was a little leverage. By April 7, 1972, the date when a new campaign financing disclosure law came into effect, this remarkable team had succeeded in raising $19.4 million for disbursement by the Finance Committee to Re-Elect the President. It provided the very lifeblood of CREEP and, as it turned out, Watergate.

Later they went on to even greater fund-raising triumphs, until the grand total in the President's re-election chest stood at $55 million—the largest campaign fund ever recorded. But it is the money that was raised before April 7 that most interests us here, as these were the funds that were to determine the whole course of the election year. The initial spadework was done by Herbert Kalmbach, the President's personal lawyer and the original chairman of CREEP's finance committee.

Kalmbach, then forty-nine, was a large, amiable Californian who had come a very long way in a very short time. His acquaintance with Nixon had come about through a close friendship with Robert Finch dating back to their days together at UCLA. Finch, considered one of Nixon's more liberal friends, was the Secretary of Health, Education, and Welfare until, bloodied by a series of losing battles with Mitchell over school desegregation in the South, he bowed out to become a kind of floating "adviser" in the White House. As he was not comfortable with the hard-nosed apostles of the "new majority," his advice was rarely taken. But while Finch's star declined, that of his protégé assumed a new importance in the political firmament.

Back in 1968 Kalmbach had distinguished himself, as Maurice Stans's deputy on Nixon's campaign-finance committee, by raising $6 million through his own personal efforts. What was good for Nixon also proved good for the firm of Kalmbach, DeMarco, Knapp and Chillingworth, with offices in Los Angeles and Newport Beach, California. Before Nixon's victory, Kalmbach was a not very remarkable lawyer in a very rich community—Newport Beach is the Millionaire's Row of the Pacific Coast. His firm's clients included the Newport National Bank, Pacific Lighting, and other primarily local concerns. After Nixon assumed office, Kalmbach's practice suddenly blossomed, as representatives from organizations such as United Air Lines, the Marriott Corporation, the Music Corporation of America, and Travelers Insurance lined up for the elevator to his new top-floor office in the Irvine Towers. There, they encountered not only a magnificent view over the yachts in the Bay, but a man with that most precious of commodities for Corporate America—political access.

While the new corporate clients rolled in from one direction, new business from the White House rolled in from another. Kalmbach was the man with custody of the $1.9 million in unspent 1968 Republican campaign funds, part of which was used to irrigate the campaign of George Wallace's opponent in the Democratic primary for Governor of Alabama. Kalmbach also handled the sensitive details of Nixon's acquisition of the $1.4 million San Clemente property, which became known as the Western White House.

In January, 1971, four months before CREEP opened its doors to voluntary contributors in Washington, Kalmbach opened a special account at the Newport Beach branch of the Bank of America, located below his office in the Irvine Towers East. Into this account he deposited the election campaign float, a mite of $500,000 that would ultimately swell, in a variety of other banks, to over a hundred times the original stake. Even in those early days, Kalmbach showed an unusually keen desire to muddy the wake of incoming funds. Many of the deposits were made in the form of cashiers' checks which he purchased with cash at a branch of the Security Pacific National Bank in Irvine Towers West, just across the way.

For Kalmbach, most of 1971 was devoted to the gentle softening-up process that is such an important preliminary of effective fund-raising. He flew all over the country talking a mixture of business and politics to those who were most interested in the mix, the directors and chief executives of the major corporations. (Though it is illegal—but not unknown—for corporations to contribute directly to political campaigns, the big-money contributions come, unsurprisingly, from individuals on the boards of the big corporations.) At this stage Kalmbach was creating a climate of interest rather than putting on the pressure. But he did have an early run of luck with his contacts in the milk industry: the consumers of milk products were less fortunate.

In early March, 1971, the Secretary of Agriculture, Clifford Hardin, pegged price supports for "manufacturing milk," which is the basis of butter and cheese, at $4.66 per hundred pounds—the same as the preceding year. A price rise might be harmful, he said. The decision was a bitter disappointment to the industry. On March 22 a dairy industry political fund (The Trust for Agricultural Political Development—TAPE) donated $10,000 to Republican committees. The next day, sixteen industry leaders were invited to the White House to meet with Nixon and Hardin; they urged reconsideration of

the price-support peg. On the next day another dairy fund paid
a further $25,000 into Republican committees. On the next
day, Hardin announced that, after all, milk price supports
would go up—to $4.93 per hundred pounds. The dairy indus-
try then began to pump an estimated $422,500 into the Nixon
campaign effort.

The dairymen did not make their contributions in the sim-
plest fashion—by handing them straight over to regular Republican fund-raising committees or CREEP. Instead they used
a somewhat arcane loophole which allowed fund-raising committees established in the District of Columbia to forego disclosure of funds received if the money is not spent "for the purpose of influencing the election in two or more states." Secrecy
for the milkmen's money was maintained on the somewhat
dubious grounds (later challenged by Common Cause) that the
committee was supporting not Nixon's re-election, which of
course influenced forty-nine more states than the maximum
for nondisclosure, but his renomination as a candidate.

As is customary in the political-finance business, whether
Republican or Democratic, most of the contributions were
divided into sums of less than $3,000 and lodged in separate
committees—a mechanism that frees large donations from the
demands of the gift tax. Eventually some 450 such committees
operating on behalf of the Republican cause were set up in the
District of Columbia; the routine expertise required to establish
them was provided in some cases by Robert Bennett, director
of the Mullen public-relations agency that employed E. Howard Hunt as one of its ace copy-writers between "moonlight-
ing" jobs for the White House. The titles of the committees
stirred the imagination, even if their purpose was to confound
the taxman and confuse the campaign-finance analyst—Supporters of the American Dream, Americans United for Objective Reporting, Committee for Political Integrity, Organization of Sensible Citizens, and Americans United for Political
Awareness, perhaps the greatest triumph of the copy-writers'
art over practical reality. All that it was necessary to know
about these high-sounding dummy organisations was who were
the treasurers: many of them turned out to be employees of the
Union Trust Company of Washington, a Republican-minded
bank where a large part of the campaign funds were deposited
in 1971.

As 1971 turned into the new year, Kalmbach's efforts became a little more urgent. A new Federal Election Campaign Act was moving through the Congress (as slowly as Republicans and some Democrats could manage it) to replace the Federal Corrupt Practices Act of 1925, which Lyndon Johnson had correctly described as "more loophole than law." The old law, which allowed contributions of any size to remain anonymous at the donor's request, had always benefited the Republicans the most, and electoral-financing reform had long been the dream of Larry O'Brien, Chairman of the Democratic National Committee. And in 1971 it was more than a dream. With the DNC $6 million in the red, it was almost a practical necessity. On November 22, 1971, O'Brien scored a great and crafty success; the Senate attached to a tax bill, which Nixon regarded as vital to the economy, O'Brien's scheme to finance all federal elections from the U.S. Treasury. This would render obsolete the dedicated work of men such as Herbert Kalmbach and ensure that the bankrupt Democrats would have no money problems in 1972.

Because the tax bill was so crucial, many Congressional leaders considered that Nixon would never veto it and that the measure would be passed. His own economic advisers thought a veto would be catastrophic. But on November 30 Nixon met with John Mitchell and other members of his political, not his economic, staff to consider how to react to the time bomb. On the basis of this meeting Nixon decided to meet what he regarded as blackmail by the Democrats head on: he would veto the bill if it was sent to him with the election provision, no matter what the consequences. Ron Ziegler publicly announced the President's private thoughts that afternoon, and in the next couple of days Wilbur Mills, the all-powerful Chairman of the House Ways and Means Committee, who had supported the measure, decided the President was not bluffing and that without the tax cuts the economy would slump. On December 2 the House-Senate conferees on the bill dropped the election provision.

Nonetheless, the more modest Federal Election Campaign Bill did continue its slow way through the Congress, and on January 26, 1972, it was sent to the President for his signature. The bill required that each party publish the sources of all contributions over $10 and report all donations of more than $100 to the General Accounting Office, the Congressional watchdog on public expenditure. The bill would take effect sixty days after the President's signature. Nixon delayed the full ten days allowed him before signing it on February 7 with a brave rhetorical flourish. The enactment of the bill, said the President, would "work to build public confidence in the integrity of the electoral process."

Nixon's men then set to work on the exploitation of a massive loophole. The change in the law, while it offered the prospect of reform in the future, provided an immediate present of blissful opportunity for the party with a candidate. At that point the Democrats, with half a dozen contenders slugging it out in the primaries, were in no shape to cash in. The Republicans, in contrast, offered a monolithic alternative in the President himself. Moreover, the delay in signing the bill had created what was virtually a legal no-man's-land between the expiration of the old law, on March 10, and the enactment of the new, on April 7. In that period literally no disclosure of contributors' names was required. Nixon's fund-raisers were in an earthly paradise.

It was time to bring on the full first team. On February 15, John Mitchell abandoned the pretenses that had previously made him CREEP's remote puppeteer by resigning from the Justice Department and becoming CREEP's full-time director. His arrival at 1701 Pennsylvania Avenue was simultaneous with that of Maurice Stans, who took over the title of chairman of the Finance Committee to Re-Elect the President. Kalmbach became Stans's deputy, a position that could be assumed without indignity even for a fund-raiser of Kalmbach's talents. Maurice Stans, after all, was the greatest.

Prior to his arrival at CREEP, Stans had been Nixon's Secretary of Commerce, a job that brought him into intimate contact with the nation's industrial barons. But Stans's contacts went deep as well as wide. In the fifties he had been one of Eisenhower's top advisers, winding up as his Director of the Bureau of the Budget. Over the years he had garnered many dazzling testimonials to his wizardry—American Accounting Association Award, 1952; American Institute of Certified Public Accountants Annual Award, 1954; the Tax Foundation Award, 1959; election to the Accounting Hall of Fame, 1960; the Chamber of Commerce Great Living American Award, 1961; and in 1971 Salesman of the Year, the highest honour accorded by the National Sales and Marketing Executives

International. For a man who had been born the son of a poor Belgian immigrant housepainter in Shakopee, Minnesota, and had started his working life as a clerk in a sausage factory, it was a remarkable record of achievement. Stans, the epitome of the American success story, was grateful to the free-enterprise system that had created him.

Even his pastimes had an energetic flavour. Whenever he could get away, Stans liked nothing more than leading a retinue of porters and gunbearers through the African bush in pursuit of rare game. He was known as the "first American to bag a bongo in the Congo" (the bongo is a rare antelope). In 1966 Stans immortalised an African safari on film. The script spoke of "boys" and "natives," and in one scene a group of the big white hunters gave an African his first cigarette and knocked themselves out with mirth when he chewed it instead of smoking it. In those sensitive times when America was confronted by the problems of the Black Revolution, some of the film's viewers failed to see the joke. When a U.S. Information Agency official denounced it as an "Amos 'n' Andy show," Stans thought it wise to take the film off the exhibition circuit.

At the Department of Commerce, Stans ran a businessman's ship. He had little time for the criticisms of the conservation and ecological lobbyists, though he did set up a National Industrial Pollution Control Council. As it was composed entirely of industrialists, it did not exhibit much interest in control; most of its reports attacked proposed legislation on environmental concerns as too costly. But if Stans had his blind spots, they were the defects of great virtues. He had the ability to simplify complex financial problems, knew the importance of crisp decisions, and was good with the kind of people who create America's industrial wealth. He also strove to bring others into the charmed circle at the top; one of his most creative innovations at Commerce was an Office of Minority Business Enterprise designed to extend business opportunities to those who felt they had been left out of the American system. He was on record with the opinion that if Blacks would only read Horatio Alger, they could eliminate most of their problems.

Stans was a total Nixon enthusiast, and his loyalty to the President was an important ingredient in his fund-raising success. There is some evidence, which Stans disputes, suggesting that his zeal for Nixon's re-election caused some conflict with

his duty as a custodian of the taxpayer's money while Secretary
of Commerce. In 1971, Jeb Magruder, then nominally in
charge of CREEP, wrote to John Mitchell describing a "discretionary fund" that Stans had built up from public funds
in his department. "He is," wrote Magruder, "using this fund
for conference, hiring, and other activities that will be bene-
ficial to the President's re-election." Magruder thought that
Stans could, if Mitchell thought the idea worth emulating, tell
other Cabinet officers how they too could go about building
similar funds in their own departments. When the memorandum surfaced publicly, Stans said that he knew nothing about
any discretionary fund.

There is no doubt, however, about Stans's leading role in the
hunt for re-election funds in the loophole period between
the two election laws. Nor is there any doubt that some of the
contributors managed to break even the exiguous requirements
of the law at that time. In their eagerness to impress Stans and
Kalmbach with their generosity, some of the corporate chieftains failed to take even the most elementary precautions. Em-
boldened by the promise of total secrecy, they shoveled the
money straight out of the corporate coffers. And that was
illegal, even in the loophole period. When the Senate Watergate committee and the Special Prosecutor's Office stripped
away the veil of secrecy two years later, various prestigious
corporations came forward with shamefaced confessions.

Phillips Petroleum Company had given an illegal $100,000;
Gulf Oil Corporation another $100,000; Ashland Oil Inc.
$100,000; American Airlines $55,000—its chairman George
Spater explained that such donations were often given simply
for fear of the consequences if they were not; Goodyear Tire
and Rubber Company $40,000; Minnesota Mining and Manu-
facturing Company admitted to $30,000. It was tough on them,
given the fact that money had been handed over on the understanding of nondisclosure, but the contributions had to be
logged for internal accounting purposes. Maurice Stans was a
stickler for accurate books, though he dutifully shredded his
list of two thousand secret contributors after the Watergate
case broke. The problem was that the file copy sent routinely
to Rose Mary Woods, the President's long-time personal secretary, survived. What became known as "Rose Mary's baby"
was an item of special interest to the Watergate Special Prosecutor, Archibald Cox.

Even in this officially anonymous period, some donors went to extraordinary lengths to further protect their anonymity. Robert Allen, president of Gulf Resources and Chemical Corporation in Houston, went so far as to route his donation through Mexico. On April 3 he withdrew $100,000 from his Houston bank and had it transferred to the account of an "inactive" Gulf subsidiary in Banco Internacional in Mexico City. The money was then switched into the account of Manuel Ogarrio, Gulf's Mexican attorney, and he converted most of it into four cashier's checks for $32,000, $24,000, $18,000, and $15,000. These were then delivered to CREEP on April 5, where G. Gordon Liddy, by this time doubling as CREEP's general counsel and espionage expert, offered to solve the problem of converting them to beneficial use. On April 20, the four checks, in well-laundered condition, were deposited in the Miami Trust account of Bernard L. Barker, Howard Hunt's loyal lieutenant on the Ellsberg psychiatrist's burglary.

Barker's bank account was also the ultimate destination of a $25,000 gift from Dwayne Andreas, a Minnesota soybean tycoon. Andreas had been a long-time Humphrey supporter but, like many other businessmen, sometimes found it sensible to hedge his bets with other candidates. In 1972 he was applying, with Kenneth Dahlberg, chairman of the Minnesota branch of CREEP, for a federal bank charter. On April 5 Andreas called Dahlberg and said he wanted to make a $25,000 contribution before the new law came into effect. He was therefore placing his money today in the hands of a third party in Miami. Dahlberg called Maurice Stans to inform him of the gift. On April 9 Dahlberg picked up the money in Miami and changed it for a cashier's check the following day. On April 11 he delivered the check to Stans in Washington. Together with his serious-minded young deputy, Hugh "Duke" Sloan, Stans decided that as he had been informed of the gift on the fifth and the money had left Andreas's hands on that day, it had been made before the April 7 deadline and need not be reported. Liddy offered his good offices again and routed the check to Bernard Barker along with the Mexican checks, bringing his total holding up to $114,000. For Andreas, Dahlberg, and their associates things turned out nicely: they received their bank charter on August 22, by which time Liddy, Hunt, and the luckless Barker faced the prospect of long jail sentences for their part in the Watergate break-in.

In the final weeks before the April 7 deadline money descended on CREEP from all directions. By this time Stans and Kalmbach were receiving enormous, if unconscious, assistance from the Democrats. On the primary trail, Ed Muskie, long considered the most serious threat to Nixon's re-election prospects, had faltered in his quest for the nomination, and George McGovern was emerging as the new front-runner. (It was a development which, as we shall see, various other operatives in CREEP had been manfully trying to engineer.) And whatever McGovern was good for, business was not thought to be it. Two of his more heretical notions were like icicles in the heart of the rich and the super-rich: one was a "take"—the idea of an inheritance tax limiting beneficiaries to a maximum of $500,000—and the other was a "giveaway"—the proposal for a $6,500 minimum family income guarantee by the Federal government. Stans would sketch out these proposals to interested contributors with the amazement of a man who did not know what the world was coming to. Only a donation to Richard Nixon's cause could save American capitalism.

A lot of the last-minute contributions were made in cash. CREEP had half a dozen "pick-up men" rushing around the country, but so many people were anxious to give that in the end they just had to refuse to collect gifts of less than $100,000—smaller sums just were not worth the effort. One CREEP employee later described this period in the life of the office as reminiscent of "a madhouse." In the last days before the deadline, the jets which fly into Washington's National Airport, swooping down the Potomac past the Watergate complex, brought a variety of swivel-eyed men carrying bulging briefcases stuffed with hundred-dollar bills.

One of the biggest bundles did not arrive at the CREEP offices on time. The consequences for Maurice Stans, who personally accepted it as "a secret contribution" on April 10, were to prove most embarrassing. The donation was the personal campaign contribution of Robert Vesco, an international financier of some reputation. Vesco was ostensibly very fond of the Nixon family. In 1968 Richard Nixon's brother Donald had helped him to make a secret gift of $50,000 to the campaign, and in 1972 the President's other brother, Edward, was the linkman who facilitated a much larger secret contribution. And since the summer of 1971, Vesco had given employment to the President's nephew,

Donald Nixon. Donald, a pleasant but somewhat aimless young man who had traveled through India and had lived briefly in a commune in the Midwest, appeared to settle down as Vesco's aide-de-camp and personal assistant: On their tours of the various sun-kissed tax havens in which Vesco's interests were deployed, a real intimacy developed. Donald once said of Vesco: "He is the one person who has never lied to me, ever." Vesco appeared to enjoy the young man's company.

By 1971, Vesco needed all the friends and friends of friends in high places he could get. Since the last election he had moved into the big time. Vesco had taken over the sickly mutual-fund colossus, International Overseas Services (IOS), from its exotic founder, Bernie Cornfeld, who, at the time of writing, is in a Swiss jail awaiting trial on several charges involving business malpractice. Shortly after Vesco moved in, many IOS investors began to feel that they were better off under Bernie. In March, 1971, three months before young Donald Nixon was taken on the payroll, the Securities and Exchange Commission launched an investigation to determine whether Vesco had misappropriated the assets of IOS.

According to an indictment handed down in May, 1973, by a Federal grand jury in New York, Vesco's attempts to fight off the SEC investigation deeply compromised Nixon's two most important campaign executives—John Mitchell and Maurice Stans. The indictment charges both men with influence-peddling, conspiracy, and perjury, listing as co-defendants Robert L. Vesco and Harry L. Sears, a New Jersey Republican leader, who acted as Vesco's go-between in contacts with Nixon administration officials.

The story in the indictment begins: "In or about June and July, 1971, defendant Robert L. Vesco, would and did arrange with defendant Harry L. Sears to have Sears speak with the Attorney General of the United States, defendant John N. Mitchell, about the SEC investigations of Vesco with the intent of having Mitchell exert his influence on the SEC on behalf of Robert L. Vesco. . . ." The indictment goes on to say that the meeting between Sears and Mitchell took place, and Sears asked the Attorney General to speak with the SEC chairman, William Casey. In January, 1972, Sears met Mitchell again, this time to complain about "harassment" of

Vesco by the SEC. On March 8 Vesco himself met with Stans and offered to contribute "at least $250,000 and possibly $500,000" to the campaign. Stans apparently said $250,000 would be enough. Vesco was then taken upstairs at CREEP to meet with Mitchell to discuss the SEC investigation. "Shortly thereafter," the indictment says, "Stans and Mitchell discussed the proposed contribution from Vesco."

Stans asked that the contribution be made in cash and paid before April 7. On April 3 Edward Nixon went to Vesco's office in New Jersey to confirm the transaction. For some reason that seemed unfathomable at the time, Vesco was unable to rustle up the hundred-dollar bills before the deadline. But on April 10 Sears handed over a brown attaché case containing $200,000 to Maurice Stans (the balance of $50,000 arrived later). Stans logged the down payment as a pre–April 7 contribution on the grounds that it had been "committed to us before that date." In any event, two hours after the money was handed over, Stans informed Mitchell that the payment had been made. And two hours after that, Sears was having his long-cherished meeting with Casey, the head of the SEC. But despite subsequent meetings with Casey and the SEC's general counsel, G. Bradford Cook, the SEC investigation ground on inexorably. In November, 1972, Vesco was charged with "looting" $224 million from IOS investors.

The SEC's complaint, however, made no mention of Vesco's handsome campaign contribution. It had been in the original draft but was deleted by the SEC's general counsel, Bradford Cook, after a discussion with Maurice Stans. From CREEP's point of view it was a useful deletion. Some time after Vesco's alleged "looting" became public, CREEP returned his money on the grounds that the SEC suit "has come to our attention" and "we believe it is in your best interests as well as ours that the contribution be returned." CREEP's hands were publicly clean, but not, as it turned out, for long.

The indictment of Mitchell, Stans, et al. provides an interesting clue to the final riddle of this whole episode—why Vesco, a man with $224 million of other people's money, should not be able to deliver a mere $250,000 on time. Paragraph "(t)" of the indictment suggests that Vesco saw some usefulness in the delay. It reads: "In November 1972, defendant Robert L. Vesco would and did attempt to submit a written memorandum to Donald Nixon, the brother of the President of the

United States, the purport and tenor of which was to threaten disclosure of the secret cash contribution and other adverse consequences unless the SEC was directed to drop all legal proceedings against Vesco. When the memorandum came to the attention of the defendant John N. Mitchell, he turned it over to the defendant Harry L. Sears and concealed its existence and contents from the SEC and other law enforcement agencies who properly should have been made aware of it."

On the story presented by the indictment it seems that what started out as just another secret campaign contribution wound up as an attempt to blackmail the President. Mitchell, Stans, and Sears deny the charges, but there is no question of the fact that the company they kept in the loophole period was not calculated to build confidence in the integrity of the electoral process. But the consequences were all in the future. Back in April, 1972, the men at CREEP could not have been happier. They announced modestly that the pre–April 7 fund-raising drive had yielded $10.2 million. In fact it had raised almost $20 million, of which $5 million was already spent and $5 million had been paid in advance for services to be rendered. The advance payments did not have to be reported, and CREEP was not anxious to deter potential donors by revealing just how rich it already was. About $1.7 million worth of donations had been made in cash and was stashed away in safes and deposit boxes, ready finance for the more unconventional aspects of the campaign. Although nobody at CREEP realised it at the time, they had a lot more money than was good for them.

CHAPTER 9

The Making of a Candidate

As PART of his 1950 senatorial campaign, Richard Nixon was scheduled to give a speech in Santa Barbara, California. Although still only thirty-seven years old, he was already a politician of national stature, with an established reputation as a hard-hitting Congressman. Some liberals might wince at the broad strokes of his anti-Communist rhetoric, but there was no doubt that Nixon expressed a powerful aspect of the national mood, and expressed it very effectively. In California his opponent for the Senate seat, Helen Gahagan Douglas ("the pink lady"), brought out Nixon's most combative, crowd-pleasing instincts. His campaign rallies were always well organized, well financed and enthusiastically attended. Until Santa Barbara.

When the candidate arrived at the huge auditorium that had been hired for him, he discovered there were only a handful of people present. A rather plump young man with a bland expression told him that he was his advance man and then stood up and made a marathon speech of introduction that emptied the hall still further. Eventually, when the few remaining survivors were practically dead with boredom, the "advance man" turned to the candidate and asked him to speak on the subject that most absorbed California and the nation—the International Monetary Fund.

Nixon struggled through the disastrous evening, but before he left he turned angrily on the plump young man with the question: "What's your name again?"

"Dick Tuck," replied the young man.

"Dick Tuck," said the candidate, "you've just made your last advance."

The candidate did not know he was talking to a fervent

supporter of Helen Gahagan Douglas. For Tuck it was the starting point of a long and creative political hobby. Over the years, Tuck has pursued Republican candidates in general, and Nixon in particular, with unabashed intensity. In the 1960 presidential campaign Nixon flew to Memphis after his first and not altogether successful TV debate against Kennedy. As he left the airplane a buxom lady wearing a huge Nixon button flung her arms around him and cried "Don't worry, son. Kennedy won last night, but you'll do better next time." She was a Tuck plant. Tuck was standing nearby hooting merrily. On another occasion Nixon was in the middle of a whistle-stop speech on his campaign train when it began to pull out of the station. Tuck had donned a railwayman's cap and signaled the driver to start up. One of Tuck's greatest technical triumphs was the infiltration of subversive fortune cookies as the final item on the menu of a political luncheon at which Richard Nixon was the guest of honour. When opened, each cookie yielded up a slip of paper with the firm prediction "Kennedy will win."

Tuck continued the pursuit in 1962 as Nixon contested the California gubernatorial election. When Nixon was at a rally in San Francisco's Chinatown, Tuck gave some children a banner which they waved aloft when the candidate approached. "Let's have a picture," Nixon himself suggested. The smiling candidate was photographed with the smiling Chinese children, blissfully unaware of the fact that the Chinese characters on the banner read "What about the Hughes loan?"—a reference to a controversial and deeply unexplained loan of $205,000 from the reclusive multimillionaire Howard Hughes to Nixon's brother Donald. In 1964, Tuck transferred his talent for creating comic catastrophies to the Goldwater campaign and will, if pressed, modestly claim responsibility for Johnson's landslide victory.

Tuck, of course, is a true original, with an artist's pride in his work, which at its best makes both a political point and adds to the precious sum of human gaiety. It is no easy task creating hoaxes that deflate but do not humiliate the victim, but then most people very properly do not try. When, in the fall of 1971, the hard-nosed men in the White House began to put together what was later described as "Dick Tuck capability" on behalf of the President, they were creating an enterprise that was bound to go rancid; hoaxes without humour are simply exercises in cruelty. But there was another element, beyond the question of taste, that made the degeneration of the idea inevitable. It derived from Nixon's traditional style of campaigning.

The President had learned his trade in a hard school. Of all the states in the Union, California is perhaps the toughest for an aspiring politician—the distances involved, the diversity and rootlessness of much of the population, particularly in the south, all conspire to make his task of getting a hearing enormously difficult. At an early stage, Nixon came under the tutelage of Murray Chotiner, an abrasive West Coast lawyer with a remarkable record of success in selling right-wing politicos. Chotiner was at Nixon's side when, as a poor and unknown ex-naval lieutenant, he first ran for Congress in Whittier, California, in 1946. With Chotiner's help and advice Nixon went on to become Senator and Vice President. Chotiner also hovered in the wings of Nixon's 1962 campaign for Governor of California; by this time Nixon was indelibly established in the liberals' lexicon as "Tricky Dick."

Chotiner's theory of campaign politics is very simple. It is that people vote against politicians, not for them. Every aspect of a politician will upset some people, so to minimise the number of people against you, you reveal as little as possible of yourself. Instead, you concentrate your campaign on those aspects of your opponent's life, record, views, and program that the voters will probably most dislike. It is not an entirely attractive approach, and many of Nixon's opponents were to complain of mudslinging and smear tactics, but it had a weird kind of integrity. People who took on Dick Nixon knew they would have a bitter, even venomous fight on their hands; if they were taken by surprise they had only themselves to blame. For Nixon, politics was always more than a debate about the issues; it was an intensely personal battlefield on which, for the period of the campaign at least, his opponent was literally the enemy. As a presidential candidate, in 1960 and 1968, Nixon sloughed part of the old image of ruthlessness to produce talk of a "new Nixon." But there were moments in both campaigns when he cut loose with flashes of the old style. And the Nixon who toured the country tongue-lashing the opposition before the 1970 midterm elections was pure "old Nixon."

The 1970 strategy proved counterproductive and gave rise, as we have seen, to the new strategy, decided at Key Biscayne, in which presidential aloofness was a key ingredient. Nixon himself would be above the battle, a statesman not just a politician, seeking endorsement not so much of himself but of the office of the Presidency. By late 1971 the construction of this image was well advanced; it was a process helped by the curious double standard which Americans impose on their political leaders. On the one hand, they do not hold politicians in general in high esteem. (A recent poll showed that politicians rank nineteenth out of twenty occupations in the public mind. One above used-car salesmen.) On the other hand, once a politician becomes President he is thought to metamorphose into a modern-day founding father, far-seeing, virtuous, and wise. From the summer of 1971, this mythology worked steadily in Nixon's favour.

It worked the more powerfully as it became clear that the myth contained a kernel of hard fact. Nixon was showing statesmanlike qualities. The old cold-war barriers between the United States and the two great Communist-bloc powers, Russia and China, were being visibly dismantled, and that was something for which the President could take genuine credit in his campaign. But it was not the whole story. The venom that had infused Nixon's earlier campaigns had not disappeared; it simply went underground.

For the "black" campaign operation there was no shortage of experienced old hands and enthusiastic beginners. Murray Chotiner himself, who had ostensibly disappeared from Nixon's orbit, was back on the team, dividing his time between the White House and a new law office just across the road, in the same block as CREEP. It was not thought to be a good thing to have Chotiner too close to the President's person, given his somewhat erratic professional and personal background (Chotiner had once had a sticky time with a Senate committee investigating influence-peddling; and his marital record—he had been married four times—aroused the active distaste of Haldeman and Ehrlichman). But personal access was not essential. In the White House Chotiner found that Colson was naturally receptive to his ideas. And after the November, 1970, Key Biscayne strategy meeting, Colson was to emerge as an intimate of the President, preceded only by John Mitchell and Bob Haldeman—and on a par with John Ehrlichman. Ehrlichman himself, of course, was by this time a seasoned spymaster, with Hunt and Liddy, ready and eager to put their talents at the disposal of the re-election cause. (He also had some personal experience of the work—back in 1960 Ehrlichman had operated briefly as a Nixon "double agent" within the Rockefeller camp when the New York Governor was tilting for the Republican presidential nomination.)

But the man who was put in overall charge of the sabotage-espionage operation, or as he later put it, "surveillance" of the Democratic threat, was Bob Haldeman. He may have seemed an odd choice, given the rugged credentials of other candidates, and his own image of boy-scout rectitude. But Haldeman was no newcomer to the black arts.

In 1962, when he was managing Nixon's disastrous campaign for Governor of California, Haldeman was directly implicated in an exceptionally dirty trick. As the battle reached its climax, 500,000 registered Democrats throughout the state received postcards from a group called "The Committee for the Preservation of the Democratic Party in California." The cards, which were constructed in the form of an opinion poll, asked recipients if they were aware that Governor Pat Brown (Nixon's opponent in the election) was controlled by the California Democratic Council, a left-wing organisation depicted as one remove from a Communist front. On the basis of this "poll" the "Preservation" committee published a report purporting to show that nine out of ten Democrats rejected Governor Brown's stance on the issues. The report was denounced by Governor Brown's campaign staff; the Republicans denied all responsibility. Two years later, Judge Byron Arnold found that "The Committee for the Preservation of the Democratic Party" had in fact been set up by Nixon's campaign staff—at a cost of $70,000. He was also satisfied that it had been established under the supervision of Bob Haldeman, and that the poll had been "approved by Nixon personally."

The extent to which Nixon personally approved all that was done in his name by his "black" operators in 1971 and 1972 may never be known; what is not in doubt is the fact that the men down the line felt they were acting in accord with his wishes. Thus, at the time when Nixon was apparently conducting the cleanest and most dignified campaign of his entire career, he was presiding over the nastiest in American history. For the "Dick Tuck capability" that was evolved was not just a practical-joke machine but the tool of a conspiracy against the effective working of the two-party system. It was, in a sense, a natural extension of the Chotiner theory of politics. Nixon's "black" strategists determined not only to display all the faults—real or manufactured—of the Democratic candidate, but also to contrive in advance that the candidate chosen by the opposition would be sufficiently flawed. To ensure the re-election of the President, the Democrat running against him must be the man in whom most electors would find most to vote against. By 1972, there was little doubt at 1701 Pennsylvania Avenue, in the White House, or in the Attorney General's office at the Justice Department about who that man was.

From the President's point of view, the opinion polls were more encouraging than they had been but they were still not pleasing. They showed that if the Democrats nominated any of their three front-runners—Ed Muskie, Hubert Humphrey, or Edward Kennedy—Nixon could be in trouble. (Kennedy, however, with Chappaquiddick still relatively recent in the public memory, was considered an unlikely contender. He had consistently maintained he had no intention of running.) But there was one outsider, who was well organised in most of the states with open-primary elections and who showed up poorly on all the head-to-head poll tests against Nixon. The outsider was the radical, antiwar Senator from South Dakota, George McGovern (it was his radicalism, not his antiwar stance, that made him publicly suspect). From early 1972 on, the "black advance" army of President Nixon's White House bent its efforts towards securing his nomination.

Within the confines of the White House, Haldeman and his men referred to the Democratic Left, represented by McGovern's wing of the party, as "the Crazies." In a rare appearance on the *Today* show that month, Haldeman caused a minor uproar by saying on the subject of Nixon's Vietnam policy, "The only conclusion you can draw is that the critics now are consciously aiding and abetting the enemy of the United States." It was tantamount to calling McGovern a traitor. Yet at the same time, Haldeman, wearing his undisclosed "surveillance" hat, was overseeing operations to help secure McGovern's nomination as a Presidential candidate. It was a piquant situation.

The first foot-soldiers for the undercover army had been assembled even before the plot was dignified by the emergence of a grand strategy. The original idea had been simply to create animosities between the various Democratic candidates in the primary and preconvention stages in order to make it difficult for them to come together unified under one candidate after the convention. The initial recruiting agent for this enterprise was the President's appointments secretary, Dwight Chapin.

Chapin supervised the minutiae of the President's daily life. It was a job that took him to many far-away places, and in all of them he won golden opinions for his efficiency at coping with a schedule. In Peking, Chou En-lai was enormously impressed. But the trip that Chapin himself found most moving was the President's visit to the Vatican. As he and the President were borne aloft in a helicopter from St. Peter's Square, Chapin looked down and saw the Pope at a window of the Vatican. Chapin relates: "The Pope was clearly blessing the helicopter as it took off. It was wonderful."

Chapin had worked, on and off, for Nixon since 1962, when he was still an undergraduate at Southern Cal. He was a close friend of Bob Haldeman, with whom he worked in J. Walter Thompson after leaving college, and he considered himself a "superloyalist." On the 1968 campaign, he described his responsibilities as "getting Nixon up in the morning, putting him to bed at night, and looking after his wardrobe, meals, and schedule." When Nixon made TV commercials, it was Chapin who led the clapping. Haldeman once described him as the man who "processes the input" to the President and the contributor of a "very sharp, creative, facile mind" to planning sessions. Chapin was very good on detail and, casting around in the belfries of his mind for Republican Dick Tucks, in June, 1971, he remembered his old friend Donald Segretti.

They had had good days together at Southern Cal, Chapin and Segretti and Gordon Strachan (a Haldeman aide) and Michael Guhin (a Kissinger assistant) and Bart Porter (CREEP's scheduling director) and Tim Elbourne (a Ziegler assistant). Almost all of them had been, in their individual ways, prominent in student Republican politics with memories of "Trojans for Representative Government" which had tried to supplant the university Establishment elite. It was rough stuff; to win their election the Trojans infiltrated their rivals' campaigns, tore down their posters, stole their leaflets, and produced others (fake). Ballot boxes were stuffed and the student court was packed. Segretti, who looked like an aging choir-boy, had been an especially active Trojan; it was perhaps natural that he should spring to Chapin's mind.

After UCLA, the diminutive Segretti had studied law in Cambridge, England, and then, after a year in the Treasury Department, was drafted and spent twelve months in the huge U.S. Army camp of Long Binh outside Saigon. Back in Fort Ord, California, he developed something of a reputation as a liberal, printed a peace symbol on his checks, hung a "Free Huey" poster on his wall, and specialised in representing soldiers who applied for conscientious-objector status. He had not, however, entirely lost his right-wing sympathies.

In the few months before he left the army in September, 1971, Captain Segretti began to take many trips away from the fort, telling friends he was looking for work. In fact he was already working for the White House. In June he had seen Dwight Chapin and agreed to organise a host of "Republican Dick Tucks" throughout the country. His other White House contact was Gordon Strachan, Haldeman's liaison man with the Committee to Re-Elect the President. Segretti was to be paid $16,000 a year plus handsome expenses by Herb Kalmbach in Newport Beach. On September 24 he flew to Portland, Oregon, and checked into the Hotel Benson. The next day he firmed up the new details of his job with Chapin, who was with the presidential party staying there with Nixon on his way to greet Emperor Hirohito in Anchorage, Alaska.

Segretti loved his new job. He traded in his old Mustang for a new $6,000 white Mercedes, got himself a chic little swinging-singles apartment in Los Angeles and, with the assumed name Donald Simmons, did a great deal of flying around the country trying to tempt other young men to become Trojan horses for Nixon inside the Democratic camp. Among those he approached were three lawyers with whom he had served in Vietnam. One of them, Alex B. Shipley, now Assistant Attorney General in Tennessee, later gave a full description of Segretti's recruiting techniques. Shipley, who did not take up the offer, was told by Segretti: "Money would be no problem but the people we would be working for want results."

Segretti also promised him that "we would be taken care of after Nixon's re-election, that I would get a good job in the government." In the meantime, Shipley would need false identification papers, and should recruit five more people—preferably lawyers (Segretti said he did not want anything illegal done)—for the job. They would set about disrupting the schedules of Democratic candidates and obtaining information from their campaign organisations. He, Segretti, would never ask Shipley the names of the five he had hired and likewise would never tell Shipley who it was who was paying them. At this point Shipley says he asked, "How in hell are we going to be taken care of if no one knows what we're doing?" To which Segretti replied, "Nixon knows that something is being done. It's a typical deal—'Don't-tell-me-anything-and-I-won't-tell.' "

Later "Donald Simmons" told Charles Svihlik, a young Republican recruit in Indianapolis, of a more specific objective. The plan was, he said, "to swing the convention to McGovern . . . to literally destroy strong candidates like Muskie."

In the latter part of 1971, Segretti traveled at least ten times across the country. His stops included Miami, New York, Houston, Manchester (New Hampshire), San Francisco, Albuquerque, Tucson, Knoxville, Portland, Salt Lake City, Monterey, and Chicago. He would explain to potential recruits what "fun" could be had in the conduct of a "negative campaign." The type of operation he tried, not in all cases successfully, to set up reached its highest organisational form in Florida, where he managed to interest Robert Melton Benz, an ambitious former chairman of the Hillsborough County Young Republican Club. The contact was made in December, 1971, when "Donald Simmons" called Benz in Tampa and asked him if he was interested in a "voter-research project." They met for a beer at a local motel and Simmons/Segretti gave Benz the old infiltration spiel. He wanted to "screw up" the Democrats, he said. Benz was taken on board at $150 a week and told he could hire assistants for $75 each. He acquired seven helpers over the following weeks. One of them got work in Muskie's campaign headquarters and passed out a steady stream of campaign information. Another penetrated the campaign headquarters of Senator "Scoop" Jackson. Yet another proved adept at the construction and deployment of stink-bombs. And somewhere along the line the requirement that all undercover activities should be "legal" became fudged. Benz would, customarily, receive his ideas and material by mail. The letters were always unsigned but were sometimes enclosed with $100 bills. He assumed that Donald Simmons was the anonymous benefactor.

While Segretti was stitching his cruddy operation together, another intelligence-gathering force was emerging from the bowels of CREEP. This was managed by Jeb Magruder, then the committee's nominal administrative chief and the recipient of numerous helpful tips from Charles Colson in the White House. Under Magruder's guidance, CREEP pieced together its own network of agents and informers. His scheduling director, Bart Porter, bought himself a 35mm. slide projector to help blow up photographs of documents taken by their resourceful operators in the various Democratic candidates' headquarters. CREEP's original star agent, a young Californian called Roger Greaves, had his reports dignified with the code name "Sedan Chair I." One of Greaves's responsibilities was to rustle up hostile pickets to give the meetings of Democratic candidates a disorderly appearance (thus, for the sake of the media, producing the phenomenon which the Nixon administration was publicly so keen on abominating). Eventually Mr. Greaves became tired of the tedious nature of the work and resigned. He was later replaced by "Sedan Chair II."

There was one small hitch. Nobody had seen fit to inform Magruder and CREEP's diligent general counsel, G. Gordon Liddy, that Segretti was running a parallel operation on behalf of Bob Haldeman out in the field. In January, 1972, "Don Simmons" called at the office of Allan Walker, a Nixon campaign official in New Hampshire, and offered his help in running a "negative campaign" against the Democrats. The bemused Mr. Walker called CREEP in Washington to ask about Mr. Simmons's qualifications for this role, and was told that nobody had heard of him. Shortly afterwards, however, Magruder was put in the picture about Simmons/Segretti and was further braced by the support of E. Howard Hunt, who had completed his "consulting" duties in the White House and was loaned by Charles Colson to help out at CREEP.

The benefit of Hunt's experience was then fed into the Segretti operation. Hunt, calling himself "Ed Warren," met and talked with Segretti and made it clear to him who was in charge. Over the next five months, Hunt provided ideas and suggestions for Segretti's undercover army, mostly by telephone. The relationship was somewhat curious as, according

to Segretti, he was never quite sure for whom Warren worked;
Warren, he later acknowledged, made him a bit "scared."
Nonetheless he carried out his orders. It was not until some
time after the Watergate break-in that Segretti discovered the
true identity of his taskmaster. While leafing through a news
magazine, he saw a picture of Ed Warren with the caption
"E. Howard Hunt."

The penetration of Muskie's campaign proved almost em-
barrassingly easy. He had, it seemed, few plumbers working
for him. Muskie workers believe that the dirty tricks began
in the summer of 1971 with the theft of a poll of New
Jersey voters from their campaign offices. Soon after, that
material, critical of Edward Kennedy, was sent out to journalists and Congressmen in counterfeit Muskie envelopes,
and Muskie was forced publicly to deny any connection with
it. An AP reporter in Boston was rung by someone claiming
to be a Muskie press aide who told him that Muskie had
declared Kennedy "a divisive influence" and that "he should
declare categorically whether or not he was going to run."
It was not true.

In December, 1971, the columnists Evans and Novak
received a copy of an interoffice memo recommending that
Muskie use the Senate Intergovernmental Relations Committee, of which he was chairman, to help his campaign. The
memo suggested that he take the subcommittee to California
for public hearings on property taxes because "property taxes
are all-important in this crucial state . . . capturing the
issue is worth a goldmine to any candidate." The memo was
published on December 12. The hearings were not held. In
February, 1972, Evans and Novak received a copy of a letter
from Muskie to an aide, suggesting that they hire a man who
was once a ghostwriter for Governor Rockefeller to write
Muskie's "personal journal" of the 1972 campaign. The
columnists pointed out that "a professional ghosted Muskie
journal might seem to violate the 'Trust Muskie' campaign
theme."

Within the Muskie camp, suspicion for the leaks centred on
Cynthia Johnston, a researcher who had once been Robert
Novak's secretary. Despite her protestations of innocence,
she was packed off to run the Muskie office in Harrisburg,
Pennsylvania. In fact many of the leaks were attributable to
a driver employed by Muskie to run documents between his

campaign and Senate offices; the driver was in the pay of CREEP. Others were the work of an employee of E. Howard Hunt. In February, 1972, Hunt asked his part-time employer, Robert Bennett at the Mullen agency, if he knew of a likely lad who could do some political work. Bennett put him in touch with his nephew, who came up with the name of Tom Gregory, a student at Brigham Young University, Utah. Under his name of Ed Warren, Hunt wrote Gregory and then sent him money and an air ticket to come to Washington. Then Hunt persuaded him, for $175 a week, to enlist in the Muskie office as a student volunteer. He would gather all possible information on the campaign and hand it over to Hunt once a week at the drugstore on Pennsylvania Avenue across the street from Hunt's office.

By now there were a lot of clandestine operatives abroad in the primary states, and with the Kalmbach-Stans axis moving into high gear, there was no shortage of funds. A proportion of CREEP's mighty cash inflow was routinely directed towards its burgeoning department of dirty tricks. The best, or the worst, were played on Muskie, though, over the ensuing months, every Democratic candidate received his share.

The gremlins in Muskie's New Hampshire primary campaign were extraordinarily resourceful. Schedules and basic polling data mysteriously went missing. A Muskie "sympathiser" was in the habit of making post-midnight calls announcing himself as a member of the "Harlem for Muskie Committee." He would then go into a number about how Muskie would deliver "full rights for the black people." New Hampshire voters are not specially exercised about the problems of black people and certainly do not want to hear about them after bedtime. Another Muskie "sympathiser" would repeatedly call the same number for polling information—again in the wee, small hours—and repeatedly apologise for his "mistake." Tony Podesta, Muskie's campaign manager in the state, found that "people were getting furious" at what they regarded as the incompetence of Muskie's staff.

On February 24, two weeks before polling day, the Manchester *Union Leader*—a paper whose publisher, William Loeb, is reputedly somewhat to the right of Louis XIV and who was very strongly opposed to Muskie—published a letter from one "Paul Morrison" of Deerfield Beach in Florida. It

claimed that Muskie had been asked in Florida what he
knew about blacks. "He didn't have any in Maine, a man
with the Senator replied. No blacks, but we have Cannocks
[sic]. What did he mean? we asked. Mr. Muskie laughed
and said come to New England and see." The letter was
perhaps slightly less damaging than being accused in Harlem
of calling the voters "niggers," but it was at least as unfortunate as labeling the electors of Queens "Yids," or the inhab-
itants of Chicago "Polacks." People of French-Canadian
descent, of whom there are a sizable number in New Hampshire, do not like being referred to as "Canucks." The letter
made the emotional Muskie very upset. So did a report, also
published in the *Union Leader,* that his high-spirited and
outspoken wife had told dirty stories on the campaign trail.
On February 26 Muskie came to Manchester to refute the
stories. The way in which he did so did a great deal to ensure
the success of CREEP's strategy.

Standing on a flatbed truck in the falling snow outside
the newspaper office, his hands in dark gloves, his scarf
wrapped round his neck, a mike in his hands, and the TV
cameras in front of him, Muskie began to speak. As he
promised that he would never slur any Americans by crude
reference to their ethnic origins and asserted that his wife
was not the kind of woman to tell dirty stories, all the
exhaustion and frustration of campaigning broke him down,
and Muskie began to cry. If there was a moment that ruined
Muskie's candidacy, that was it.

It seems to be an accepted convention of the English-
speaking peoples that men do not cry, especially not if they
are men who seek public office. Although the American
public, like the British, treasures definite suspicions of politicians, judging them not to be amongst the least corruptible
band of men and women, they do not, for some reason, expect
their frailty to extend to their emotions. Weak financial or
moral standards are deplored but often accepted; apparent
emotional weakness is less easily tolerated. Overnight Muskie's
image changed from being that of a big, craggy, angry, and
honest man to being something of a crybaby. One legacy of
the New Hampshire incident was the taunting flyer which
surfaced in later primary campaigns: "If you don't vote for
Muskie, he will cry."

It later turned out that "Mr. Paul Morrison," the presumed

author of the "Canuck" letter, did not exist. And much later
Ken Clawson, employed as deputy communications director
in the White House, reportedly bragged to a former colleague
on the *Washington Post* that he was the true author (Clawson has since denied the boast). But by then the damage
was long done.

Muskie had started on the primary trail with the expecta-
tion of at least 60 percent of the Democratic vote in New
Hampshire. In fact, on March 7 he sneaked home ahead
of George McGovern with only 49 percent—it was the signal
to all the other Democratic contenders that Muskie was
vulnerable. Meanwhile the gremlins stayed in attendance.
While they were snowing on him in New Hampshire, they
were frying him in sunny Florida. In the weeks before the
Florida primary, signs appeared on trees asking people to
"Help Muskie, support bussing our children." Muskie was in
favour of school desegregation, but even the dimmest members of his staff were alert to the fact that vigorous emphasis
on the "bussing" issue was not the way to win votes south of
the Mason-Dixon line. Other Muskie cards bearing the
legend "If you like Hitler you'll love Wallace" were placed
by Segretti's agents under the windshield wipers of those
who drove to a mammoth Wallace rally near Tampa. Another
batch invited the public to a free lunch at the Muskie headquarters on the top floor of the Key Biscayne Hotel. Several
stinkbombs were placed in his Tampa headquarters.

On March 11, with the primary election only three days
away, Florida voters were mailed letters which began "We
on the Sen. Ed Muskie staff sincerely hope that you have
decided upon Senator Muskie as your choice. However, if
you have not made your decision you should be aware of
several facts." The "facts" were that two of Muskie's rival
candidates, Hubert Humphrey and conservative Democrat
"Scoop" Jackson, were guilty of a variety of sexual impro-
prieties stretching back as far as 1929. No substantiation was
offered for these charges and none has been forthcoming
since the letters' delivery. As "black" propaganda it was
brilliant, in that it effectively smeared Humphrey and Jackson
while ensuring that the purveyor of the information, whom
the voters wrongly imagined was Senator Muskie, would lose
all respect. George Wallace won a handsome victory in the
primary while Muskie finished a poor fourth.

The Muskie "several facts" letter was the product of
Segretti's Florida operation. Segretti, at the time of writing,
is under indictment in Florida for certain abuses of the mails
during the state's primary election. One of his men, George
A. Hearing, is serving a year in a Federal prison for his help
on the "stop Muskie" enterprise.

Muskie took his limping campaign off to Wisconsin,
where further embarrassments were in store. Segretti and
Robert Benz, who had done so well in Florida, were waiting
for him. By now the Muskie enterprise was so close to ruin
that only the most lighthearted pranks were needed to send
it spiraling into despair. To cheer up his staff, Segretti and
Benz started to order a lot of stuff in the name of George
Mitchell, a Muskie advance man. Most of it the Senator did
not really need—bunches of flowers, fifty pizzas, fifty buckets
of chicken, a brace of limousines. They were having a lot
of fun. On April 4, Muskie finished last in the Wisconsin
primary.

Over in California, potential contributors to the Muskie
campaign received a fabricated letter saying that the candidate
was not interested in "the usual fat cats" but wanted to rely
on small donations. By this time, too, Humphrey's campaign
was beginning to feel some of the heat. In Wisconsin, Segretti
composed a handbill, under Senator Humphrey's name, which
invited recipients to a gala lunch with Humphrey, Lorne
Greene, star of the *Bonanza* TV series, and Martin Luther
King's widow. In Milwaukee's black ghetto fake leaflets were
distributed promising free food and drink and "balloons for
the kiddies." In California, Humphrey was attacked as a war-
monger and "opportunist" in leaflets produced by such
groups as "Democrats Against Bossism" and "Democrats for
a Peace Candidate." No members of these groups have ever
been located. A bogus news release, on Humphrey stationery,
was sent out accusing Shirley Chisholm, the black Congresswoman, of being mentally unbalanced.

Muskie's Washington office spent much time and effort
in March and early April organising a massive fund-raising
dinner to carry him through the Pennsylvania and New York
primaries. Thirteen hundred guests were invited for April 17,
and very careful small-table plans were drawn up. On the
morning of the seventeenth the headquarters were called by
the Embassy of Niger, told that the chargé had accepted his

invitation from the campaign director Jack English, and asked "when would the hired limousine arrive?" Only Democrats had been invited, but the Muskie staff felt that they could not insult the chargé and so told him to come anyway.

He did. And so did fifteen other ambassadors or chargés, all of them from African or Middle Eastern countries. "Since this was a seated dinner it caused us a bit of pain trying to seat them without causing embarrassment," said Madalyn Albright, the dinner's organiser. During the evening, a $50 bunch of flowers arrived COD. Then $300 worth of liquor. Then two hundred pizzas; finally two magicians appeared saying that they traveled all the way from the Virgin Islands "to perform for the children." They warned the exhausted Muskie staff, "If you don't let us in, we'll turn you into something terrible."

On April 27, Muskie withdrew from the presidential race. The destruction of his candidacy had taken little more than two months. In February, 24 percent of Democrats and independents polled by Harris wanted Muskie as their candidate, whereas only 5 percent were rooting for McGovern. And at that time Muskie was running level with Nixon in the head-to-head polling tests—both with 42 percent of the potential vote, with the balance going to George Wallace (who was expected to run as a third-party candidate after he had finished trampling on the Democrats in the primaries). By the time of his withdrawal, Muskie had dropped nine points in the test with Nixon; and among Democrats he was the first-choice candidate among only 6 percent; McGovern, in contrast, was now the choice of 21 percent. Their roles had been reversed. McGovern was the new front-runner, with Muskie out and Humphrey thrashing about in his wake. It was a development that delighted CREEP's "black" operators, and made most of the Democratic Party's traditional bosses pray for a sign, if not from God then at least from Teddy Kennedy. No sign ever came.

Muskie's early collapse may well have prevented another of Hunt's "surreptitious entry" operations. Early in 1972 it became the subject of wild rumour on Hunt's political grapevine that there was some explosive dirt on Muskie locked away in a safe in Las Vegas. The safe happened to belong to Hank Greenspun, the free-wheeling editor and proprietor of the Las Vegas *Sun*. Greenspun also had another claim

to fame as a mortal enemy of Howard Hughes, the invisible
billionaire, who owned a fair chunk of Las Vegas. When
Hughes left Las Vegas back in 1970, Greenspun, a resourceful newsman, managed to persuade one of the billionaire's
lieutenants to turn over a large portion of his master's private
archive—it was said of Greenspun that he owned "the
largest collection of Howard Hughes memoranda in cap-
tivity." The memos lay in the same safe as the explosive
Muskie dirt.

Hunt hit upon the seemingly brilliant idea of combining
public and private service. The Hughes organisation, as a
client of the Mullens agency, might be interested in recovering their boss's documents from Greenspun's safe. Their
removal could be used as a "cover" for the real motive of
the burglary—the Muskie dirt. Unfortunately, when the idea
was put up to Hughes's attorney, Hunt was told that Hughes
felt he could live without recovery of the documents. Which
in some ways was a pity, as it might have been fascinating
to know the effect of Greenspun's "explosive" material on
Hunt's entry team. The only stuff on Muskie in Greenspun's
safe was information on his conviction in 1965. While hunting
ducks with Eugene McCarthy, he had violated the local game
laws. Both he and McCarthy, the records showed, were fined
$27.50.

Hunt's Cuban-American mercenaries were, however, not
entirely inactive during this period. Early in May, both
Bernard Barker and Eugenio Martinez, veterans of the
psychiatrist's office burglary, came to Washington with
seven henchmen from Miami. They carried out instructions,
emanating from Charles Colson in the White House, to break
up and generally disrupt an antiwar demonstration. One of
them managed to thump Daniel Ellsberg as he was addressing
the protesters from the Capitol steps.

Meanwhile, back in the national-security area, Nixon and
Kissinger were having problems with the choreography of
"peace with honour" in Vietnam. Hanoi had launched its
spring offensive and invaded large areas of South Vietnam:
strong measures were required to make the North Vietnamese
see the Nixon version of sense at the conference table in
Paris. In May, Nixon sanctioned a massive bombing campaign
and the mining of Haiphong Harbour, potentially a deeply
unpopular escalation.

The McGovernites were naturally aghast, but Nixon's re-election servants managed to defuse some of the more general outrage. CREEP employees did a manful job of getting sympathetic organisations and individuals to ring and telegraph their support. The response enabled the White House to claim with perfect honesty that messages of support eclipsed those of criticism in a five-to-one ratio. In less perfect honesty, CREEP bought advertising space in the *New York Times* to state the case of "The People vs. the *New York Times*." The *Times* had criticised the Haiphong operation but the "People" thought it was right. There was no mention of CREEP or any White House interest in the advertisement, although its author was none other than the ubiquitous Charles Colson. The original "Dick Tuck capability" had come a very long way since its birth less than a year earlier.

A year later, after much of this mire had been revealed by the Senate Watergate Committee, Tuck tells the story of an encounter he had with Bob Haldeman in the Senate Office Building. Haldeman was by this time Nixon's former chief of staff, and he evidently felt bitter about it. He is said to have addressed Tuck as follows: "You son-of-a-bitch, you started this." To which Tuck replied: "Yeah, Bob, but you guys ran it into the ground."

It is impossible to know whether the "black advance"–inspired hazards that afflicted Muskie made the difference between his success and failure. McGovern was on a moving band wagon, attracting the highly motivated antiwar element in the party that had brought Eugene McCarthy close to nomination back in 1968. Muskie, in contrast, had the front-runner's problem; he could only, in relationship to his pursuers, appear to go back. But the speed with which he went back broke all known political records. The exceptional harassment which he and his staff—on paper the most in the field—experienced was certainly a major factor in this decline. For Nixon's strategists, the task of stopping Muskie had proved unexpectedly easy. George Wallace was more of a problem.

CHAPTER 10

"The Southern Strategy"

BACK IN 1971 some expert readers of the political tea leaves inclined to the view that George Wallace had achieved his life's ambition. They reasoned that his bid for the Presidency in 1968 which had scared the life out of the American political Establishment had satisfied his thirst for glory. He had left his mark on history, married a young and attractive wife; now he seemed happily settled in cultivation of the luxuriant garden of Alabama state politics.

Early in 1972 a raucous voice was heard coming out of the South. It spoke of a government run by "hypocrites and uninterested politicians," the kind of men who could not "even park their bicycles straight." It spoke of "briefcase-totin' bureaucrats" with nothing to do but waste the tax-payers' money. It informed the electorate "if you opened all their briefcases you'll find nothing in them but a peanut-butter sandwich." George Wallace was back in form, and back in the running.

For Nixon's strategists in the White House, the news caused chagrin but not complete surprise. George Wallace had, after all, been on their "enemies list" since the summer of 1971 and closely watched ever since 1968. Most people who were on the enemies list had offended because of something they had said or written or endorsed. George Wallace was in a somewhat different category: he was the blot on the landscape of the new Republican majority, or, to be more accurate, the new Nixon majority.

To understand the dismay that the prospect of a Wallace candidacy caused, it is necessary to go back to the White House's favourite psychological work, *The Emerging Repub-*

lican Majority by Kevin Phillips. In his last chapter, Phillips discusses the future implications of trends revealed in the election result. He begins: "The long-range meaning of the political upheaval of 1968 rests on the Republican opportunity to fashion a majority among the 57 percent of the American electorate which voted to eject the Democratic Party from national power." (I.e., Nixon's 43.4 percent plus Wallace's 13.5 percent.) Phillips then goes on to note that one of the most decisive elements in the fragmentation of the Democratic vote was "that fifteen million or so conservative Democrats who shunned Hubert Humphrey to divide about evenly between Richard Nixon and George Wallace. Such elements stretched from the 'Okie' Great Central Valley of California to the mountain towns of Idaho, Florida's space centers, rural South Carolina, Bavarian Minnesota, the Irish sidewalks of New York and the Levittowns of Megalopolis."

And later: "Although most of Wallace's votes came from Democrats, he principally won those in motion between a Democratic past and a Republican future." Phillips goes on to say: "Only those fully alienated by the national Democratic Party stuck with Wallace in the voting booth. Offered a three-party context, these sociopolitical streams preferred populist Wallace; a two-party context would have drawn them into the GOP. Three-quarters or more of the Wallace electorate represented lost Nixon votes." Phillips's conclusion: ". . . the appeal of a successful Nixon Administration and the lack of a Wallace candidacy would greatly swell the 1972 Republican vote in the South, West, Border and the Catholic North. . . ."

Stopping Wallace was, almost from the start of the Nixon Administration, a matter of prime political concern. Whatever was done to the Democrats, they were bound to find a candidate somewhere—they could not be prevented from running in the election altogether. The same was not true of the American Independent Party. It could run no one but Wallace. If Wallace could be deterred his party would be out of the race altogether. Only then would the much-vaunted "Southern strategy" pay maximum dividends.

A secret "Stop Wallace" drive, coordinated by Bob Haldeman, had been underway since 1970 when the little Southerner was running again for Governor of Alabama. Before the election, James Martin, the National Republican Committeeman from Alabama, reportedly visited Wallace and, passing himself off as Nixon's personal emissary, tried to induce the Governor to sign a pledge not to run as an Independent in 1972. The story was later reported in the Atlanta *Constitution*, but Martin has denied using the President's name. In any case, when it became clear that Wallace's ambitions were as grand as ever, Nixon's strategists threw their financial support behind Albert Brewer, his opponent in the race for the governor's mansion.

Secret payments totaling $400,000 were made by Herbert Kalmbach out of residual 1968 Nixon campaign funds to the Brewer campaign. Kalmbach flew across the country to hand over the first $100,000 to an unknown "bagman" in New York's very smart Sherry-Netherland Hotel. Soon afterwards, Haldeman's brother-in-law, France Raine, delivered another $200,000 at the same place. The final $100,000 was handed over by Kalmbach at the Los Angeles branch of the Bank of California. It seems that neither Kalmbach nor Raine knew the purpose of the payments or the identity of the bagman; they simply followed their orders to make the deliveries. The investment almost paid off; Brewer ran a surprise lead in the first primary. But he failed to gain a clear majority and Wallace won the runoff.

At the same time, Haldeman was seeking to damage Wallace by revealing that his brother Gerald had defrauded the Internal Revenue Service. He demanded of the Justice Department a full report of the IRS audit of the Wallace brothers' law firm; the audit alleged that Gerald had omitted legal-fee income from his tax returns in 1967 and 1968. This income, so the charge went, was largely from political kickbacks. In early 1970 Gerald Wallace complained bitterly to a visiting newsman from Washington: "They have got forty-seven agents on me right now. You all are trying to beat George Wallace. You're not interested in my tax returns." He said that Federal agents had been chasing him ever since his brother "scared the hell out of Nixon and Humphrey."

After the failure of the 1970 effort to destroy Wallace's political base in Alabama, it seemed that the best that could be done was to persuade him to apply his divisive strength to the Democratic Party, and to run as a Democrat rather than an Independent. In May, 1971, Nixon, on a visit to Alabama, had Wallace ride with him on a flight from Mobile to Birmingham. What they said to each other is not known, but it was not long afterwards that the case against Gerald Wallace was dropped and that George Wallace announced that he would run as a Democrat, not an Independent, in 1972.

This ensured that the Democratic primaries would be nicely disrupted, but it did not do much to lessen the eventual threat of Wallace himself. He was quite happy to do what he could to weaken his opponents, but he had no intention whatsoever of withdrawing the AIP from the race. He would spend the first six months of 1972 establishing what a force he was amongst Democrats in both the North and the South and then, when he inevitably failed to win the nomination, he would fall back upon the AIP and launch his own drive for the Presidency. There was, therefore, every reason for Nixon's lieutenants to intensify their drive against his party. At the end of 1971 they went so far as to undertake a bizarre scheme which involved the help of the American Nazi Party.

The idea was to remove Wallace's AIP from the ballot in California, Nixon's home state. Under California law a party's registration must exceed at least one-fifteenth of the total statewide registration for it to be included on the ballot. If enough AIP members could be persuaded to change their registration, the AIP could take no part in the elections. The scheme was outlined to Attorney General John Mitchell and Jeb Magruder by Glenn Parker, a Nazi sympathiser, in the Los Angeles Hilton in October, 1971. According to Parker, Mitchell opened the conversation by outlining the strategic problem: "He said he had heard there was a way to remove the AIP from the ballot. He said they had run a poll between Muskie, Nixon, and Wallace that showed that without Wallace, four-fifths of the Wallace vote would go to Nixon. He emphasised that they thought they were in trouble, and that Nixon especially wanted to win California."

Mitchell liked the registration idea, and Magruder authorised the payment of $10,000 for its implementation. "Duke" Sloan, the CREEP treasurer, handed the money over in an envelope to Lyn Nofziger, who later became CREEP's director in California, and he passed it on to Bob Walters, the right-wing advertising man and friend of Parker who had dreamed up the scheme in the first place. But Parker and Walters found the drive a little more difficult than their enthusiastic outline to Mitchell had suggested. It involved persuading all but 10,000 of the AIP's 140,000 registered California voters to change their allegiance. In mid-November they decided they needed more help and called on the services of Joseph Tommassi, twenty-two-year-old head of the Southern Californian branch of the American Nazi Party. In his swastika-decorated house in the El Monte suburb of Los Angeles, they offered Tommassi $5,000 to have his men help in the drive. He agreed, and twenty Nazis, neatly dressed in plain clothes, began to scour the state.

The plan was not enormously successful. During this period, AIP registration actually increased by 6,500. And even if Walters, Parker, and all the Nazis in California had actually managed to persuade 130,000 voters to desert George Wallace, the AIP would still have remained on the ballot. Another provision of the state law allows any party which received more than 2 percent of the vote at the previous gubernatorial election, as the AIP did, to be placed automatically on the ballot. Magruder and Mitchell had not bothered to find this out when they embarked on the venture.

So George Wallace stormed into the new year of 1972 with every chance, and every intention, of making life difficult for both his Democratic and Republican rivals. "Send Them a Message" was his campaign slogan. The targets were familiar from his barnstorming days in 1968—the liberal twisters in the press, super-fatted bureaucrats, pointy-headed intellectuals, two-timing politicians in Washington. On race, the issue that had first brought him to prominence as a fiery segregationist, he spoke with the oblique caution that was required after a decade of civil-rights legislation. It was an issue that had to be dealt with in code, and in 1972 the code was "Bussing."

In January, 1972, Judge Robert R. Merhige, Jr., of the Federal District Court of Richmond, Virginia, ordered that a racial balance must be attained in the now 70-percent-black public schools of the city. It was impossible to achieve this from within the city itself, so he ruled that the two suburban counties adjacent to the city must send their children into the urban center until the racial mix was correct. Fifteen of the fifty-one largest cities of the United States then had a majority of nonwhite pupils in their public schools; according to this decision all of them would have been entitled to reach into the suburbs and force lower-middle- and middle-class whites—many of whom had retreated from the cities for the sole purpose of sending their children to predominantly white schools —to watch their kids being bussed back into the decaying black city centers. Predictably enough, the decision aroused a furor throughout the country—one which George Wallace exploited to the full and to which Nixon felt compelled to respond.

The Merhige decision (reversed in June, 1972) was only the culmination of a series of court orders which had, throughout 1971, needled anxieties, and by early spring, 1972, bussing was one of the main campaign issues.

While he was preparing his China trip, the President had his staff prepare him a statement to Congress setting out more categorically than ever his opposition to bussing. With George Wallace setting fire to Florida on his return from Peking, Nixon decided that the first draft they sent him was not nearly strong enough; two days after Wallace blazed to victory in Miami on March 15, the President sent the final version up to the Hill. It was strong stuff. "I am opposed to court-ordered bussing for the purpose of achieving racial balance in our schools," he wrote. "I have spoken out against bussing scores of times over many years. And I believe most Americans—white and black—share that view. But what we need now is not just speaking out against more bussing, we need action to stop it."

As Nixon was publicly trying to defuse Wallace's most potent issue, his loyal supporters in CREEP were privately trying to make Wallace's third-party candidacy more problematic. In March, 1972, methods of removing the American Independent Party from the various state ballots were the subject of intensive study in the office of CREEP's general counsel. Gordon Liddy abandoned the work only in April, when Watergate planning made more pressing demands on his time.

Wallace, meanwhile, went from strength to strength in the Democratic primaries. Even though he had no chance of achieving the nomination (one of the few things on which the radical McGovernites and traditionalist Humphreyites could agree was that the party of Franklin Delano Roosevelt should never be led by a segregationist), Wallace was proving that he had grass-roots support North and South. By mid-May, he was running second in terms of committed delegate support at the convention, with 324 to McGovern's 560. In terms of actual votes cast in the primaries, he was ahead of both McGovern and Humphrey. If he could not be the Democratic candidate, Wallace was certainly going to be a power-broker at the convention and, after that, a strong third-party candidate.

And if McGovern was nominated, anything might happen. For McGovern was weakest in those areas of the North where Wallace was showing the most strength—among white, working-class Democrats. Wallace had threatened the North in 1968, but the brilliant work of Humphrey's supporters in the labour unions had drawn most of the potential defectors back to their Democratic allegiance by election day. As Kevin Phillips put it in his book: "In the last few weeks of the campaign, labour union activity, economic issues and the escalating two-party context of October, 1968, drew many Wallace-leaning Northern blue-collar workers back into the Democratic fold." In 1972, given the sour relations between McGovern and George Meany, the all-powerful chief of the AFL–CIO, the union leadership seemed much less disposed to make a similar effort. Wallace was moving into a situation that gave him real potential, not just in the South and Border states, but as a national candidate.

At 4:15 on the afternoon of May 15, such speculations became academic. Wallace was gunned down after a campaign rally in Laurel, Maryland. The five bullets fired into the Governor of Alabama from close range have left him paralysed from the waist down ever since. The would-be assassin, Arthur Bremer, a twenty-one-year-old Milwaukee busboy, was immediately arrested.

According to a *Washington Post* story published in June, 1973, the attempted assassination of Wallace caused perturbation in the White House. The *Post* story quotes a "White House source" as saying that when the President heard of the shooting that afternoon he voiced concern that the attempt on Governor Wallace's life might have been made by someone with ties to the Republican Party or his campaign. Such ties, he is alleged to have said, could cost him the election. According to the "source": "The President was agitated and wanted the political background on Bremer." This alleged episode ties in with an odd aspect of Howard Hunt's testimony in secret session with investigators on the Senate Watergate Committee staff. Hunt reportedly said that about an hour after the Wallace shooting, he was called by Charles Colson from the White House, asked to fly at once to Milwaukee and break into Bremer's apartment, where he should try to find anything that might be useful in linking Bremer to left-wing political causes. Hunt said that he told Colson that this was impossible; he could never arrive before the police. Colson denies making the request in the first place.

Out of this thicket of contradictions it is difficult to be certain what happened. But, with hindsight, it is easy to see why there should have been concern in the White House. By this time CREEP's excessive loose change had financed so many dirty tricksters that it was just conceivable that one of them might have been Arthur Bremer. As it happened, such concern proved superfluous. Left-wing literature was found in Bremer's apartment, and in his car was a handwritten diary; it demonstrated that he was no friend of Nixon. According to the diary —a transcript of which was produced in evidence at Bremer's trial in August, 1972—the unhappy young man had stalked Richard Nixon himself in the apparent hope of killing the President of the United States (press and Secret Service photographs showed how close to the President he had approached on this mission). In his diary Bremer said that it was frustration at his inability to kill Nixon that led him to pick on the less heavily guarded George Wallace.

Wallace's personal tragedy simplified the politics of the Republic. It would be essentially a two-party election after all, and it looked increasingly as if Nixon and McGovern would be the respective party champions. This meant that CREEP's strategists no longer had to entertain the uncomfortable prospect of political war on two fronts; they could begin to bore in on McGovern without fear of exposing a flank to Wallace. And by May, 1972, preparations for McGovern's comeuppance were already far advanced: plans for bugging his every political move had already been drafted, financed, and approved.

CHAPTER 11

Dinner Is Served

J. EDGAR Hoover died in his bedroom on the morning of May 2, 1972. The Washington Medical Examiner, Dr. James L. Luke, reported that Hoover had been suffering from a heart ailment for some time. The cause of death was officially described as "hypertensive cardio-vascular disease." Hoover was seventy-seven years old and, after a career as FBI chief spanning almost half a century, he can have had few complaints about the fullness of his life. He did not, however, die a contented man.

Shortly before his death, Hoover revealed some of his concerns, on a strictly off-the-record basis, to Andrew Tully, a friendly newspaperman. Hoover said he was worried about the future of the bureau, particularly in its relations with what he described as "the President's kindergarten." He told Tully that he had been forced "to put the kibosh on one crazy intelligence scheme against subversives"; but similar schemes kept coming back. But what worried him most was the development of a new investigative-cum-intelligence force which appeared to be working directly for the President ("the plumbers"). "By God," said Hoover, "he's got some former CIA men working for him that I'd kick out of my office. Some day, that bunch will serve him up a fine mess." At the time he was conversing with Tully, in January, 1972, Hoover was simply expressing a hunch. He did not know that "that bunch" had already served up the hors d'oeuvres— the Ellsberg psychiatrist's office burglary—nor did he know that plans for the main course—the Watergate burglary— were already almost half baked. Death, perhaps mercifully, spared him from contemplation of the full repast.

Like many of history's more remarkable ideas, the origins of the Watergate burglary seemed comparatively innocuous. Around the summer of 1971, Jack Caulfield began seriously to consider his future. After his failure to go along with the idea of burgling the Brookings Institution, he and his friend Tony Ulasewicz found they were getting less and less work from the White House. Caulfield thought it might be a good idea to go into the security business on his own, with CREEP as his first customer. He began to develop a plan.

By September, 1971, he had submitted his grand design, which he had named "Operation Sand Wedge," in a manila folder to John Dean and John Ehrlichman. It envisaged his setting up a firm called "Security Consulting Group, Inc." with offices in New York, Chicago, and Washington. Its overt side would do normal security business, with CREEP just the first of its hopefully many clients; its covert side—based in New York—would provide "bag men" to carry money and be able, if required, to engage in electronic surveillance. But nobody seemed very interested in the idea. Realising that he would find it very hard to get his firm off the ground without the prestige of CREEP as its baptismal client, Jack Caulfield determined instead to get the best possible security work on the staff of CREEP, and he asked John Dean to arrange an interview for him with John Mitchell.

On November 24, Caulfield saw Mitchell in the Justice Department and explained to the Attorney General that he would like to do for him the kind of job that Dwight Chapin did for the President. Mitchell was noncommittal, and gave him the temporary task of sleuthing Paul McCloskey, one of the few California Republicans who opposed Nixon and who later ran briefly in the Republican primaries as a presidential candidate. It was not the kind of work that Caulfield wanted; as he left, he was not much encouraged to see G. Gordon Liddy, the man who had supplanted him as the White House's top investigator, sitting in the Attorney General's outer office.

Liddy had a rather successful meeting with the Attorney General. He had come, highly recommended by Egil Krogh, to apply for the post as CREEP's general counsel, a job which Mitchell had already decided should carry responsibility for CREEP's intelligence-gathering operation. Liddy evidently impressed Mitchell more than the battered ex-cop who had preceded him. For Liddy emerged with the job and with the understanding that he should prepare plans for a major intelligence operation—a glorified version of Caulfield's humble "Sand Wedge."

On December 12, Liddy finally joined CREEP and met for the first time with his new boss Jeb Magruder. Magruder, who did not know that Liddy had been a "plumber," was told by his new general counsel that he had been discussing "a broad-gauged intelligence plan" with people at the White House. Liddy said that he had been promised $1 million to carry it out. Magruder advised Liddy to prepare the background documents necessary to justify such a large budget. A scheme of that size would have to be approved by John Mitchell.

As Liddy began to fashion his plan, he found that another recent recruit to CREEP's staff was proving enormously helpful. James W. McCord, Jr., CREEP's new director of security, was in many ways the antithesis of Liddy. He was a quiet, unassuming middle-aged man who wore his accomplishments lightly. In conversation he was polite but reticent, yielding his opinions and observations only when specifically asked. In January, 1972, Liddy began to ask McCord whether he knew anything about recent developments in the art of electronic surveillance. He found McCord was a mine of information.

Beyond the fact that McCord had once been in the CIA and that he had come to CREEP highly recommended as a Republican with security experience, little was known about the new director of security. There was nothing in his earnest and diligent demeanour that suggested he would emerge as the most dramatically intriguing character in the whole Watergate drama. But McCord had always been a remarkable man, and rather more careful checking into his background by CREEP at the time might have forewarned them about the dangers of using such a man.

The details of McCord's CIA-sanctioned curriculum vitae do not give much away. But even its bald, carefully screened facts indicated a man of quality. It reads as follows: JAMES McCORD; BORN: January 26, 1924, Waurika, Oklahoma. HIGH SCHOOL: McLean and Electra, Texas. EDUCATION: Master of Science, George Washington University,

1965. Bachelor of Business Administration, University of Texas, 1949. Graduate class of 1965, Air War College. 1942–43: FBI, Washington and New York. Radio intelligence duties. 1943–45: U.S. Army Air Corps officer. 1948–51: FBI special agent, San Diego and San Francisco, California. 1951–70: CIA, chief, Physical Security Division, Office of Security. From 1962–64, CIA senior officer in Europe. MILITARY: Lieutenant Colonel, USAF Reserve. Former commander, National Wartime Information and Security Program detachment, Washington USAFR. CIVIC AND OTHER: Member, National Legislative Affairs Board, National Association for Retarded Children, and member board of directors, Cerebral Palsy Association and Montgomery County Workshops for the Handicapped, Montgomery County, Maryland. AWARDS: Distinguished Service Award for outstanding performance of duty from director of CIA, Richard Helms. Retired August 1970 after 25 years Federal service.

The flesh on this skeleton makes McCord, if anything, more impressive. The security jobs with the CIA were not simply those of a glorified "house dick" sweeping rooms for bugs and so on. He cleared personnel as well; under the charter of the organisation, the CIA screens its own staff. He was, therefore, a good judge of character as well as electronic gear. He was part of the CIA–FBI team which debriefed U-2 pilots shot down in 1959 on a mission over the Soviet-Iranian border. According to Colonel L. Fletcher Prouty, who has written a book about the CIA, McCord was such a good interrogator that, from the questions he asked the crew on their release, he was able to find a picture and identify the Soviet intelligence agent who questioned the fliers. A former number-two man in the CIA described McCord's work as "highly responsible requiring great accuracy with details." Allen Dulles, a former CIA chief, once referred to McCord as "my top man."

In August, 1970, McCord resigned from the CIA, and after a few months' traveling around the country set up his own security business, McCord Associates, near his home in Rockville, Maryland. He also offered a course of lectures at the nearby Montgomery College. His course, Criminal Justice 234, was listed in the college catalogue as "introduction to historical, philosophical, and legal basis of government and industrial security programs in a democratic society." McCord would spend a half-day each week running a "social fellowship" for older members of the Rockville United Methodist Church. McCord Associates, however, was not doing much business. He was, therefore, very much available when in the fall of 1971 the offer of a job came up at CREEP.

McCord was recommended for the job by Jack Caulfield and Al Wong, an old friend who was then deputy assistant director of the Secret Service. (One of Al Wong's specific jobs as the technical-security expert in the Secret Service was to supervise the installation of President Nixon's elaborate bugging mechanisms in the White House.) McCord was taken on as CREEP's part-time "security coordinator" in October, and on January 1, 1972, was given the full-time post, while his firm, McCord Associates, was given a contract to provide security services for the Republican National Committee. He had already proved his worth.

But from the White House's point of view, CREEP's supremely competent physical-security man held two highly dangerous opinions. In the first place, he was intensely loyal to the CIA, with a strong belief that it should be totally free of partisan control in its intelligence-gathering function. Secondly, he was a profound admirer of Richard Helms, whom McCord regarded as the best guardian of the CIA's integrity. McCord's arrival at CREEP—just one month after Helms had told the White House that the CIA would have nothing more to do with its "plumber" E. Howard Hunt—was fraught with ominous possibilities. Given McCord's background, the CIA could be sure that, if its interests were ever trampled on by the growing army of CREEP's dirty-tricksters, it would have a friend at court. And that is precisely what McCord became, with catastrophic consequences for the White House.

It was perhaps only natural that McCord should evince helpful interest in Gordon Liddy's plans, and by the beginning of January, 1972, they were discussing the general counsel's responsibilities in some detail. As McCord later told the story, it became increasingly clear to him that Liddy was less concerned with the minutiae of the election laws than with intelligence-gathering problems—especially those involving the forthcoming Republican convention. Liddy, it seemed, was very, very worried about the problems of demonstrators. "He began," said McCord, "seeking from me certain information regarding the costs and the types of electronic devices that could be used in bugging." In mid-January he showed McCord a package of large charts wrapped up in brown paper; he was going to use them in his presentation to the Attorney General.

On January 27, Liddy humped his package over to the Justice Department and up in Mitchell's private elevator to the Attorney General's fifth-floor office. At 4 P.M. he carried it through the seventy-five-foot-long, blue-carpeted, wood-inlaid, formal office into Mitchell's private office beyond. He set the charts up on an easel in the corner and then he began to explain his immodest proposals to Jeb Magruder, the assistant director of CREEP, John Dean, the President's legal counsel, and John Mitchell, the Attorney General of the United States.

Each of Liddy's charts, which were professionally drawn in living colour, bore names like "Gemstone" and "Target." He envisaged the use of mugging squads, kidnapping teams, well-trained prostitutes, and electronic surveillance. The mugging squads were to rough up demonstrators, the kidnapping teams were to round up radical leaders and ship them to camps in Mexico for the duration of the Republican Convention in San Diego, and the prostitutes were to be used at the Democratic convention both to obtain information and to compromise leading Democrats. Liddy said that he would hire a yacht on which the girls would operate. It would be specially wired for sound and fitted with hidden cameras. The girls, he assured his distinguished audience, would be very high class, "the best in the business." Moving on to the problems of electronic surveillance, Liddy said that after consultation with one of the best authorities in the country, he had decided that this should be far more extensive than mere bugging and tapping of phones. He declared that his plan included the interception of communications between aircraft and the ground. For thirty minutes Liddy enthusiastically outlined his proposals, moving the charts on and off the easel, eloquently expounding the advantages of each and every component, and ending by saying that it could all be done for just $1 million.

Dean recalled the whole thing was "mind-boggling." Magruder later said they were all "appalled." Mitchell subsequently described it as "beyond the pale." But he did not say so at the time. His reaction then was, according to Dean, characteristic. During Liddy's presentation he sat back in his chair impassively sucking his pipe, and when he once caught Dean's eye, he winked. When Liddy had finished, Mitchell took some long reflective puffs and said, "It's not quite what I had in mind." Liddy was told to "go back to the drawing boards and come up with a more realistic plan." As he left the building, Dean told Liddy to destroy his charts. Altogether, Liddy seemed rather discouraged.

He soon returned to his normal cheery self. A few days later he told McCord that Dean said that things "looked good" for the plan, that the only problems were that "some means would have to be found for deniability for Mr. Mitchell" and that "a method of funding should be arranged so that the funds would not come through the regular committee." Liddy, without telling his supervisors, also asked McCord, for the first time, if he would like to join the operation to bug the Democratic National Committee. McCord, apparently impressed by this high honour, agreed to do what he could.

Over the next week Liddy revised his plans. He dropped the idea of the call girls and, although Mitchell had said that it was the demonstration problem in which he was most interested, he abandoned the plans for kidnapping squads as well. His new, streamlined, $500,000 version concentrated on wiretapping and photography, and at 11 A.M. on February 4, Mitchell and Magruder and Dean gathered once again in the Attorney General's office to hear him out.

In keeping with the more modest nature of his proposals, Liddy had reduced his charts to eight-by-ten-inch sheets which he passed around. They then discussed specific targets, says Magruder (Mitchell does not remember this)—amongst them the DNC Headquarters and the Fontainebleau Hotel, where the Democrats would have their headquarters during the convention at Miami Beach. Magruder also recalls discussing material damaging to Edmund Muskie in the safe of a Las Vegas newspaper editor—Hank Greenspun of the Las Vegas *Sun*. McCord described this information as "blackmail type," and says that a plan was later developed whereby "the entry team would go directly to an airport near Las Vegas where a Howard Hughes plane would be standing by to fly the team directly into a Central American country." This mission, as we have seen, was aborted, partly as a result of the Hughes organisation's reluctance to provide a "cover" and partly as a result of Muskie's fast receding viability as a candidate. (At the time it was discussed, Howard Hughes was living in Managua, Nicaragua; he is currently London's most invisible resident.)

Magruder says that Mitchell still "didn't feel comfortable" with the plan, and that Liddy was sent away to refine it just a little further. Mitchell says he rejected the plan completely. After the meeting, which he himself had cut short, says Dean, because "these discussions could not go on in the office of the Attorney General," Dean sought out Haldeman. He told him of the "incredible, unnecessary, and unwise" schemes Liddy had proposed. He says that Haldeman agreed that Dean should have no more to do with them. Haldeman does not remember any such conversation, though if his staff work was as good as its reputation, Haldeman should already have known of the schemes. Magruder was supposed to keep Haldeman's liaison man, Gordon Strachan, regularly informed of all that went on at CREEP, and he says that he told him of both meetings after they occurred. He claims that he even sent over to the White House copies of the diagrams that Liddy produced on February 4. Strachan denies any knowledge of the planning sessions.

While Liddy's intelligence-gathering plans were being refined under the supervision of Nixon's all-powerful Attorney General, the President's dignified approach to his re-election was reaching new levels of distinction. On the day Liddy's $500,000 proposal was being discussed in Mitchell's office, the sixth round of the SALT talks with the Soviet Union was completed. Two weeks later, the President boarded his plane, *The Spirit of '76*, and flew to Peking to the public celebration of the secret diplomatic edifice constructed by Henry Kissinger. The U.S. table-tennis team had paved the way to the Forbidden City, but Nixon's visit provided the real imprimatur on the new world order. Without a doubt, it was the high point of his Presidency and an impressive personal performance—right from the opening banquet when Nixon proposed in his toast that the two countries "start a Long March together." Before the final communiqué was issued, it was clear that the President's journey had achieved significant results: the door to China was wide open; it was difficult for Americans now to regard China as the bogeyman of the East; and other nations, particularly Japan, were having to readjust their own policies to the impact of the new dialogue.

At home, a nationwide Louis Harris poll showed that 73 percent of the American people approved of Nixon's trip to China, and even the Democratic-controlled Congress, on its own initiative, granted him a ten-day period of grace on his return to consider new legislation. His political opponents, campaigning in the New Hampshire and Florida primaries, found themselves struggling for media attention. Nixon had prepared well for his journey; he quoted Mao Tse-tung's poetry at a banquet and greeted Chou En-lai before one talk session with a hearty *Ni hau* ("How are you?"), and he was happy to disclose that he "used to play a little Ping-Pong years ago."

As this era of international amity was being ushered in, various disagreeable tensions were opening up among Nixon's secret strategists. For one thing, Mitchell was finding Haldeman increasingly hard to take—he never did much like John Ehrlichman. (There is an accumulating weight of evidence that suggests that many of Nixon's senior advisers never much liked anybody—except of course Nixon, to whom they owed their high eminence.) Relations between Mitchell and Chuck Colson were close to poisonous. Further down the line things were even more claustrophobic. Strachan, Haldeman's liaison man, was terrified of Haldeman—who made him wear a bleeper for instant summonses—and resentful of Jeb Magruder, who he felt did not put him fully in the picture. Magruder found that Colson's helpful prompting from the White House was getting on his nerves. According to one CREEP official, Magruder once received an idea from the President's special counsel with the observation: "That goddam Colson, he just sits there and dreams up this crap!" Relations between Magruder and Liddy verged on the murderous.

Liddy resented taking orders from the imperious, younger Magruder, in the same way that Magruder resented working with the junior Strachan. Because Liddy was so preoccupied with his espionage plans, his legal-counseling work had fallen somewhat behind. One day Magruder came up to him in the corridor, put his hand on his shoulder, and asked him "to be more cooperative in producing the work that we needed quickly." Liddy turned around and told Magruder that if he didn't take his hand off him, he would kill him.

Magruder now says he did not consider this a serious threat, that it was just Liddy's picturesque way of expressing his dislike. However, Magruder decided he could work with him no longer. Liddy seemed to accept it and suggested that his friend Howard Hunt—who had started working with him at CREEP—could take over the intelligence work. But afterwards, says Magruder, Liddy went to his friends at the White House to complain, and in the next few days Dean and Strachan called him to ask him to keep Liddy on. In the end the problem was settled by moving Liddy two floors down to the Finance Committee; he could continue his intelligence work and he and Magruder would no longer get in each other's hair.

Before he left Magruder's field of vision, Liddy was well established as the office freak. Several of the office secretaries had been the astonished recipients of life-size posters of G. Gordon Liddy posing beside a police squad car with a bullhorn in his hand. Once, when accompanying Hugh Sloan, the CREEP treasurer, to the bank, Liddy became concerned about the build-up of pressure in his gas-operated pellet gun. He solved the problem by discharging the weapon into the bowl of the men's lavatory in a nearby hotel. On another occasion Liddy demonstrated the mastery of his unusual mind over matter by holding his hand over a burning candle until it seared his flesh. The young lady who observed this remarkable feat enquired, "What is the trick?" Liddy replied, "The trick is not minding." For women pacing the terror-ridden streets of Washington, he was an encyclopedia of useful information. He once told the attractive wife of a CREEP official that she should always carry with her a sharpened pencil, but to be sure the eraser was in excellent condition. This precaution, Liddy observed, "will protect the palm of your hand when you drive the pencil into the attacker's throat."

On yet another occasion, Liddy startled one of Magruder's aides by indicating that he had orders to kill Jack Anderson. Though Anderson was a prominent "enemy" the aide thought this a bit extreme, told him to wait a minute, and contacted Magruder. It turned out that Magruder had thrown out an oblique reference to the fact that Anderson was giving the organisation a hard time. Liddy was advised that the figure of speech did not qualify the man for execution status. CREEP's general counsel took it well but advised Magruder to be more careful in the future, as "Where I come from, that's a rub-out."

Meanwhile, Liddy continued to refine plans for the intelligence-gathering operation and was becoming increasingly irritated with the bureaucratic delays. His old "plumbers" partner, E. Howard Hunt, was also keen to get going. Hunt was visiting Barker in Miami with increasing frequency, keying up the old team for a new job. One evening in early March, Hunt and Liddy sought the assistance of Charles Colson and asked him to persuade Magruder to get a move on. Colson then rang Magruder and said "Gordon Liddy's upset. He's trying to get started on an intelligence operation and he can't seem to see anybody." Magruder remembers him as asking him to "get off the stick and get the budget approved for Liddy's plans." Colson acknowledges making the call but denies any knowledge of what Liddy's plans actually were.

On March 30, Liddy's final proposal, now costed at an insignificant—by CREEP standards—$250,000, was put up for approval. By this time, Mitchell had left the Justice Department, transferred to CREEP, and was taking a short break at a holiday home in Key Biscayne. Magruder flew down to Florida with the Liddy proposal on his agenda list. Versions of the final authorisation meeting vary considerably. What is not in doubt is the identity of those present. Dean was not there. His place in the final strategy session was taken by John Mitchell's close and mysterious friend, Fred LaRue, the quiet Mississippian.

For three years Frederick Cheney "Bubba" LaRue worked in the White House as an aide without portfolio, without title, without a listing in the White House directory, and without pay. At the end of the first term he was almost as completely unknown as when he had arrived from the South in 1969. His father, whom LaRue shot in a hunting accident in 1957, was a first cousin of Sid Richardson, the Texas oil tycoon. Ike LaRue had gone to jail in Texas for bank violations. He then moved to Mississippi, searched for oil, and found a lot of it. The oil money that Fred was able to spread around Mississippi made him something of a power in the politics of the state.

LaRue first met Nixon in 1965 when LaRue was Republican National Committeeman for Mississippi and was attending a Western Republicans' Conference in Albuquerque, New Mexico. Nixon was just beginning to devise his "Southern strategy." LaRue, who had supported Goldwater in 1964, said later that

"Nixon's dilemma was that he had to win the nomination basically with the same forces Goldwater had in 1964 but without associating with them or being associated." Nixon was impressed with the quiet shrewdness of the man, and LaRue was apparently equally taken with Nixon. Later LaRue played a large part in keeping the Republican South from Reagan and winning it for Nixon.. With Richard Kleindienst he played a key role in getting Strom Thurmond, South Carolina's ferociously segregationist Senator, to swing his influence behind Nixon at the 1968 Republican convention.

Throughout Nixon's first term, LaRue continued massaging the President's Southern friends. Not all of them were Republicans; in fact, segregationist Democrats were often more congenial allies. For example, Fred LaRue was a close friend of James Eastland, Mississippi's Democratic Senator who had been so good to Nixon appointees when they came before his Judiciary Committee, and in 1972 he persuaded the White House to withhold effective support from Eastland's Republican rival.

When CREEP was established he moved to 1701 Pennsylvania Avenue as John Mitchell's personal envoy, and shared a suite with Magruder. They became so inseparable that some of the CREEP junior staff referred to the leadership as "Magrue." Down in Key Biscayne on March 30, LaRue was running errands and answering the phone. He was not in the room all the time Mitchell and Magruder talked.

Liddy's scheme was the last of some thirty issues which Magruder brought up for a decision from Mitchell. He had, he says, as usual made three copies of the proposal. One he had sent to Strachan, the second he now gave to Mitchell, and the third he kept for himself. The project now called simply for breaking into the DNC, photographing documents, placing bugs on the phones, and setting up a monitoring unit. There was a supplementary proposal that "if funds were available," bugs should also be placed in the Fontainebleau Hotel, where the Democratic Party's high command would be staying during the convention in Miami Beach, and in the campaign headquarters of the Democratic Party's nominee (who, by this time, looked increasingly like George McGovern). Magruder remembers the idea being gone over very thoroughly. "We discussed it," he said before the Senate Watergate Committee, "brought up all the pros and cons. I think I can honestly say that no one was particularly overwhelmed with the project. But I think we felt that the information could be useful and Mr. Mitchell agreed to approve the project."

Mitchell denies this emphatically. He says that he still doesn't understand who kept sending the Liddy plan back to him, and that he told Magruder, "We don't need this. I'm tired of hearing it. Let's not discuss it any further." Fred LaRue has yet another recollection. According to LaRue, Mitchell said of the Liddy proposal: "Well, this is not something that will have to be decided at this meeting."

Whatever was said, Magruder went back to Washington with the firm impression that the Liddy plan was approved and, he later claimed, called Gordon Strachan and told him that he could pass on the news to Haldeman that the plan was ready for "go" status. Strachan and Haldeman do not recall any such message. However, Robert Reisner, Magruder's assistant, does recall being instructed by Magruder in early April: "Call Liddy and tell him it's approved. Tell him to get going in the next two weeks."

Watergate was under way. It is perhaps understandable that memories should be so disorientated on the subject of approving an enterprise that involved burglary of the largest political party in America. But at least one of those present at the Key Biscayne meeting might not have been paying too much attention. Before we break and enter, it is worth examining the contemporary problem of John Mitchell, who had the best of all reasons for being abstracted during the months of February and March, 1972. The ITT scandal had just broken.

CHAPTER 12

"Destroy This, Huh?"

ON FEBRUARY 29 columnist Jack Anderson published a memo written nine months before by Dita Beard, the indomitable Washington lobbyist of the giant International Telephone and Telegraph Corporation (ITT). Dated June 25, 1971, it was marked "personal and confidential" and addressed to her boss, Bill Merriam, the head of ITT's Washington office. The subject was San Diego, a city where ITT had three hotels (another was under construction) and which the Republicans were on the point of choosing as the site for their forthcoming convention to nominate Richard Nixon for his second presidential term. These facts were public knowledge. What was not known was that shortly before Dita wrote her memorandum, the company's president, a slight, bespectacled, English-born accountant named Harold S. Geneen, had secretly offered the Republicans $400,000. For nearly two years Geneen had been fighting an attempt by the Justice Department to block what would, if successful, be the biggest corporate merger in American history: the acquisition by ITT of America's fifth-largest insurance company, an old, established, and highly profitable concern called Hartford Fire Insurance. Interestingly enough there were a number of references to this problem in Dita's memorandum.

"Other than permitting John Mitchell, Ed Reinecke [the Lieutenant Governor of California], Bob Haldeman and Nixon . . . *no one* has known from whom the 400 thousand commitment had come," Dita wrote.

"I am convinced . . . that our noble commitment has gone a long way toward our negotiations on the mergers eventually coming out as Hal [Geneen] wants them. Certainly the President has told Mitchell to see that things are worked out fairly. It is still only McLaren's mickeymouse we are suffering." (This was a reference to Richard W. McLaren, head of the Department of Justice's antitrust division and the main architect of the attempts to block the ITT–Hartford merger.)

"I hope, dear Bill, that all of this can be reconciled . . . if all of us in this office remain totally ignorant of any commitment ITT has made to anyone. If it gets too much publicity you can believe our negotiations with Justice [over Hartford] will wind up shot down. Mitchell is definitely helping us, but it cannot be known." The memorandum ended with a request: "Please destroy this, huh?"

The impact of the Anderson revelations was colossal, for his column is syndicated across the country. Here, apparently, was evidence that the White House and many of the most senior members of the administration had been induced by ITT to influence the Department of Justice to make a crucial antitrust decision in ITT's favour. The President himself was implicated. So, more directly, was the Attorney General, John Mitchell. Furthermore the memorandum seemed to show that Richard Kleindienst, then Mitchell's deputy, had been lying the previous December when he publicly denied that there had been any pressure at all in the Hartford case. In the wake of the disclosure, the Senate hearings into Kleindienst's nomination as Mitchell's successor, confirmed only the previous week, were reopened.

The Anderson story was one of his best scoops ever. To his young assistant, Brit Hume, who wrote the original story, the memo was "the single most incriminating piece of paper" he had ever seen. But was it genuine? Shortly after acquiring the memo, Anderson sent Hume to see Dita Beard to find out.

Yes, Dita said, she had written the memo. But there was no trade-off. "All we ever did," she told Hume, "was to offer to help raise that money." The following day she telephoned Hume to invite him to her house in Virginia. There she changed her story. Yes, there had been a settlement which she had personally negotiated with John Mitchell during a lunch given by the Governor of Kentucky during the Kentucky Derby in May, 1971. Mitchell had asked her, "What do you want?" She replied they wanted to keep Hartford and part of another company called Grinnell, but were prepared to let the others go. Mitchell apparently agreed: the settlement negotiated then was, so Dita claimed, exactly the one the Justice Department offered a month later. But, she insisted, it had nothing to do with the $400,000 pledge.

This was the last anybody was to hear from Dita for a little while. Two days after the publication of the Anderson story she was whisked away from Washington to a secluded private hospital half a continent away, in Denver, Colorado. There she was placed under the care of a Hungarian-born heart specialist named Dr. Radetsky. The man who organised Dita's disappearing act was none other than G. Gordon Liddy, the legal counsel to CREEP.

While the FBI and a posse of newspapermen scoured the country for Dita, the PR men at ITT were busy cranking the publicity machine. "Neither Mrs. Beard nor anyone else except legal counsel was authorised to carry on such negoti- ations," said ITT. Mitchell too put out a denial. It was less than comprehensive. He said he had "no knowledge of any- one from the [convention] committee or elsewhere dealing with ITT." Later during the Senate's re-examination of the Kleindienst nomination, he went further and denied com- pletely that he had ever reached any agreement of any kind with Dita Beard or ITT during Kentucky Derby week. Nor, he said, had he specifically discussed the ITT–Hartford merger during his frequent meetings with Geneen in 1970 and 1971; the conversations were of a general nature and dealt with the administration's antitrust policies only in the broadest of terms.

ITT was not content with issuing a simple denial; by then the issue was far too serious. The day after the Anderson story broke, the company mounted a search-and-destroy operation. Every document it could find relating to the San Diego convention and the secret negotiations over Hartford was fed into the shredding machine. To prove the Beard memo a forgery, ITT recruited two teams of typewriter experts who subjected the memo (which ITT succeeded in recovering) to a whole battery of tests. These showed, the experts claimed, that the memo was not written in 1971, as its date indicated, but early in 1972. The FBI made similar tests. But its analysts came up with a different conclusion. "On the basis of the chemical tests possible within the time available," the FBI re- ported, "the typewriting ink appears to be substantially similar in composition to typewriter ink appearing on all submitted

comparison documents [from Mrs. Beard's typewriter] bearing
dates June 28, 1971, and earlier."

Meanwhile Dita Beard, still confined to bed in the Rocky
Mountain Osteopathic Hospital, Denver, had had a visitor
from Washington. But he did not come to offer best wishes
for a speedy recovery; nor was his appearance calculated to
improve a heart condition. Dita's son Robert recalls him as
wearing an outsize red wig which canted over one eye—"like
he had put it on in a dark car." In an attempt to disguise
his complexion, the visitor had smeared his face with pancake
makeup which, during the course of the interview, began to
trickle down one cheek. According to Robert his entire appearance was "mysterious . . . very eerie." Robert never
discovered exactly who he was or what he had come for. The
mysterious visitor was in fact E. Howard Hunt, who had
been sent by Charles Colson to discover exactly what Dita
intended to say when her pursuers eventually caught up with
her. Shortly after Hunt's visit Mrs. Beard changed her story:
the Anderson memo was a hoax and her initials had been
forged.

The following week a special subcommittee of the Senate
Judiciary Committee, then in the throes of re-examining the
Kleindienst nomination, flew to Denver to get Dita's story
at first hand. It was a macabre scene. Dita was wired up to an
electrocardiograph and after two hours of inconclusive questioning—during which she stuck to her new story—Dr. Radetsky called a halt to the proceedings, insisting that his patient
was too ill for further questioning for at least six months.

It was all very unsatisfactory. The Beard memorandum was,
as Hume had said, highly incriminating. But by itself it was
not conclusive. And in the absence of hard evidence that
Kleindienst had behaved improperly, the Senate felt it had no
option but to reconfirm his nomination as Mitchell's successor as Attorney General. In June, 1972, the longest nomination hearings in the Senate's history finally ended: only
nineteen Senators voted against the Kleindienst nomination.

The result might have been different if the Senators had had
the opportunity of reading a private memorandum that White
House aide Charles Colson had written to the President's chief
of staff, Bob Haldeman, on March 30, 1972. In it Colson expressed anxiety about a whole series of White House and ITT
memoranda written between April, 1969, when the Justice

Department first began to make warning noises about the ITT–Hartford merger, to May, 1971, shortly before McLaren at Justice gave ITT the green light and allowed it to keep Hartford. Colson told Haldeman that he thought that most, but not all, of the memoranda had been retrieved. But he was afraid that if the contents of one in particular ever got out, "that revelation would lay this case on the President's doorstep."

He was therefore concerned by the threat the hearings posed. "Kleindienst is not the target," Colson wrote, "the President is, but Kleindienst is the best available vehicle for the Democrats to get to the President. Make no mistake, the Democrats want to keep this case alive—whatever happens to Kleindienst—but the battle over Kleindienst elevates the visibility of the ITT matter and, indeed, guarantees that the case will stay alive. . . .

"Neither Kleindienst, Mitchell, nor Mardian know of the potential dangers. I have deliberately not told Kleindienst or Mitchell since both may be recalled as witnesses and Mardian does not understand the problem. Only Fred Fielding [a White House aide on the legal counsel's staff], myself, and Ehrlichman have fully examined all the documents and/or information that could yet come out."

ITT's friend at the White House was John Ehrlichman. Since 1969 he had been pressuring McLaren to drop his opposition to the merger. In September, 1970, Ehrlichman wrote to John Mitchell complaining about McLaren's attitude and referring to an "understanding" with Geneen. However, even with the White House and the Attorney General on its side, ITT could not be sure of success. Although McLaren was new to the political game, he *was* head of the antitrust division of the Justice Department and he *had* made it clear he was prepared to fight the issue right up to the Supreme Court. ITT kept trying.

By the spring of 1971 the Hartford case was still unresolved, but on May 5 Ehrlichman wrote to Mitchell, referring to a conversation the Attorney General had had with the President in which they had discussed the "agreed-upon ends" in the ITT case. Exactly a week later, ITT held its annual general meeting among the palm trees of San Diego. And there at an open-air dinner party Geneen made his $400,000 pledge to the Republican Party. At the end of July the settlement was announced. ITT was forced to disgorge six companies but

Geneen kept what he most wanted—Hartford Fire Insurance. "Quite clearly," said *Fortune* magazine, "Harold S. Geneen has achieved something of a victory."

Yet another victory, of sorts, was effected by the Nixon administration in the spring and summer of 1972; most of the embarrassing details of the Justice–ITT trust negotiations were kept from the prying eyes of the Senate during the Kleindienst hearings. Jack Anderson's story and Dita Beard's cavorting had caused a storm but, for want of further evidence, it had quickly passed. The President emerged untouched; Kleindienst's nomination was accepted; and John Mitchell could now return his full attention to the business of the Committee to Re-Elect the President, where the next item on the agenda was the Watergate break-in.

CHAPTER 13

"Gemstone"

THE WATERGATE complex of apartments, hotel, and offices, towers like a huge modern fortress over the left bank of the Potomac. During the first Nixon administration it came to be known as the "Republican Bastille," for many of the men Nixon brought to town preferred its immediate comfort and safety to the dark little streets of Georgetown favoured by the permanent and largely Democratic residents of Washington. John Mitchell lived in the Watergate; so did Maurice Stans; and on the sixth floor of its office block was the main target of CREEP's clandestine operation—the headquarters of the Democratic National Committee.

Even after months of testimony before the Senate Watergate committee, nobody has satisfactorily answered the question of why bugging the DNC and attempting to bug George McGovern's campaign headquarters were worth the money, time, and energy put into the task. Jeb Magruder, so far the only man who has admitted to consciously approving the project, suggested it was a very low-priority operation, sanctioned almost as an afterthought. The only specific objective he mentioned was a desire to get something on the DNC chairman, Larry O'Brien, then reckoned the shrewdest political general in the opposition camp. O'Brien had also been a moving spirit behind Democratic exploitation of the ITT scandal in the Kleindienst hearings. According to Magruder, CREEP had received a tip from Kevin Phillips, the author of *The Emerging Republican Majority*, that O'Brien was involved in a kickback scheme involving a business exhibition to be held at the Democratic convention. The tip on O'Brien turned out to be a dud. But digging up a scandal on O'Brien, even presuming one existed, was essentially detective-agency work. It did not require the expenditure of $250,000, nor did it explain the attempt to bug McGovern's headquarters.

The explanation favoured by most commentators is that by this time Nixon's loyalists in CREEP had reached such a pitch of paranoia that they were adopting a scatter-gun approach and bugging everything that moved, just in case it might turn up something useful. Since none of the operators from Hunt down to the Cuban-exile legmen has actually stated what was the precise purpose of the bugging (they may not, of course, have known), this has been a practical, but perhaps too comforting, hypothesis. It is one, for example, that fits in with President Nixon's subsequent explanation of Watergate and associated dramas as examples of "excessive zeal" by low-level personnel. But bugging the DNC was very high-grade criminality indeed, even for zealots. Or perhaps, high-grade "national security." And as Hunt and his Cuban-exile associates, who actually did the burglary, say they were involved in a "national security" operation, it is at least a proposition worth exploring. Once again the clue may be in Vietnam. For Nixon's "peace with honour" strategy throughout 1972 would be vitally influenced by the Democratic attitude. It is possible that the early bugging-plan sessions may have been no more than contingency discussions. But by the end of May, 1972, when the bugging actually began, there was a very good reason why Nixon's men might have considered it necessary as a "national security" operation.

Muskie had been cut down and McGovern had emerged, but in somewhat more potent form than Nixon can have felt happy with. A Harris poll taken on May 10 showed McGovern only 7 percent behind Nixon in a two-way race, and Nixon had a reputation of dropping support as election day approached. For the men around Nixon this must have been deeply disturbing. In part, McGovern was a "monster" of their own creation, but he was also the kind of man who could interfere with "peace with honour."

Indeed, there were some in the White House who felt that he had even done so already by his mobilisation of critics of the Vietnam policy. Although there were many on the left who saw Vietnamisation followed by "peace with honour" as cynical stage-management of a civil war to save American face in Southeast Asia, no one in Nixon's White House considered it in those terms. They believed in the policy and, more importantly, believed that those who interfered with it were rendering a disservice to the nation. They also knew, from the polling evidence, that if Americans did not see some prospect of Nixon's bringing the war to an end, his re-election chances would be much diminished.

But it takes two sides to make peace, with or without honour, and as long as Hanoi saw a reasonable prospect of getting what it wanted from a new administration it might not feel inclined to conclude a peace short of its objectives with Nixon. Indeed, it was precisely this thinking that informed Haldeman's surprise appearance on the *Today* show in January, 1972, when he said that Nixon's war critics were "consciously aiding and abetting the enemy." And shortly after Haldeman's broadcast, Nixon added his own caution by asking Democratic candidates for the Presidency to say nothing which "might give the enemy the incentive to prolong the war until after the election." For McGovern, of course, and to an extent for all the Democratic presidential candidates, with the possible exception of Senator Henry "Scoop" Jackson, this was literally impossible.

Moreover, McGovern had already shown himself ready to make his own unilateral soundings of Hanoi's position. Back in September, 1971, he had stopped off in Paris for three days to talk with the North Vietnamese negotiators at the Peace Conference. McGovern scrupulously passed on the content of these talks, which were largely about POWs, to the U.S. Embassy in Paris and the State Department, but the White House was not amused. Indeed, for Nixon's men anything that detracted from an image of monolithic American determination to protect the Thieu regime was harmful to Kissinger's negotiating position vis-à-vis North Vietnam.

The spring offensive of Easter, 1972, which led to the fall of Quang Tri and a new threat on Hue, complicated the situation still further. On the one hand, it gave an extra impetus to McGovern's candidacy just as the Tet offensive of 1968 had assisted Eugene McCarthy. On the other hand it jeopardised Nixon's own plans for phased withdrawal of American troops, which by this time were down to 63,000. Nixon, as we have seen, extricated himself from the military difficulty by an escalated bombing campaign and the mining of Haiphong Harbour. After initial disarray, the South Vietnamese forces held. The political problem, however, was more complex. All through 1971 Nixon had told his aides that the war would not be an issue in 1972, implying that it would be as good as over by the election. It was one of the main reasons why McGovern was welcomed as the opposition candidate, there being not much point to "peace" candidates in time of peace. But with the war in an escalatory phase, McGovern became a political force. And if McGovern became a viable presidential candidate, the readiness of Hanoi to talk peace specifics with Kissinger would be diminished. From where Nixon's men were standing, McGovern was a potential danger to their idea of "national security." Much the most logical explanation of the plan to bug the DNC, McGovern's headquarters, and the Democratic convention is that it was designed to ensure that McGovern as a presidential candidate did not outflank Nixon on the war, through secret contacts of his own with Hanoi. (Some such contact did, as we shall see, take place after McGovern's nomination.)

Early in April Liddy collected the first installment of his allotted $250,000 from "Duke" Sloan—a small matter of $83,000. Sloan was startled by the size of the demand and checked with Magruder and Stans, who passed the query on up the line to John Mitchell. Magruder explained that this was the "front-end load" (a mutual fund term, much favoured by Bernie Cornfeld) and that the initial outlay, involving the purchase of expensive equipment, was bound to be heavy. This explanation, Magruder says, was accepted by Mitchell. Mitchell denies this. Either way, the authorisation for the expenditure soon came down the hierarchy. The way was clear for the detailed planning to begin.

The key members of the team, Hunt, Liddy, and McCord, were already in Washington and ready to go. On April 12, Liddy gave McCord $65,000 and dispatched him on a six-week shopping expedition. It was at this point that the whole operation nearly came unstuck. Among the places McCord visited was New York. Besides picking up some bugging equipment, he called at the headquarters of the November Group, the consortium set up to produce CREEP's campaign advertising, to check out its suspicion that its telephones were being tapped. He never did discover whether this was true. But very

President Richard M. Nixon

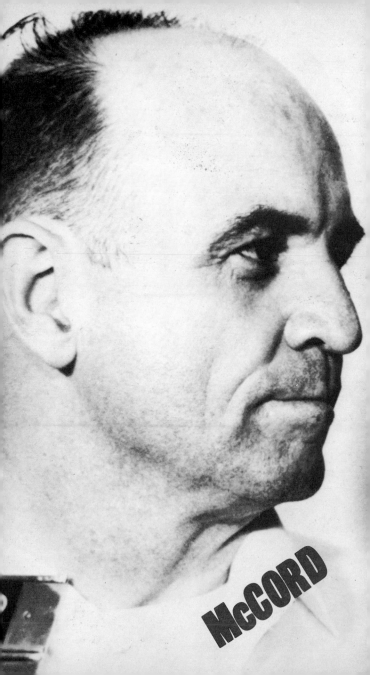

James W. McCord Jr., ex-CIA
and Watergate wireman

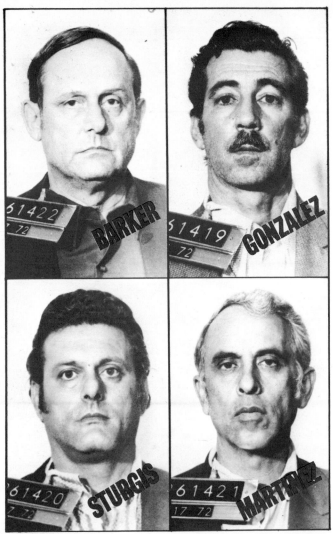

The Watergate burglars as they appear in police files. Top left, Bernard L. Barker, ex-CIA and Bay of Pigs veteran; right, Virgilio R. Gonzalez, locksmith and exiled Cuban. Bottom left, Frank A. Sturgis, former Marine; right, Eugenio R. Martinez, ex-CIA and Bay of Pigs. Opposite, telephone of Spencer Oliver in the Democratic headquarters in Watergate. Arrow points to the black box bugging device

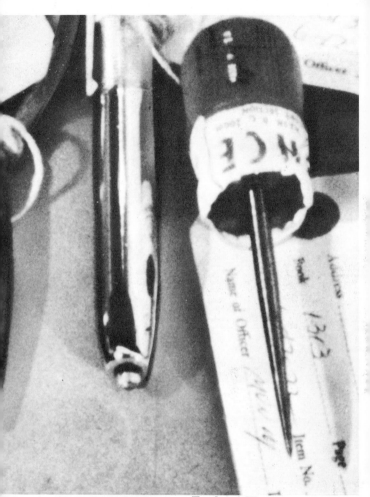

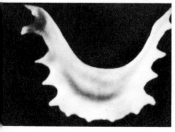

Tools of Watergate: above, items confiscated from the burglars by Washington police — tape, screwdriver, pliers, flashlight etc. Far left, receiver used by the bugging unit. Near left, metal mouthpiece that disguises the voice when speaking on the telephone

The watchers and the watched: from the Howard Johnson Motel room (arrow left), CREEP operatives monitored the phone taps on Democratic offices (arrow right) in the Watergate Building

Frank Wills,
Watergate janitor,
who called the police

LIDDY

CREEP spymen Howard Hunt
and Gordon Liddy

Tennis at the top: Bob Haldeman (right) and John Ehrlichman

Bob Haldeman, crewcut Christian Scientist who headed Nixon's White House staff. Above with his boss and (circled) below among Beta Theta Pi fraternity members as a student at UCLA

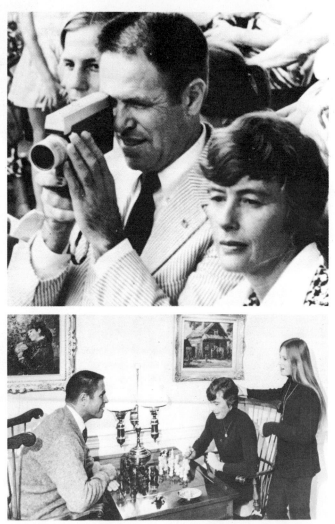

As White House chief of staff, Bob Haldeman had few opportunities to relax. But he found time to indulge his passion for home movie making and for weekend games of chess with his wife, Jo. Standing right (in lower picture), Haldeman's youngest child, Ann, aged 15. Opposite, Haldeman's closest friend in student days at UCLA, John Ehrlichman, who showed a taste for behind-the-scenes political work

Pulling wires behind the scenes has kept Kappa Sig John Ehrlichman out of the limelight but he was a potent political power nonetheless. As Executive Secretary of IFC, Johnny split his talents between the Ad. Building and Kerckhoff.

John Ehrlichman shortly after the Watergate revelations forced him to resign his post as President Nixon's chief Domestic Affairs Adviser in the White House. He used to work a regular 12 to 14 hours a day. Now he has time to unwind and play stick pitching with the family dog and (right) get down to running repairs in the garden of his Great Falls, Virginia, home where vital equipment like the mower somehow never managed to get fixed

Jeanne Ehrlichman, attractive wife of Nixon's White House Number Two, and mother of five children aged 13 to 23. The Ehrlichmans were more outgoing than most of the withdrawn and suspicious White House families. Jeanne's influence was the key

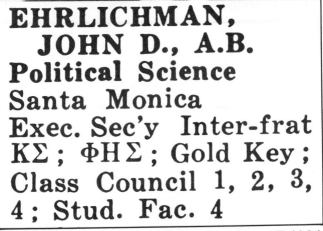

EHRLICHMAN, JOHN D., A.B.
Political Science
Santa Monica
Exec. Sec'y Inter-frat
KΣ; ΦΗΣ; Gold Key;
Class Council 1, 2, 3,
4; Stud. Fac. 4

Ehrlichman at UCLA (above); John Wesley Dean III (right)

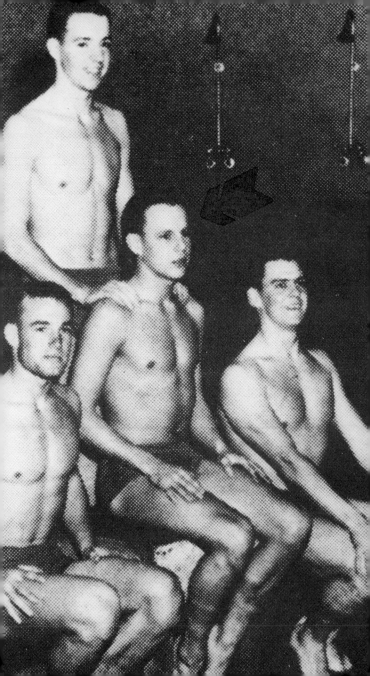

John Dean and wife Maureen, watch the Senate hearings on TV

Dean (arrow) as a military-school cadet

The Dean home in Washington. President Nixon's resourceful Legal Counsel in embryo: as a free-swinging schoolboy golfer (right) and (opposite) as lissome member of the college swimming team

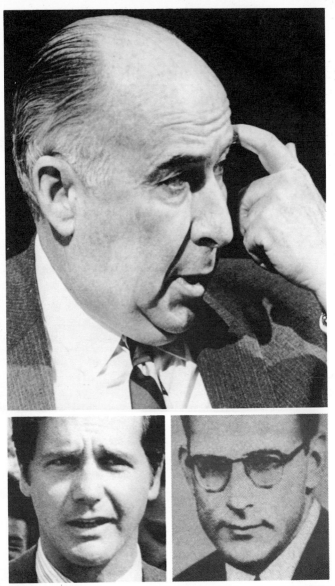

Watergate high command: John Mitchell (above) and CREEP aides Jeb Magruder (left) and Fred La Rue. Right, Martha Mitchell

Charles Colson, Special Counsel

Patrick Gray   **Maurice Stans**

Don Segretti   **Gordon Strachan**

Opposite, Dwight Chapin, Nixon's Appointments Secretary (right), with Henry Kissinger and Chou En-lai on Peking visit in 1971

Blacklisted: a selection from the 200 "enemies" and "oppo-

Huey Newton

Jack Anderson

Barbra Streisand

Leonard Woodcock

Joe Namath

Robert McNamara

Harold Gibbons

Walter Hickel

William Fulbright

Leonard Bernstein

Dan Schorr

Noam Chomsky

Edward Kennedy

Jane Fonda

Carson Blake

Mary McGrory

Daniel Ellsberg

Dick Gregory

Paul Newman

Ralph Abernathy

Ken Galbraith

Allard Lowenstein

Kingman Brewster

Steve McQueen

ENEMIES

The undoing of Nixon's presidential opponents: Senator Edmund Muskie weeps in the snows of New Hampshire; above right, George Wallace is the victim of an assassination attempt in Maryland (insert: the would-be assassin, Arthur Bremmer); below, George McGovern (right), the Democratic party candidate, with his biggest liability, new running-mate Tom Eagleton

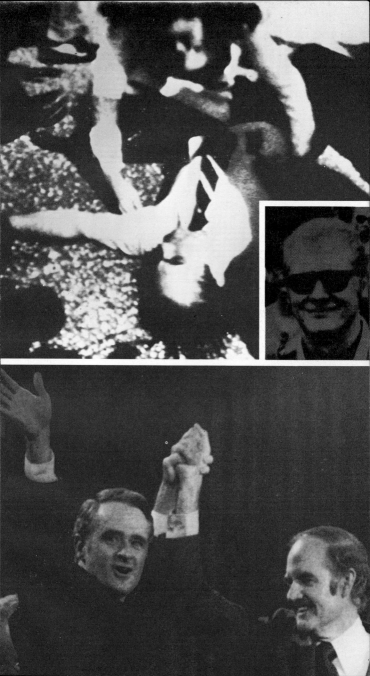

The Inquisitors: Senator Sam Ervin (above), chairman of the Senate committee inquiry. Below, sitting with co-chairman, Senator Howard Baker. Other committeemen standing behind, from left to right, Senators Weicker, Inouye, Talmadge, and Gurney

shortly afterwards a strange rumour began to circulate in New York: the November Group was planning to bug the DNC.

One of the people who picked it up was William Haddad, a New York entrepreneur and former prize-winning investigative reporter for the *New York Post*. He says that he got the story from a private investigator who had good contacts with the FBI. On April 15 Haddad, an old Kennedy liberal, passed this information on to Jack Anderson and to Larry O'Brien, the chairman of the Democratic Party. O'Brien took the story seriously, but as the Democrats' finances were in very poor shape he eventually concluded it would be too expensive to mount a full-scale de-bugging operation. Anderson, whose own house was under surveillance at the time by agents from Robert Mardian's Internal Security Division at the Justice Department, was equally intrigued. He tried hard to check the story out. But he was misled by the reference to the November Group and, not surprisingly, drew a blank.

It is possible that McCord himself, who has many friends in the FBI, was the unwitting source of the leak. What is certain is that somebody talked. "Operation Gemstone" had got off to a distinctly shaky start.

Meanwhile the team was being assembled. On May 1 an ex-FBI man named Alfred C. Baldwin III received a telephone call at his home in Hamden, Connecticut, from McCord. He had been looking through the register of the Society of Former Special Agents of the FBI in search of a suitable assistant. The fact that Baldwin was unmarried was, McCord later explained, the main recommendation in his favour. Beyond stressing the urgency of the mission, McCord said little on the phone. Later that evening, Baldwin arrived in Washington, and next morning McCord revealed that his first job was to be a security guard for Mr. and Mrs. John Mitchell. Now that Mitchell was no longer Attorney General, this was a CREEP rather than an FBI responsibility. Baldwin was not overjoyed with the offer, but was tempted when McCord dangled the possibility that this temporary job might be "a stepping stone to a permanent position."

The formalities were quickly completed. McCord marched Baldwin, who was dressed in the standard FBI uniform—conservative suit, white shirt, and black wing-tipped shoes—to see Fred LaRue. After a cursory once-over, LaRue nodded. "OK, that's fine." Baldwin was then given a .38 police special ("You'll need this while you are with Mrs. Mitchell," McCord said) and told to report for duty. That afternoon with the revolver and $800 in expense money, he left Washington to accompany Mrs. Mitchell on a six-day trip to Detroit and Westchester County, New York. The trip was not an unqualified success. Martha complained that in Detroit Baldwin had led her without any warning straight into the middle of a demonstration, and that in New York he insisted in walking barefoot about her Fifth Avenue apartment and telling all her friends he was a Democrat. "He is," Martha later declared, "probably the gauchest character I have ever met in my whole life." On his return Baldwin was informed by McCord that he would not be traveling with Martha again. But there would soon be other work for him.

While Baldwin was on his travels with Martha, additional forces were preparing to come to Washington from Miami, where Howard Hunt had been doing some recruiting. On one of his frequent trips to Miami that spring, Hunt had told Bernard Barker to prepare for a "double operation" that would last about a week. But beyond saying that it would involve an Ellsberg-type break-in he offered no details. He advised Barker to "get your men in training by going up and down stairs. They must be in good physical condition." On April 19 Barker's account in the Republic National Bank, Miami, became healthier by $114,000 as he deposited the four Mexican checks and the Dahlberg check that Liddy had routed to him from the CREEP offices.

McCord, meanwhile, was having loyalty problems. As part of his duties as CREEP's security chief, he would make daily calls over to the Justice Department to obtain the best hot news on the domestic subversion situation. Part of this intelligence convinced the Republicans that holding their convention in San Diego might not be such a good idea after all. California was thickly populated with peaceniks, many of whom seemed ready to make a mockery of Nixon's inevitable nomination as the Republican Party's election candidate. The Republicans eventually decided to have their convention in Miami. This kind of information was useful to McCord in his security work, but some of the things he heard in the Justice Department did not please him at all. His main contact on this level was Robert Mardian, the hard-driving head of the ISD, who also worked on Nixon's Intelligence Evaluation Committee. Mardian worried McCord. At the Senate Watergate hearings, McCord later confided: "Based . . . on a discussion with Robert Mardian in May, 1972, it appeared to me that the White House had for some time been trying to get political control over the CIA assessments and estimates in order to make them conform to 'White House policy.'" Despite this fastidious perception, McCord stayed on as part of one of the hairiest political-espionage operations of modern times. However, his touch seemed to get less certain. Hunt later described him as a bungler.

By the end of May, however, there was no shortage of bunglers involved in the enterprise. On May 22 a group of Cuban exiles flew from Miami to Washington and checked into the Hamilton Manger Hotel under assumed names. There was the Ellsberg team: Barker as "Frank Carter," Martinez as "Jene Valdes," and DeDiego as "José Piedra." Plus three other newcomers to this type of "national security" work: Frank Sturgis, a former Marine and soldier of fortune who had fought both with and against Castro; Reinaldo Pico, another Bay of Pigs veteran; and Virgilio Gonzalez, a locksmith. For hotel-registration purposes Sturgis was "Joseph D'Alberto," Pico was "Joe Granada," and Gonzalez was "Raul Goday."

It was in Barker's room at the Hamilton Manger that Hunt finally explained just what the "double operation" really involved: the objective was the DNC at the Watergate and McGovern's headquarters on First Street in the southwest district of Washington. To enlist maximum cooperation Hunt constructed an ingenious rationale. According to Barker he told his team, all passionate anti-Castroites, that if they helped the White House now "it would be a decisive factor at a later date for obtaining help in the liberation of Cuba." It was, in the circumstances, a remarkably generous promise, but its validity was not questioned. "I was not there to think," Barker said later. "I was there to follow orders."

On May 26 the Barker group moved into new quarters at the Watergate Hotel. Baldwin, meanwhile, had been installed across the street in the Howard Johnson's motel, where a room had been reserved for him under the name of McCord Associates, McCord's private firm. That afternoon, Baldwin, returning to the Howard Johnson's from a short trip to his home in Connecticut, found McCord in his room hunched over an expensive and complicated radio receiver housed in a blue Samsonite case. Scattered around the room was an array of walkie-talkies, bugging equipment, and tape recorders. "I want to show you some of this equipment and how we are going to use it," McCord said. After inserting a bug in the hotel's phone to test the receiver, McCord pointed across the street to the Watergate. "We're going to put some units in there tonight," he said, "and you'll be monitoring them." Baldwin was also equipped with an alias. He was to be known as "Bill Johnson." But when Hunt and Liddy arrived later, also sporting aliases (Hunt was supposed to be "Edward Hamilton" and Liddy "George Leonard"), McCord muddled everybody up and finished by introducing the conspirators to each other by their real names.

That evening, in anticipation of their triumph, everybody except McCord and Baldwin went down to the dining room of the Watergate Hotel and had a blowout. As CREEP was providing the money they saw no reason to stint themselves. So they ordered a banquet and washed it down with fine wines, specially selected by Hunt. The bill came to $236—nearly $30 a head. Thus replete, the burglars set to work.

Hunt did not have far to go. Behind the dining room there was a corridor leading into the first floor of the Watergate office building. Hunt and Gonzalez, the team's locksmith, hid there until the waiters had cleared away the meal and then went to work on the door. It refused to open. Unable to go forwards or back, the two men spent the night on the floor at the back of the Continental Room.

Meantime, the rest of the party set off for McGovern's headquarters. As they approached the building they discovered the area was illuminated by a bright street light. Liddy had brought his gun with him and offered to shoot out the light (as he had done once before) but was dissuaded by McCord, who was much more concerned by the presence of a wandering drunk. They hung about for several hours waiting for the drunk to go away but eventually gave up and drove back to the Watergate. It had not been a very successful night. On the next evening they tried another strategy.

Like many modern office buildings, the Watergate offices are built round a central stem which rises through the building like the trunk of a tree; the floors are the branches. The base of the stem is in the garage, and on either side of it doors lead into two stairwells. On many floors the stairwells open onto corridors, but as the Democrats had taken the entire sixth floor there were no corridors. The door from Stairwell 1 was always locked from the stair side, but it opened straight into the offices themselves; Stairwell 2 opened into the elevator lobby which was separated from the DNC office by a glass front door. The garage is open twenty-four hours a day.

On the evening of May 27 Hunt took the elevator up to the sixth floor and then walked down Stairwell 2 and taped the garage doors so that anybody could enter without using a key or forcing the lock. Hunt then rejoined Liddy in their room at the Watergate Hotel and much later sent four of the Miami group into action, equipped with rubber surgical gloves, flashlights, cameras, and walkie-talkies. McCord stationed himself on the balcony of the Howard Johnson's opposite. At about 1:30 A.M. he saw pinpoints of light moving around the DNC. Minutes later Hunt called him to say, "My people are in; you can go in now."

McCord planted two bugs. One went on the phone of Larry O'Brien's secretary, Fay Abel, and one on the telephone of R. Spencer Oliver, executive director of the Organisation of State Democratic Chairmen. After Barker had made an abortive search for papers indicating that the Democrats were being financed with contributions from Communist Cuba or "from leftist organisations or those inclined to violence," the team photographed a few random documents and one on security for the Democratic Convention. By 3:30 A.M. the first half of the "double-header" was complete.

That night they tried George McGovern's headquarters again. Hunt's "inside" contact on this operation was Tom Gregory, the student who had first worked as a CREEP spy in the Muskie headquarters but later switched to the McGovern camp. Instead of leaving with the other volunteer workers that night, Gregory hid in the furnace room until around midnight, waiting for an opportune moment to let in the entry team. When he emerged, Gregory was surprised by a man sitting on the floor, who said, "What are you doing here?" Gregory could offer no very convincing reply so he made an excuse and left. The Cubans now returned home to Miami. They never did manage to place the tap on McGovern.

The results from the Watergate taps were, to put it mildly, disappointing. The signals from the DNC were so faint it took McCord and Baldwin two days to pick any up at all. And when they did they learned little of political consequence. What messages they did receive came from Spencer Oliver's phone—which, it turned out, was widely used by the DNC secretaries for what Baldwin later described as "intimate conversations." The other bug did not work at all. Sitting in his motel room, Baldwin monitored some two hundred conversations, which he typed up almost verbatim and handed to McCord. McCord took them over to CREEP where Liddy's secretary, Mrs. Sally Harmony, was instructed to retype the choicer and more sensitive passages for consumption by Liddy's superiors. Mrs. Harmony used stationery headed "Gemstone." According to Magruder, the Gemstone transcripts were shown both to Gordon Strachan, the White House liaison, and to John Mitchell at CREEP, but both deny this. Magruder also says that Mitchell was disappointed at the meagre haul, and complained that the results were "worthless" and that the money had been wasted. He therefore insisted, says Magruder, that Liddy and his men return to the Watergate for a second attempt. This Mitchell contests even more vigorously. It is "a palpable, damnable lie," he told the Senate Watergate Committee.

In any event, in the first week in June plans for a repeat performance were laid. To make certain there was no mistake about the phone this time, McCord asked Baldwin to reconnoitre O'Brien's office. This Baldwin did, successfully masquerading as the nephew of the Democratic chairman of his home state, Connecticut's Jim Bailey. On his return he drew McCord a plan.

On June 16 Barker, Sturgis, Martinez, and Gonzalez were summoned from Miami to Washington. On his arrival Frank Sturgis bumped into an old friend with whom he had once written an article describing his adventures with the Cuban "freedom-fighters." It was none other than Jack Anderson, on his way to Cleveland. Anderson asked Sturgis what he was doing in Washington. "Private business," Sturgis replied, intro-

ducing Anderson to Martinez, the team's official photographer. For the second time Anderson had missed quite a scoop. On the following day he learned the nature of Sturgis's "private business."

Barker and his group again booked into the Watergate, Barker and Martinez in Room 214 and Sturgis and Gonzalez in 314; and again they treated themselves to a hearty meal. But this time it was McCord who taped the garage doors. He then returned to Baldwin's room in the Howard Johnson's to work on the electronic gear. The place was littered with screwdrivers, wires, batteries, and soldering irons which he had bought that afternoon. "The room looked like a small electronics factory," Baldwin later recalled.

Normally there are two guards on duty at the Watergate. But on the night of June 16/17 there was only one, a young man named Frank Wills. At 12:45 Wills made his rounds and discovered the tapes on the garage door. Thinking that they had been left there by the maintenance staff, he removed them and then strolled across the street to have a cup of coffee at the Howard Johnson's. Minutes before, the watching McCord had seen the lights go off in the DNC offices as the last hard-working volunteer decided to call it a day. The coast was clear.

After getting the go-ahead from Hunt, McCord joined the others, crossed the street to the Watergate, and headed for the garage. They found the tapes gone and the door locked. While Gonzalez got to work on the lock, with Sturgis standing guard, the others retired to their rooms to discuss the development. At this point, continuing with the operation was clearly a foolish risk. There had been any number of aborted missions before, and it is still unclear why this one was not immediately consigned to that category. Within the team itself there are two versions about who most influenced the fatal decision to go on. As lines of authority on the team were never clearly defined it is difficult to know which is true. McCord's position in the hierarchy was never clear at any time. At the Senate Watergate hearings, he maintained that he was simply a member of a team of which Barker was the leader; he had no independent authority of his own. Barker, however, held that McCord was more a fellow-traveler of the team than part of it. Hunt later described McCord's role as that of "an electronic hitchhiker" who, he felt, should never have been on the team. He was essentially Liddy's man and Liddy had certainly not told his superiors that a CREEP staff member was involved in the actual burglary.

According to Barker it was McCord who pressed for the operation to go forward after the discovery of the locked garage door. Barker himself wanted to call the whole thing off and recalls being skeptical of McCord's argument that the tape was routinely removed by a maintenance man. McCord claims that he, too, was reluctant to go on, but that the final decision was made by Hunt and Liddy, who were keeping watch from the Watergate Hotel. It is certainly true that without Hunt and Liddy's say-so the operation could not have gone forward again. When Gonzalez reported over his walkie-talkie that the lock had been successfully picked and the doors retaped, the raiding party went in.

By this time Wills had finished his coffee and was back on his rounds. He quickly discovered the garage door had been retaped; this time he called the police. At 1:52 A.M. Wills's call was relayed to Metropolitan Police Car 727, which at the time was cruising only a few blocks from the Watergate. Sergeant Paul Leeper and Officers John Barrett and Carl Schoffler, the crew of car 727, were members of the Washington Police's plainclothes division, the so-called "Bum Squad." They were using an unmarked car and dressed in clothes not normally associated with the police. Leeper, who was at the wheel, was wearing a golf hat, a light blue V-necked T-shirt, light blue trousers, and a dark windbreaker emblazoned with the legend "George Washington University." The others looked as little like policemen as he did.

When the police arrived, Baldwin was standing on the balcony of the Howard Johnson's keeping a lookout. But as all he saw was three casually dressed men strolling into the building, he thought nothing of it. It was only when the lights appeared on the eighth floor that he grabbed the walkie-talkie. "We have got some activity here," he reported. "What have you got?" a voice Baldwin could not identify inquired. Baldwin mentioned the lights, and the voice said: "OK, we know about that. That's the two o'clock guard check. Let us know if lights go on any other place."

Meanwhile, finding nothing on the eighth floor, the police had made their way down to the DNC, where they found some further tapes that the burglars had placed on their way in. Cautiously the police drew their guns and moved out onto the balcony and into full view of the watching Baldwin. "Base one to unit one," Baldwin radioed to Hunt in Room 214 of the Watergate Hotel. "Are our people dressed in suits or dressed casually?" "What?" asked Hunt. Baldwin repeated the question. "Our people are dressed in suits," Hunt replied. "Well, we've got problems," said Baldwin. "We've got some people dressed casually and they've got guns. They're looking around the balcony and everywhere but they haven't come across our people."

At this Hunt began to sound, says Baldwin, "absolutely panic-stricken." Frantically he tried to raise the men in the Watergate. "Are you reading this, are you reading this?" he shouted. But there was no reply. After the message about the two o'clock guard, the economical Barker had switched off the walkie-talkie to save the batteries. McCord was just getting down to O'Brien's phone when the police arrived. Seeing part of one arm behind a glass partition they shouted, "Hold it. Stop. Come out!" To their amazement not two but ten arms came into view. "Are you gentlemen the Metropolitan Police?" McCord inquired. On being informed that they were, the Watergate five agreed to come quietly.

Hunt's reaction was anything but quiet. After failing to raise the burglars on his walkie-talkie, Hunt radioed Baldwin, "Stay there; I'll be right over." Baldwin saw Hunt and Liddy emerge from the Watergate Hotel, climb into their car, and drive around the block. Hunt called Baldwin again to say that he was on his way up. "You better not park near this building," Baldwin warned. "Police are all over the place." "OK," said Hunt.

Soon afterwards, a breathless Hunt arrived in Baldwin's room. He took one look at the scene below and fled to the bathroom. In the half-darkness of a summer night the street seemed to be filled with motorcycles, squad cars, paddy wagons, and men running in all directions. In the middle of the melee were his men being led away from the Watergate in handcuffs. When Hunt emerged from the bathroom he made straight for the white phone by the bedside. "I've got to call a lawyer," he explained, and dialed a local number. "They've had it," he said.

He put the phone down and turned to Baldwin. "Do you

know where McCord lives?" Baldwin said that he did. Hunt pointed to the litter of electronic gear and wiretap logs that were scattered about the room. McCord's wallet, car keys, and loose change were still lying on the bed where he had left them. "Well, get all the stuff out of here," Hunt ordered. "And you get out of here too." With that Hunt unhooked his walkie-talkie, threw it on the bed, and rushed from the room. Baldwin called after him: "Does that mean I am out of a job?"

CHAPTER 14

Operation Houseclean

SIX HOURS after Hunt darted from Baldwin's room, the machinery of the press was set in motion. At 8 A.M. on that Saturday morning, Howard Simons, the managing editor of the *Washington Post*, was called at home with a tip. There had been a break-in at the DNC. The burglars were wearing surgical gloves. Simons was intrigued, called the Metropolitan Editor, Harry Rosenfeld, and the *Post*'s publisher, Katherine Graham. "You will not believe what is going on," he told her.

Rosenfeld called Barry Sussman, his District of Columbia editor; Sussman sent Al Lewis, a veteran police reporter, to the Watergate (he saw the ceiling panels were out and immediately suspected bugging), and Robert Woodward, a younger recruit to the paper, was dispatched to the District of Columbia's Superior Court to cover the arraignment of the arrested men. Woodward sat up in the front of the court and heard Associate Judge James Belson ask McCord what he did for a living. "Security Consultant," said McCord. The judge asked who he had worked for previously. "CIA," said McCord in a near-whisper. The information appeared on Sunday morning in a story on the identity of the suspects written by another young reporter named Carl Bernstein.

It was not only the *Washington Post* reporters who were busy that summer Saturday. After he left Al Baldwin to drive the equipment out to McCord's house and then to make his way home through the dawn to Connecticut, Howard Hunt rushed downtown to his office at the Mullen agency. He called Barker's wife in Miami and told her the news. Then he made off to a friend's home and together they searched for a suitable lawyer for Hunt, eventually coming up with Joseph Rafferty, an attorney with experience in criminal work.

At the Second District Police Station the five burglars initially gave false names to the police. McCord said his was "Ed Martin." They were searched and, apart from their break-in and bugging and photographing equipment, the police found on them $1,300 in consecutively numbered $100 bills. In Barker's pocket they found a check made out to the Lakewood Country Club and signed by an E. Howard Hunt. A search of the register of the Watergate Hotel showed that four of the men had checked into Rooms 214 and 314; there the police found another $3,200 in neat packages of consecutively numbered bills. They also found an address book with the initials H.H. in it. Beside them was a telephone number and an inscription "W. House."

Before breakfast Harold Titus, the U.S. Attorney for the District of Columbia, was told of the burglary. He immediately called Henry Petersen, a lifelong career member of the Justice Department who had worked his way up from clerking with the FBI to the position of Deputy Attorney General and head of the Department's criminal division—one of the few men at such a level not to be a political appointee, and also, incidentally, a Democrat. Startled, he called his boss, Attorney General Richard Kleindienst—very much a political appointee. "I thought he ought to be forewarned," said Petersen later.

Over at the CREEP headquarters, Robert Odle, the young head of administration, heard news of the break-in, but no details, with mingled incredulity and relief. He told another CREEP employee: "That could never happen here, because I have this guy working for me named Jim McCord, and he has got the place really tight, and all I can say is, I'm glad McCord works for me." Shortly afterwards Odle was rung by Mrs. McCord, who told him that her husband was in jail and asked if Odle could recommend a lawyer. Around 9:30 A.M., G. Gordon Liddy burst upon the scene.

The first person he met was Hugh Sloan, CREEP's treasurer. "My boys got caught last night," said Liddy. "I made a mistake. I used somebody from here, which I told them I would never do. I am afraid I am going to lose my job." Shortly afterwards Liddy bumped into Odle in a corridor. "Where is the office shredding machine?" Liddy asked. On being told it was on the second floor, Liddy disappeared for a moment and then re-emerged carrying a foot-high pile of papers en route to the shredder. Seconds later he was back again: "How do you work this thing?"

Once he had the hang of the machine, Liddy closed the door and started his own personal cover-up operation. He fed into the shredder every scrap of incriminating evidence, including every consecutively numbered $100 bill, he possessed. Liddy had made a habit of collecting paper soap wrappers from every hotel he had visited. These too disappeared into the machine. By the time he had finished, all that was left was strings of multi-coloured paper.

The next job was to tell Jeb Stuart Magruder that the job had been blown. This involved a long-distance telephone call as Magruder, together with John Mitchell and other senior CREEP officials, was in Los Angeles for a series of campaign meetings. Thanks to the time difference it was still early in the morning when Liddy's call to the Beverly Hills Hotel came through. Magruder was having breakfast with Fred LaRue and about eight or ten other people.

Magruder took the call in the dining room.

"Can you get to a secure phone?" Liddy asked.

"No," Magruder replied. "What's the matter?"

"There has been a problem."

"What kind of problem?"

"Our security chief has been arrested at the Watergate."

"Do you mean Jim McCord?"

"Yes."

Magruder blanched and hurried back to where LaRue was sitting. "You know, I think last night was the night they were going into the DNC," he muttered. LaRue told him to find a pay phone and call Liddy back. Magruder did just that, but beyond the fact that McCord and four others had been arrested in the middle of the previous night while trying to break into the DNC there was not much more that Liddy could tell him. It was enough.

LaRue then hurried off to break the news to former Attorney General Mitchell. "This is incredible," said Mitchell.

At this point, Magruder, LaRue, and Mitchell should, as law-abiding citizens, have taken the nearest cab down to the nearest police precinct station and reported that they had evidence that might be needed in connection with a burglary committed the previous night; and that three other men called John Dean, then employed as legal counsel to the President of the United States, E. Howard Hunt, then employed as a White House consultant, and G. Gordon Liddy, then general counsel to the Committee to Re-Elect, might also be in a position to provide further information. They might also have added the names of Charles Colson, the President's special counsel, Bob Haldeman, the President's chief of staff, and Gordon Strachan, a White House assistant, all of whom had, to their collective knowledge, been apprised of an expensive intelligence-gathering operation, that seemed to have ended unlawfully in Watergate. The thought does not appear to have occurred to them.

Over the next year many thousands of man-hours and millions of words were devoted to an attempt to answer the question: who ordered the Watergate cover-up? As it turned out it was one of history's most irrelevant questions. For it all became so obvious after Jeb Magruder's testimony before the Senate Watergate Committee in June, 1973. "I don't think," said Magruder, with a puzzled frown, "there was ever any discussion that there would not be a cover-up." It was instinctive from the very beginning—and once started, there was no way back without the risk of compounding the original felony.

The immediate problem was not what to divulge but how to explain away McCord's presence at the scene of the crime, or, better still, remove him from the roster of suspects. (They did not yet know about the discovery of the money or the address book.) Someone suggested that Liddy, invoking Mitchell's name, go find Kleindienst in Washington and ask his help to get McCord out of jail. Magruder says Mitchell ordered Robert Mardian, a former deputy attorney general and now CREEP's political coordinator, to call Liddy with this instruction. Both Mitchell and Mardian deny this; however, somebody in the group did call Liddy with this instruction almost immediately.

Shortly before midday Washington time (9 A.M. California time), Liddy, in the company of Powell Moore, a CREEP public-relations man, arrived at the Burning Tree Country Club in search of the Attorney General. He was found having an early lunch in the club's main dining room. Liddy motioned to Kleindienst to come over and asked if there was somewhere they could talk in private. Kleindienst drew the two men into a locker room which led off the lobby. Seeing that it was empty he said: "Gentlemen, come in here. I think this would be a private place in which to talk." Liddy then told Kleindienst about the break-in and explained that some of the people involved might be employed either by CREEP or by the White House. He had, he said, been sent by Mitchell to ask Kleindienst to get McCord out of jail. At this point Moore, who was standing behind Liddy, vigorously shook his head to indicate that Liddy was exceeding his instructions. Whether Liddy was or not made little practical difference.

As soon as he had grasped the drift of the conversation, Kleindienst rushed out of the locker room to phone his assistant, Henry Petersen, to tell him that on no account were the Watergate burglars to be offered any special treatment. This order struck Petersen as rather strange; it had never crossed his mind that they would be. On his return Kleindienst ordered Liddy and Moore to leave the premises. Then he went back to his lunch, having, it seems, forgotten to pass on Liddy's incriminating suggestion to the head of his criminal division.

Back in California, CREEP's high command was trying manfully to make it appear as if all was, as always, for the best in the best of all possible campaigns and that nothing in the least surprising or disturbing had occurred. Mitchell went ahead with a meeting with Governor Ronald Reagan, and the others carried out their own schedules faithfully. Opportunities to get together to discuss the crisis were snatched when and where a break in the long-planned calendar allowed. In the middle of the morning the four top men of CREEP—Mitchell, Magruder, Mardian, and LaRue—met in the banqueting hall of the Airporter Hotel in Englewood, with a young CREEP official, Bart Porter, standing guard outside the door.

It was Magruder who both collected and disseminated most of the information. On arrival at the Airporter he drew Mardian aside to tell him that Liddy was a "nut" and he regretted not firing him weeks before. From Magruder, Mardian, who was new on the team, also learned that CREEP had been given a budget to finance dirty tricks and to carry out "a black advance." Mardian was not familiar with the term. "What's that?" he asked. "Countermeasures against opposition candidates," Magruder explained. Nothing much was decided at the Airporter, as they were still waiting for more information. Soon after, Magruder learned that the Washington police had discovered the burglars' $100 bills and were asking awkward questions about their origins. He also learned that Kleindienst was not being cooperative about McCord's release. Things were getting complicated.

At 2:45 P.M. the California party reassembled at the Beverly Hills Hotel to discuss the drafting of the press statement which would explain away McCord. They decided, after a deal of anxious debate, that less than total candour was the better part of valour. Mitchell's statement, issued that afternoon, was not very accurate.

Mr. McCord, he said, "is the proprietor of a private security agency who was employed by our committee months ago to assist with the installation of our security system.

"He has, as we understand it, a number of business clients and interests, and we have no knowledge of those relationships. We want to emphasise that this man and the other people involved were not operating on either our behalf or with our consent. I am surprised and dismayed at these reports. There is no place in our campaign or in the electoral process for this type of activity, and we will not permit or condone it."

This statement did little to impress Larry O'Brien—"No mere statement of innocence by Mr. Nixon's campaign manager will dispel questions of CREEP involvement," he said that afternoon—but it took care of the McCord problem for the moment. At least as worrying, however, to Magruder, were the contents of his own desk.

Among his papers was the "Gemstone" file. A light grey folder, an inch and a half thick, it contained the transcripts of conversations held on Spencer Oliver's phone. And the Democrats were already threatening legal action to force CREEP to turn over all documents that could possibly relate to the break-in. Late on Saturday afternoon, Magruder called his assistant, Robert Reisner, in Washington.

"Bob," said Magruder, "there is a file that has some Gemstone papers in it." Would he kindly make sure that it was removed to some safe place over the weekend? Magruder explained he was worried that the Democrats might retaliate and raid CREEP. Reisner had already filled his own briefcase full of other papers, so he passed the Gemstone file to Robert Odle, who took it home and put it in a cupboard with his golf clubs. At no time, said Odle later, did he ever look to see what the file contained; he was under the impression it was "advertising" material. The following Monday he gave it back to Magruder, who by this time had returned from Los Angeles.

Although the story was on the wires all Saturday long it was not, it seems, until late afternoon that the White House became interested in the affair. The police had worked out with the help of the check in Barker's pocket that the initials "H.H." in his address book might stand for Howard Hunt, and that "W.H." and "W. House" just could refer to the White House. They traced Hunt to his home in Potomac, Maryland, where he had anxiously lain low most of the day. Two FBI agents arrived on his doorstep at 5:30 P.M. and asked to interview him. Hunt refused, saying he would answer questions only in the presence of his lawyer. Between six and seven o'clock the FBI officer in charge of the Washington field office spoke to Alexander Butterfield, a Haldeman aide who was in charge of liaison with the Secret Service. He told him that the FBI had learned that Hunt was involved in the break-in and asked what Hunt did at the White House. Butterfield replied that he thought Hunt had been employed as a security consultant some time ago but would check.

At about the same time John Ehrlichman was called at home, first by Patrick Boggs of the Secret Service, and then by John Caulfield. Boggs, he says, told him that the only connection found between the White House and the burglary was Hunt's name in the address book. Caulfield was more forthright: "John, it sounds like a disaster of some type," he said. "My God," said Ehrlichman, "I can't believe it. I had better call Mitchell." Caulfield replied that this might be "appropriate." Mitchell simply told Ehrlichman, whom he cordially loathed, that he didn't know what it was all about and he would get back to him.

Ehrlichman also called Ron Ziegler, Nixon's press secretary, down in Key Biscayne, where Nixon was resting after his Moscow trip, and then Chuck Colson. He knew that Hunt was a Colson protégé, and wanted to find out whether or not he was still on the White House staff. Colson said he was unsure and would enquire. He had his answer when Hunt rang him himself the next morning and told him that it was desperately important that the contents of his White House safe be removed at once.

Henry Petersen, at his own request, was kept abreast of the police and FBI investigations all day, and amongst the things he learned was the Hunt connection. He gradually became more and more alarmed. He began to realise what Kleindienst had meant when he called at noon to say that these burglars must be treated the same as any others. "I realised," he said, "that immense political repercussions were possible." That evening he called Kleindienst at the Statler Hilton, where he was making a speech, to bring him up to date on the CREEP and White House links. Kleindienst's response was, says Petersen, "guarded." Kleindienst, says Petersen, never did remember to pass on the details of the Liddy locker-room conference.

On Sunday morning the fruits of the *Washington Post*'s labours appeared as the second lead of the paper; eighty-three inches were devoted to the story. (The *New York Times,* by contrast, had thirteen inches buried on an inside page under the headline "Five Charged with Burglary at Democratic Quarters.") That morning Haldeman called Magruder from Key Biscayne and, says Magruder, gave him very precise instructions: get back to Washington immediately, find out the exact status of those $100 bills, talk to Dean, CREEP treasurer Sloan, Haldeman's own assistant Gordon Strachan, and anyone else who could throw some light on what had happened. Magruder, of course, assumed that Haldeman knew all about the operation and that the instructions were designed to assist the cover-up. (Haldeman maintains that assumption was incorrect.)

John Dean was not in the best of positions to help. He arrived in San Francisco on Sunday morning on a flight from Manila, where he had given a lecture at a drug conference. He had intended to stop over on the West Coast and recover from some of his jet lag, but when he learned of the burglary from his assistant, Fred Fielding, he flew straight on to Washington and arrived in a state of both confusion and exhaustion. "My first thought," he later recalled, "was that Colson was responsible." By this time many of the other principals had also returned to the capital. Monday promised to be quite a day.

For John Dean the pace was particularly hectic. The phone never stopped ringing; everybody seemed to want to talk to him. Magruder was among the first to call. "It's all Liddy's fault," he complained. Then Ehrlichman came on with a long string of instructions: discover what it's all about, find out if Colson's involved, talk to Kleindienst and ask him what the Justice Department is doing, get hold of Liddy. Then report back. "Yes," said Dean and promptly rang Colson, who said he knew nothing about it. He still could not say whether Hunt was on the White House payroll, but was worried about Hunt's safe.

Haldeman remained in Key Biscayne, but his assistant Gordon Strachan spent much of Monday going through his boss's files looking for anything that seemed to have the slightest connection with Watergate or wiretapping or, indeed, with any CREEP intelligence operation. As the White House contact with top levels of CREEP, Strachan had received from Magruder any or all material of importance, and Strachan's job was to make sure that Haldeman saw it too.

Much to Magruder's annoyance, Strachan often also sought information elsewhere, and then summarised everything he had in what he called "Political Matters memoranda" for Haldeman, who initialed or ticked each paragraph as he read it. Strachan also prepared "talking papers" which listed the points he thought Haldeman should cover in conferences wtih his visitors. In the course of his short career at the White House Strachan had written twenty-four Political Matters memos and any number of talking papers.

In Political Matters Memorandum No. 18 Strachan found what he was looking for. The memo was based on a conversation with Magruder and had been written shortly after Magruder had returned on March 30, from Key Biscayne, where the financing of the Watergate operation had been discussed. It contained a three-line paragraph, which Haldeman had ticked, reporting that CREEP has "a sophisticated political intelligence-gathering system with a budget of 300." Strachan later explained that this meant $300,000. "We were dealing in such big figures I always left off the last three noughts." Strachan also found a reference to an operation

called Sedan Chair II (the code name for one of Magruder's
political espionage agents) which contained the phrase "confidential sources indicate. . . ." Strachan thought (incor-
rectly) that this might refer to wiretap information, so he
pulled it out. Finally he discovered a Haldeman memo telling
him to call up Segretti and say that Liddy would be giving
him instructions, and a "talking paper" which he had prepared
for a Haldeman-Mitchell meeting the previous April. In this
he had suggested that the two men should discuss CREEP's
intelligence-gathering program.

Later Strachan recollects showing Haldeman, on his return
from Key Biscayne, what he had discovered. He found his
boss in a surprisingly mellow mood. After asking, almost
jokingly, what "we knew about events over the weekend,"
Strachan says that he was told to "make sure the files were
clean." Haldeman has no recollection of the episode. Nonetheless, Strachan did promptly shred the political memo, the
talking paper, and Sedan Chair II. He then went over to John
Dean's office and told him what he had done. Operation
Houseclean, he reported, was complete.

On Monday lunchtime, Dean took a stroll with Gordon
Liddy. As they walked down the street towards the Corcoran
Gallery, Liddy did some explaining. It was all Magruder's
fault. He, Liddy, hadn't wanted to go into the DNC again,
but Magruder had pushed him into it because one of the bugs
placed earlier was not working properly. McCord had been
used, Liddy said, only because Magruder had cut his budget
so badly. Still, Liddy was very sorry for what had happened.
"I am a soldier and will never talk," he said. "If anybody
wishes to shoot me on the street, I am ready." At this the
two men parted. "I am afraid I will be unable to discuss
this matter with you further," Dean murmured. Liddy said
he quite understood.

The time had come for Dean, who had by now faithfully
carried out the morning instructions, to report back to
Ehrlichman. In mid-afternoon the two men met in Ehrlichman's office. There, according to Dean, Ehrlichman was
told about the Liddy chat and the fact that in late January
and early February Dean had attended two meetings in
Mitchell's office to discuss early versions of the Watergate
plan. Dean remembers that Ehrlichman was more interested
in the present situation than in delving into its origins. "I'm

getting Colson in. Come back later. Meanwhile keep trying the Justice Department," he said.

Dean returned to Ehrlichman's office just before 5 P.M. This time Colson was there too, and the question of what to do about Hunt was on everybody's mind. Ehrlichman had no doubts, says Dean. Even before the meeting had started he told Dean to get Liddy to order Hunt out of the country. Dean hurried away to make the call. But on his return he had second thoughts. "Was it really wise for the White House to give orders of this kind?" he says he asked Ehrlichman. "Why not?" Ehrlichman replied, "He's not a fugitive from justice." Colson chimed in; he too agreed it was not a very bright idea. And so, says Dean, Ehrlichman backed down and Dean went out to call Liddy again and rescind the order. Ehrlichman says he never made any such suggestion in the first place.

In any case, Liddy did try to call Hunt at the Mullen agency, but Hunt had already left, telling Bennett, his superior, that he was departing Washington "until all this blows over." He had good reason. Sometime that day Eugene Bachinski, a *Washington Post* police reporter, had heard through his police contacts that Barker's address book had given rise to an official interest in a man called Howard Hunt, who was thought to have some kind of job in the White House. He passed the information on to Bob Woodward. Woodward called the White House switchboard and asked to speak to Mr. Howard Hunt. An operator rang Hunt's extension in the Executive Office Building. No answer. Obligingly, she said to Woodward, "There is one other place he might be—in Mr. Colson's office." She tried it; a secretary said, "Mr. Hunt is not here now." So the White House operator suggested that Woodward call the Mullen PR firm across the street. Woodward did so and he found Hunt there and told him his name had been found in Barker's address book. "Good God," exclaimed Hunt and slammed down the phone. As he left, he did tell Bennett where to reach him, and when Liddy called the second time Bennett agreed to pass on the instruction that "the signals had changed and that he was to stay put" (i.e., not leave the country). "I wish they would make up their minds," snapped Hunt on receiving Bennett's message. Bennett also told him that, from his own point of view, he would like an explanation of what was going on: Hunt should come into the agency and tell him or face suspension.

The next day, Tuesday, Hunt left for New York, supposedly to make a TV film. There he decided to ignore Bennett's ultimatum. That evening he disappeared to California, where he hid out for the next ten days in the house of a lawyer friend. After his departure, Bennett asked a secretary at the agency to clear out the desk in Hunt's windowless office. She found nothing but an empty whisky bottle and a pillbox with a couple of Librium tranquilisers left in it. Hunt's spoor at the White House was more positive.

For it was not so much Hunt's whereabouts that worried Nixon's men as was what he had left behind. After the brief skirmish over Hunt's travel plans, Dean, Colson, and Ehrlichman got down to a detailed discussion of Hunt's White House status and the contents of his office safe. A quick inspection of White House personnel records confirmed Ehrlichman's and Colson's worst fears: they clearly showed that Hunt was still on the payroll. (Earlier in the day a White House spokesman had been asked about this. He replied that Hunt had worked as a White House consultant for 63 days in 1971 and 24½ days in 1972 but, he added, he had not been on the payroll since March.)

The conversation then turned to the safe. It was decided that the General Services Administration should assume the role of cracksmen and hand over the contents to Dean, who was to inspect and report. That evening the GSA men, supervised by Dean's assistant, Fred Fielding, carried Hunt's safe to a fifth-floor storeroom at the Executive Office Building and set to work.

For John Dean it had been a long, tiring day, but there was still more work to be done. On leaving Ehrlichman's office, Dean hurried over to John Mitchell's apartment at the Watergate, where a meeting between Mitchell, Magruder, Mardian, and LaRue had already started. Just before it began, Mitchell had a twelve-minute conversation with the President, who was now back from Florida. The President inquired about Watergate, and Mitchell says he replied that he did not know what had happened but was sorry he had not kept "a stronger hand" over things. Nixon, recollecting the conversation at a press conference in August, 1973, said Mitchell "expressed great chagrin that . . . some of the boys, as he called them, got involved in this kind of activity which he knew could be very, very embarrassing to—apart from the illegality—to the campaign."

Accounts of what was said at the ensuing meeting of CREEP strategists conflict. Everybody agrees that Watergate was discussed, but no one agrees on just what they decided should be done about it. Magruder says that they talked about a number of problems. One suggestion was that the Gemstone file which had been returned to him that morning, unread, by the incurious Odle should be destroyed, and LaRue remembers Mitchell saying it would be "a good idea if Magruder had a fire." Mardian, Mitchell, and Dean have no such recollection. However, the general consensus of the meeting was that Watergate was very bad news indeed.

It was a view that was not shared, at least officially, by the chief presidential press spokesman, Ronald Ziegler. Earlier that day Ziegler had appeared in the White House press room for the routine briefing that is held every day at 11 A.M. for the benefit of the White House press corps. The press already knew about McCord, but nothing had yet appeared about Hunt. Most of the questions were straightforward ones about the break-in. Ziegler was in one of his most disdainful and dismissive moods. He did not even expand on Mitchell's statement, which had appeared in full in that morning's papers. Ziegler said: "I am not going to comment from the White House on a third-rate burglary attempt. This is something that should not fall into the political process."

On Tuesday, the GSA men, accompanied by Fred Fielding, arrived in John Dean's office carrying a large cardboard box, sealed with tape and marked "Top Secret," and a black attaché case. The contents of the attaché case were subsequently itemised as follows:

—Four walkie-talkies—a technical manual and operating instructions.
—Four rechargeable Bell and Howell nickel-cadmium batteries.
—One tear gas canister—General MK VII.
—Two microphones.
—Two earphones.
—One shoulder harness with white lead wire and phone jack.
—Three shoulder harnesses and three belt harnesses and assorted road maps, antennas, and lead wires.

The contents of the cardboard box were even more interesting; amongst them were:

—A folder marked "Pentagon Papers."
—A pile of papers dealing with Ellsberg, including the CIA's "psychological profile."
—The fruits of Hunt's investigations *re* Chappaquiddick and Edward Kennedy.
—A series of State Department cables relating to Vietnam, stretching back as far as 1963; two of them were Hunt's efforts to link President Kennedy directly with the assassination of Diem.
—A memo to Colson about Hunt's talk with William Lambert, the *Time-Life* reporter, over the forged Kennedy cables.

Altogether it was a strange collection of material to be found in the safe of a White House consultant, and John Dean was suitably impressed. After looking through Hunt's archive, Dean looked up at Fielding. "Holy shit!" said the President's legal counsel.

CHAPTER 15

The Pilot Fish

IN THE fullness of time John Wesley Dean III became known as the viper in the trusting bosom of Nixon's White House. From the vantage of the President's spokesmen in the summer of 1973, the things he had done were really rather terrible. Almost single-handed, he had managed to conceal the facts of Watergate from an enquisitive President and his top aides. Dean had deluded them with false assurances that there was nothing to worry about—the Watergate stain, Dean had maintained, began and ended at a level well below Nixon's high command in the White House and the Committee to Re-Elect. Worse, he had done this at a time when, on the President's instructions, he was supposed to be carrying out a full investigation and keeping John Ehrlichman, Nixon's chief domestic adviser, fully abreast of the facts. Neither Haldeman nor Ehrlichman naturally had any knowledge that Dean himself had sat in on two of the three high-level Watergate planning sessions, a fact that somewhat compromised his impartiality. Dean said that he had told them, of course, but that just showed how unscrupulous was his handling of the truth.

It made an interesting theory. For were it true, Dean would be the kind of man at whose feet Machiavelli himself would have been delighted to sit. It does not, however, accord with a number of well-corroborated facts, nor with Dean's known track record. Dean was certainly covering up from the moment he returned to Washington after the Watergate break-in, but in this, as in everything else in his previous political career, he operated with a firm sense of what pleased his masters.

John Wesley Dean III was the perfect staff man. Bright,

hard-working, ambitious, anxious to please, and discreet. Born in 1938 of middle-class, middle-western parents—his father worked for Firestone Tire Co. and became vice-president (production) of Blazon, once the world's largest manufacturer of backyard toys for children—John Dean had a fifties up-bringing. Known now as the "silent generation," young people of his age and class were profoundly apolitical but not without energy. John Dean was then, as he has always been since, nothing if not typical. His concerns at college were dating, clothes, the fraternity group, cars, and careers. All of them had to be just so. He was an orthodox young man, but he liked the best of what the orthodox had to offer. His room-mate at Staunton Military Academy, Virginia, where Dean made the swimming team, was Barry Goldwater, Jr. He says Dean was hard-working, and "regular."

But he did have two slight irregularities for that conformist era. One was his hobby—Dean was an accomplished amateur magician. The other was the fact that he was more ambitious than most of his peers. The classmates whom he sought to emulate might be looking forward to going home to their small towns, settling down, finding a nice girl to marry, raising a family, and becoming perhaps a bank president or chairman of the local Rotary Club. John Dean wanted more than that. "John," says his sister, "always went first class."

He liked Brooks Brothers suits, drove the most expensive car he could afford, and washed his hair with the pungent Grandpa's Wonder Soap because he was told it would stop him going thin on top. When he was still at Wooster College, Ohio, he fell for Karla Hennings, a very rich Senator's daughter. They were married in 1962 and Dean, who once had thoughts of becoming a writer, decided instead to become a lawyer. He enrolled in Georgetown University Law School.

His grades at law school were middling, just as they had been at the other schools he had attended. He was liked well enough, though no one remembers him as outstanding in any way: a sweet-looking, earnest, and very well-groomed young man who still seemed almost apolitical (he had supported Nixon in 1960 and was distraught at the candidate's perform-ance in the TV debates). Most of his contemporaries imagined he would become a corporation lawyer.

After law school he found himself a job with Welch and Morgan, a Washington law firm which specialises in acquiring

TV licenses for its clients. After only six months Dean was fired for "unethical conduct." He had joined a group competing with the firm for a license in St. Louis. He had taken outside legal advice as to the ethics of the move, and had been advised that it was all right, but the senior partner, Vincent Welch, was furious and fired him at once. Dean asked his brother-in-law, Robert McCandless, whether he should take the matter to the ethics committee of the Bar Association, and McCandless recommended instead that he bury himself in another job. Welch later retracted the charge of "unethical conduct." But for the young man in a hurry it appears to have been a cautionary experience. In his subsequent career, he was more careful in handling his superiors.

The old Wooster tie helped him to get a job as minority counsel on the House Judiciary Committee, working for Representative William McCulloch of Ohio. He impressed all those he met on the Hill as the ideal political aide—always ready to work hard for his boss's interests, always ready to suppress his own ego, never likely to make a wrong move—indeed, unlikely to make any move at all without clearing it. At the same time, says McCulloch, "he was in a hell of a hurry."

So much so that within five years he had moved from his $7,800 job with McCulloch, through a $25,000 post on the National Commission for the Reform of Federal Criminal Law, and into the Justice Department with Richard Kleindienst, who had been impressed with the law-and-order position papers he had produced on request during the 1968 campaign. Kleindienst and Mitchell thought Dean, with his young good looks, would be an ideal front man to negotiate with radical groups on crime legislation. "I'm too young," said Dean. But he accepted all the same.

Then in June, 1970, "out of the blue" Egil Krogh, Ehrlichman's aide, called and asked if he would like a job at the White House. Dean's first reaction, he says, was "No. I had had enough dealings with people in the White House to know it was the toughest place in the city to work." But Ehrlichman was keen on the idea. Now that he was graduating from the job of Counsel to the President to Chief Domestic Counsel, Ehrlichman wanted his old job to be filled with an able but pliant young man whom he could control. He called Dean and asked him to fly out to San Clemente to talk to the President.

In California he was met by a helicopter and saluted by a
Marine guard. He was overwhelmed. "Looking back on it now,
I see what they were doing to me," he said later. Haldeman
took him through a four-hour interrogation. "Very thorough,"
says Dean. "He took me apart on my beliefs, my way of doing
things, and then put me back together again." Thus patched,
he was ushered into the presence of the President and was
surprised by Nixon's sporty red jacket.

The temptation was too great; he grasped the President's
hand gratefully and flew back to Washington to break the news
to Mitchell and Kleindienst. Kleindienst was very sad to see
him go. "I wonder if John Ehrlichman will put his foot on
you," mused John Mitchell.

Dean had parted from Karla, his wife, but, now worth
$42,500 a year, he bought himself a chic little townhouse in
the suburb of Alexandria, a Porsche car and, like Henry Kissinger, became something of an eligible bachelor. But he found
that his title on the door did not mean very much else. "I was
Counsel to the President but I didn't really counsel the President." He was set to work preparing legal justifications for
policies already decided, and he was involved in plans for the
Richard Nixon Library. He worked on Tricia Nixon's wedding
and the somewhat arcane financing of the San Clemente White
House. All of his work was presented through John Ehrlichman; he hardly ever saw the President, and one of the few
occasions he spoke to him was when Nixon asked him to help
one of his daughters prepare a talk on presidential succession.

But however menial the task might appear, John Dean
always fulfilled it willingly. He never grumbled; he just went
ahead with the job and carried out his instructions, never
going out on a limb, always clearing any decision with his
superiors. A former colleague described him as "a pilot fish.
You know, the little fish who swim beside the sharks."

Dean had shown that he was not only reliable but adept in
times of difficulty. He had already been used several times as
a White House firefighter. He had helped douse the sparks
when the FBI's investigation of Daniel Schorr was revealed,
and he played a large part in putting out the larger flames of
ITT—during the Kleindienst hearings he had spent most of
his time in the Vice-President's office on Capitol Hill, briefing
administration witnesses before they went down to testify. He
was the ideal choice to try and contain the burning Watergate.

With his prior knowledge of the Watergate planning sessions, he was already unusually well equipped. Even Dean, however, did not, until he examined the contents of Hunt's safe on the morning of Tuesday, June 20, realise the potential scale of the conflagration. Containing it was going to be more than a one-man job. In the early, crucial phases of Watergate fire-fighting, he received rather exceptional assistance not only from his old chief John Mitchell but also from his White House superiors, John Ehrlichman and Bob Haldeman.

CHAPTER 16

"Deep Six"

AFTER LEAFING through Hunt's secret files and itemising the bugging equipment in his briefcase, John Dean knew he was in possession of a hoard that might do the President's chances of re-election some considerable harm. The public implications of what the White House had already designated "a third-rate burglary attempt," unworthy of its comment, would escalate dramatically if it was revealed that a White House "consultant" had suddenly gone missing, leaving behind random bugging gear and a couple of juicy political forgeries. Dean responded to the situation with his customary caution. After seeing that the "politically sensitive" documents were locked away in his safe and depositing the briefcase of electronic gear in his closet, he sought the advice of John Ehrlichman.

Dean tells this story of their encounter. Ehrlichman's reaction was to order him to shred the sensitive documents and "Deep Six" the briefcase. "What do you mean by Deep Six?" asked Dean. Ehrlichman leaned back in his chair and said, "You drive across the river on your way home every night, don't you?" "Yes," said Dean. "Well, when you cross over the bridge on your way home, just toss the briefcase into the river." Dean apparently replied—jokingly, of course—that Ehrlichman also crossed the river to get home and so he could do it instead. Ehrlichman was unamused: "No thank you," he said.

As Dean considered it very risky to destroy evidence, particularly in this case (there were other witnesses to the opening of Hunt's safe), Ehrlichman's instructions placed him in a quandary. He did remove the briefcase from his office. He did place it in the trunk of his car, and he did drive it, several times, across the Potomac, each time wondering whether he really should stop on the bridge and fling it into the water. After a few days, he decided that he could not; he returned the case to his office and tried to work out a plausible excuse for his disobedience. (Ehrlichman maintains that he never suggested destroying evidence, though Dean's assistant, Fred Fielding, remembers his boss agonizing over a "Deep Six" instruction at that time.)

The matter became more pressing on June 22, as Dean sat in on Charles Colson's interview with the FBI. The agents asked Colson if Hunt had an office in the White House complex. He did. They naturally asked if they could see it. Dean stalled by telling them he would check and let them know later. After that the agents called several times to ask about the office and its contents. On June 25 or 26 Dean went to see Ehrlichman again to discuss the problems posed by the materials found in Hunt's safe. By this time there was little hope of containing the case at the five original burglars; with the FBI on Hunt's tail and Liddy arousing suspicion by refusing to talk to the bureau's agents, it was evident that they would eventually go down as well. The only strategy now was to minimise the consequences of their inevitable arrest. Dean's view was that as the GSA men, the Secret Service men, and his own assistant Fielding had all seen at least some of what was in Hunt's safe, it would be crazy to destroy any of it. But that raised the problem of what was to be given the inquisitive FBI agents.

At his meeting with Ehrlichman, Dean suggested a two-tier approach. The most sensitive documents—the forged State Department cables linking President Kennedy to the murder of Diem, the Ellsberg material, the Chappaquiddick data, and the details of other plumbers' enterprises—be extracted, and the rest handed over to the FBI agents on the case. In order for Dean to be able to swear that everything had been given to the FBI, the potentially damaging documents should be handed straight to the new acting director, L. Patrick Gray III. Ehrlichman agreed. Pat Gray was a man on whose discretion the President could rely.

On June 27 Dean and Fred Fielding gave the FBI agents Hunt's briefcase and the more innocuous files from his safe. On the afternoon of June 28 Pat Gray came to see John Ehrlichman in his office, where he also met John Dean armed with the delicate documents in two folders. They told Gray they wanted him to take the files, that they were from Hunt's safe, that they in no way related to Watergate but did contain information which could be "political dynamite" in an election year. Gray remembers Dean telling him that they "should never see the light of day." He obtained a clear impression from both Ehrlichman and Dean that he was being asked to destroy them. Ehrlichman cannot understand how he received such an impression. And from the subsequent history of the documents, it seems there may well have been some imprecision in the discussion. Gray took the files away in two large envelopes and first hid them for maximum security under a pile of shirts in his Washington apartment. Several weeks later he decided they might be better locked in his office safe. Later still, he took them to his home in Connecticut and hid them in a cupboard. Throughout this time he never looked through them because, he explained, "I didn't have the natural curiosity of the cat—or the female." Just after Christmas he took them downstairs and out into the garden to the incinerator where he was burning all the Christmas rubbish. Then and only then, he says, did he glance at the top sheet in one file. It was the Diem cable. Horrified, he thrust both files into the flames.

L. Patrick Gray III was in many ways the most tragic of the characters fouled by Watergate. But there is a certain symmetry in his tale: loyalty to Nixon had raised him slowly up and it was the same quality that was responsible for his rapid decline. Gray had been a Nixon fan since 1947, when the young Congressman from Whittier was grabbing headlines with his pursuit of Alger Hiss. In 1960 Gray retired from the Navy early—thus losing several retirement benefits—in order to handle candidate Nixon's staff logistics. He then joined a New England law firm, and in 1968 gathered intelligence for Nixon on his Republican rival, Governor Nelson Rockefeller. He was not immediately snapped up after Nixon's victory. In fact he had to fill out a routine job application before he was given work in HEW, moving to the Justice Department as an assistant attorney general in January, 1970. But in May, 1972, his loyalty was finally rewarded.

Initially, his appointment as Acting Director of the FBI seemed to breathe new life into the bureau. Agents who had for years been subjected to Hoover's rigorous and often petty regulations were suddenly allowed to grow their hair and wear coloured shirts for the first time in their lives. They were even given permission to drink coffee at their desks. One FBI veteran described the joy at these reforms by saying, "The agents thought they had died and gone to heaven."

They were soon brought back to earth. Gray's problem, it turned out, was an exaggerated desire to please. He later explained that much of his career was built on the watchwords "Aye, aye, sir." And as he was desperately anxious to be made permanent director of the FBI, he was abnormally receptive to guidance from above. He even started making political speeches in favour of Nixon's re-election, a chore that those below thought took up rather too much of his time. He became known in the bureau as "Two-Day Gray." One of the things for which the architects of the White House cover-up had reason to be grateful after June 17 was that J. Edgar Hoover had died in May.

From the start of the FBI investigation, Dean was given the job of liaising with Gray. The principle was immediately established that Dean should sit in and take notes whenever the FBI wanted to talk to White House staff members. He would also give them guidance before the FBI men arrived. This was done, on specific instructions from the President, in order to protect the White House against unwarranted disclosure of "national security" information. Gray was very cooperative on this issue.

The only snag occurred when the FBI said they wanted to interview David Young's secretary, Cathy Chenow. She was on holiday in England and there was some concern that, if she were reached by an FBI agent before she could be briefed, she might let fall information on Hunt's and Liddy's activities as "plumbers." (From the White House viewpoint, of course, the President's "national security" concern provided instant justification for covering up the burglary of Ellsberg's psychiatrist's office.) Dean dispatched Fred Fielding to England to bring her back. Fielding had what he thought was a London address for her in "Kings Heath, Birmingham." When he arrived at Heathrow Airport in London he had some difficulty in discovering just where in the capital this Birmingham district was. It was some time before he found out that Birmingham is Britain's second-largest city, over one hundred miles from London. When he eventually arrived at the address, he just managed to catch Cathy Chenow before she left for a holiday in Wales. She was whisked back to Washington and told what she should not say, had her interview with both Dean and Fielding sitting in on it, and was then allowed to return to Britain to resume her travels.

But monitoring the interviews and listening to the drift of the FBI's questioning was not enough. By the end of June both the White House and CREEP were anxious to see what the agents were actually writing in their reports. Mitchell, Haldeman, and Ehrlichman, Dean says, all thought he should be given access to the reports, and in early July he asked Gray to let him see them. Gray complied with the request, but with some reluctance. By this time even his massive reserves of loyalty were dwindling. He was getting a hard time from his own agents. And he himself began to feel that some people in the White House might be serving up red herrings. The largest of these was the CIA connection, which had already stalled a key aspect of the FBI's investigation for over two weeks. It was dished up soon after the FBI's first major break on the money side of the Watergate operation.

On June 20, only three days after the break-in, the FBI field office in Miami had examined Barker's account and found the April 20 deposit of $114,000. The bank supplied copies of the original checks, and four of them were seen to be signed by Manuel Ogarrio on a Mexican bank, the fifth by Kenneth Dahlberg. The information was immediately forwarded to Washington and was in Pat Gray's hands on June 21. That same day John Dean came to see him and told him he had been told to keep abreast of the investigation: Gray told him of the leads. Although Gray did not know it at the time, the trail of Barker's checks if pursued through Mexico would establish an undeniable link between CREEP and the burglars. For Dean it was a worrying piece of information.

As four of the five burglars had worked for the CIA (Martinez was still on a retainer), suspicion of agency involvement was understandable. On June 22 Gray called Helms and asked him about this possibility. Helms, who had already had the burglars' CIA records checked, said they were not operating on behalf of the CIA. That evening, Dean came to see Gray again to discuss, in particular, the Mexican connection. Despite his call with Helms, Gray and Dean discussed the possibility that the CIA might be involved. Gray remembers Dean pointing out that an investigation into the Mexican checks might reveal a covert CIA operation.

Such fears had occurred almost simultaneously to the President himself. Nixon asked Haldeman and Ehrlichman to ascertain whether there was any CIA involvement. On June 22 he met with Haldeman, and they discussed, says Haldeman, the risks to national security (not, he says, to CREEP's reputation) that the inquiry posed. Nixon says he wanted justice to be done in the Watergate case, but in the scale of national priorities in which he dealt it was important not to expose either any CIA or any "plumbers" operation. So he instructed Haldeman and Ehrlichman to tell Gray to liaise with the CIA to make sure this did not happen. Gray, Nixon specifically said, was to work with General Vernon Walters, Richard Helms's deputy.

General Walters, who had recently succeeded General Cushman as the CIA's Deputy Director, was considered a good friend of the White House. He had known Nixon for a long time, and they were exceptionally close during the fifth of the six crises described in Nixon's book. (Walters had been Vice-President Nixon's interpreter on his hair-raising tour of South America when he was mobbed by left-wing students.) On June 22 Walters and Helms were invited over to the White House for a high-level meeting to discuss the ramifications of Watergate.

The meeting took place in Ehrlichman's office at 1 P.M. on June 23. Haldeman did most of the talking. He pointed out that the administration was taking a lot of flak on account of the break-in, that the opposition was capitalising on it. Haldeman told them of Nixon's concerns. Helms assured him that there was absolutely no CIA involvement in Watergate despite the fact that so many of the burglars had been former employees of the agency. A thorough FBI investigation could not harm the CIA.

Despite Helms's assurance about there being no CIA involvement, Haldeman seemed convinced that there might be. At this, apparently both Helms and Walters began to wonder whether there really was such an operation about which the White House had exclusive knowledge. In an agency employing 18,000 people, a third of whom are clandestine operators, there are times when even the Director and Deputy Director do not know everything that goes on. According to a memorandum prepared by Walters—on Helms's instructions —shortly after the meeting, Haldeman's instructions were quite specific. "Haldeman," he wrote, "said the whole affair was getting embarrassing and it was the President's wish that Walters call on Acting Director L. Patrick Gray and suggest to him that since the five suspects had been arrested, this should be sufficient and that it was not advantageous to have the enquiry pushed, especially in Mexico." (Haldeman said later that he was making a request, not giving an order; he does not recall mentioning Mexico.) As they left the White House, Helms told Walters just to remind Gray that the FBI and the CIA have a delineation agreement whereby neither will upset the other's applecart; if one runs into the operation of the other, it simply discreetly passes the information along. Walters agreed and went straight over to the FBI without returning to CIA headquarters in Langley, Virginia.

Gray was glad to see him. The two men shared, said Walters later, "a long association with the President and a desire to protect him." Walters told Gray that he had just come from the White House, where senior staff members were concerned that the FBI investigations in Mexico would uncover covert CIA activities. He reminded Gray of the delineation agreement; Gray had not heard of it. But Walters then went beyond Helms's instructions and told Gray that "if the investigations were pushed south of the border it could trespass on some of our covert projects." Gray then, according to Walters, proceeded to tell him that his problem was "how to low-key the matter now that it was launched." But Gray did the best he could. After Walters's visit, the FBI's acting director told his agents not to pursue the laundering of the money that they discovered in Barker's bank account. Ogarrio and Dahlberg were not to be interviewed, he instructed.

John Dean was such a good staff man that his very thought processes were often the same as his superiors. He did not know of Ehrlichman and Haldeman's meeting with Helms and Walters, but on June 26 he suggested to Ehrlichman that maybe the CIA could help the White House a bit. Ehrlichman told him of the moves that had already been made and advised him to go ahead and call Walters, not Helms. Dean did so, and after Walters had checked out with Ehrlichman that he should deal with his unknown young man, they met in Dean's office at noon that day. Dean told Walters that the investigation was very embarrassing and could lead to some important people; he asked if the CIA could not help in some way. Walters replied that it might, but that he knew the director would not countenance anything that might compromise the agency, and that he, too, would resign rather than be party to any such scheme. Dean was impressed. But Ehrlichman, says Dean, told him to try a little harder. Dean recalls Ehrlichman saying something like: "General Walters seems to have forgotten how he got where he is today."

Gray, too, was becoming a little unhappy. His agents were pressing him to lift the ban on interviewing Manuel Ogarrio. On June 27, he called Helms and asked specifically whether the CIA had any interests in Ogarrio: should the FBI hold off? He wanted CIA confirmation of the instructions to stay out of Mexico—preferably in writing. He asked Helms and Walters to come down the next day to talk about the case. In the afternoon Helms called back, said the CIA had no interest in Ogarrio whatsoever, and confirmed the next day's meeting. Seven minutes later, says Gray, Dean called him and asked once again that the FBI stay away from Ogarrio and Dahlberg because of "CIA interest in these men."

Dean then called Walters down to the White House again and once more asked if there wasn't the slightest CIA involvement in the case. But by now, Walters was operating on very much the same wavelength as his director. He said there was not. And when Dean asked if the CIA could provide financial support for the Watergate burglars, Walters's response was immediate. "No way," said Walters, and reported the conversation to Helms.

Next morning, a thoroughly bewildered Pat Gray returned a call to John Ehrlichman and was promptly told: "Cancel your meeting with Helms and Walters today. It isn't necessary." Gray asked him why, and Ehrlichman simply repeated that it was unnecessary. Gray then enquired just who it was who made decisions as to who should be interviewed, and Ehrlichman replied, "You do." He told Gray that he should deal in future with Walters, not Helms. Gray dutifully canceled the meeting with Helms. Ehrlichman says he made his demand because aides to Gray who were to attend the meeting were considered to be news leaks.

A few minutes later Dean again called Walters to the White House for a final overture. Dean told him that there was a problem of the FBI enquiries leading to Dahlberg and his campaign gift. Again he asked what Walters could do. According to Walters's memorandum on this meeting, he replied that "the idea I act independently [of Helms] had no basis in fact." Walters realised the affair was very embasrassing at the moment but he thought that Washington was a town where scandals were always quickly superseded. "I said that this affair already had a strong Cuban flavour and everyone knew the Cubans were conspiratorial and anxious to know what the policies of both parties would be towards Castro." He suggested that the White House pursue the possibility of strengthening the Cuban connection. Dean thanked him for the advice. (In fact, much of the White House's private "guidance" to reporters already indicated that they were wasting their time probing what was nothing more than a nutty Cuban escapade.)

The whole weird episode reached a weirder climax when Pat Gray returned from a San Diego inspection trip in the middle of the first week in July. Gray found his agents very unhappy with the way in which the investigation was being held up. In response to their insistence that they must interview Ogarrio, Gray promised that if the CIA would not put a request in writing they could do so. On July 5 Gray called Walters and told him of his requirement. Walters said they should not discuss it over the phone, and they agreed to meet the next morning. Walters was prepared to do a lot to protect the White House from embarrassment in an election year, but he was not prepared to write Gray a completely false letter claiming a CIA proprietary interest in Ogarrio. When he arrived at Gray's office the following morning he gave him a letter which said exactly the reverse—that the agency had no interest at all in either Ogarrio or Dahlberg.

Gray and Walters then had a heart-to-heart talk about the whole case, about their mutual desire to protect the President and how this should be best achieved. Both agreed that the integrity of their organisations was something that took precedence over the reputation of certain figures in the White House. According to yet another of those useful Walters memoranda that surfaced with all the other Watergate revelations a year later, Gray felt very bitter on this issue. "He [Gray]) did not see why he or I should jeopardise the integrity of our organisations to protect some mid-level White House figures who had acted imprudently. He was prepared to let this go to Ehrlichman, to Haldeman, or to Mitchell for that matter. He felt it important that the President be protected from his would-be protectors."

Towards the end of their talk, Walters told the acting FBI director that he had come into an inheritance and was not going to let "those kids" in the White House kick him around any more. As Walters stood up to leave, they discussed whether one of them, and which one, should not call the President and tell him of the disruption that the CIA red herring was causing.

Gray had already been told by several FBI agents that there was a cover-up in progress. One of them recalls that he "just didn't get the message to the President because he was apparently afraid to make it appear he didn't know what he was doing." But now he plucked up his courage. "After General Walters left the office," says Gray, "I sat at my desk quietly and mulled over our conversation. I was confused, uncertain, and uneasy. I was concerned enough to believe the President should be informed."

At 10:51 A.M. on July 6, Gray recalls telephoning his concern to Clark McGregor, the new director of CREEP (McGregor had replaced John Mitchell, who, five days earlier, had resigned, citing "personal reasons" for the decision). Gray told McGregor that he had to speak to the President about the way in which the FBI investigation was being hampered. Half an hour later, Nixon called Gray from San Clemente, and congratulated him on the way in which the FBI had just foiled a hijacking attempt in San Francisco. Gray then said, "Mr. President, there is something I want to speak to you about. Dick Walters and I feel that people on your staff are trying to mortally wound you by using the CIA and the FBI and by confusing the questions of CIA interest in, or not in, people the FBI wishes to interview."

Gray at this point expected an answer reflecting surprised concern from the President on the other end of the line. He was ready to let go with names and facts about the White House staffers who he felt were trying to wound the President. The one thing he was not expecting was the response he got. There was a pause. Then the President's voice came through: "Pat, you just continue to conduct your thorough and aggressive investigation."

A year later when evidence of a massive cover-up was laid out before the Senate Watergate Committee, Nixon expressed total astonishment at the revelations. He had, he said, repeatedly asked his aides about this. Yet on July 6, only three weeks after the burglary, he had passed up a golden opportunity to have it all laid out. Whether by accident or design, the President had preserved personal "deniability" about knowledge of a Watergate cover-up. When asked about Pat Gray's warning, a subject on which only he and Gray had first-hand knowledge, the President said: "Whether the term used was mortally wounded, I do not know. Some believe it was. Some believe it wasn't."

CHAPTER 17

The Tough Get Going

HAD THE President been really interested in finding out about Watergate, he would have had no problems. His close friend and campaign manager, John Mitchell, had most of the relevant information at his fingertips and ample opportunity to convey it. Prior to the break-in, they were in the habit of meeting almost daily to discuss campaign developments. But after the most important development of all—the Watergate burglary—they did not seem anxious to talk about it.

Mitchell, unlike Pat Gray, had an excellent appreciation of the rules of the "deniability" game. He was not about to tell the President something he would be better off not knowing—unless asked, of course. Meantime, Mitchell had more than enough to do handling his own personal war on two fronts. Not only did he have the mess at CREEP to contain, but there was also the problem of his wife, the volatile Martha, a lovable but impossible woman. Pat Gray did, eventually, achieve some dim understanding of the rules—albeit too late to save his reputation. Mrs. Mitchell, however, was a dead loss—she believed in speaking her mind. Fortunately for the success of the cover-up, it was not a mind to which people paid very much attention.

The story of how Mrs. Mitchell got the news of Watergate is the subject of a deposition which she prepared for her lawyers in May, 1973. It reads like a Feydeau farce with Lucille Ball in the starring role. Martha tells how she was with John in California on the Saturday of the break-in: but he never mentioned it to her, either on that day or the next. On Monday he persuaded her to stay on while he went back to Washington; he threw away the morning papers before he left.

Later she had her security guard, Steve King, go out and buy some more, and then she learned about the break-in and her husband's comments on Jim McCord. "My first thought," she says in her deposition, "was that McCord had been a double agent." Her second appears to have been that her husband was not being entirely frank about McCord's position with CREEP. She was "dazed," and called her husband for an explanation but, according to the deposition, could not remember what he said. She was horrified, she says.

She remained incommunicado until Thursday. Then, deciding that she must get John out at once, and that the best way was to make a public announcement, she called her friend Helen Thomas, UPI's White House correspondent. Martha told her that if Mitchell didn't leave politics, "I will leave him." The conversation, wrote Ms. Thomas, ended "abruptly when it appeared that somebody had taken the telephone from her hand." Martha is more graphic. Steve King, she says, rushed into the room and pulled the receiver away from her. He later jerked the phone from the wall. He did the same with all the other rooms in the motel villa where they were staying. For the next three days, she claims, he kept her prisoner there, and when her protests became too shrill he held her down on a bed while a doctor injected a sedative into her bottom.

Martha's public ultimatum to her husband was not treated with great seriousness. John Mitchell expressed his "amusement" that his wife had resumed her telephonic habits and said that he fully intended to leave politics after the election anyway. No one else seemed to think, as she did, that she was being kept away from Washington because her husband and his colleagues were "afraid of my honesty." (John Mitchell used their Watergate apartment for many crucial cover-up meetings during that first week after the break-in.) Most papers pointed out that Martha had always made funny phone calls: it was all a bit of a lark.

The joke, however, could get embarrassing. And did when Martha finally made it to a phone for her second blast, complaining, "I am a prisoner. . . . I won't stand for this dirty business." Mitchell flew off to join her and then brought her back to Washington, where Martha got her way. After a lunchtime meeting with the President on July 1, at which Watergate, says Mitchell, was not discussed, Mitchell resigned.

In a public statement of regret, Nixon said he understood what a toll politics could take on men's families.

Mitchell later told the Senate Watergate Committee that he had embraced a policy of total silence so far as the President was concerned. Not because he considered the Watergate episode itself so very damaging, but because he had learned of such previous Hunt and Liddy exploits as the Ellsberg psychiatrist break-in. Had he told the President the truth, he argues, Nixon would have been compelled to "lower the boom" and reveal not only the extent of CREEP involvement in the break-in but also what John Mitchell called "the White House horrors." He thought this might be damaging to Nixon's chances of re-election, which he considered far more important than anything, including the law. However, Mitchell testified, had the President ever asked him about any of these matters: "I would have spelled it out chapter and verse." He considered it very fortunate that the President never mentioned them.

Mitchell's formal departure did little to lessen his participation in the cover-up. He continued his frequent meetings with all his former colleagues right up to the moment the indictments were handed down. The topic of discussion was, throughout, the need to minimise the damage done. One problem was how to explain away the $199,000 which Liddy had spent on clandestine activities. Magruder says that at one point he volunteered to "take the heat" for authorising it, but the idea was rejected because the trail would then inevitably lead higher. The safest cut-off point was Liddy. The burglary had, after all, been bizarre enough to be explained away in terms of his rather idiosyncratic character.

The scheme devised, therefore, was to inflate the sums of money given Liddy for legal intelligence activities and to say that he had, on his own bat, used this money for illegal purposes. Next, everyone had to agree to go along with the story. Magruder went to talk to his scheduling director Bart Porter about it. He told Porter that he was known as "someone we can count on," a "team player," and Porter did agree to perjure himself and swear that he had given Liddy $100,-000 to infiltrate radical groups. While John Dean was doing his bit stalling the FBI investigation, some nicely structured perjured testimony was settling into place. There was only one real problem within CREEP; the young treasurer, Hugh Sloan, was found lacking in team spirit. It caused him a lot of personal anguish.

Earnest, competent and straightforward, "Duke" Sloan was the image of what an accountant should be. He had served in the White House as an aide to Dwight Chapin, married a White House social secretary, and was at CREEP right from the beginning. As treasurer he was to Magruder what Stans was to Mitchell. But he soon found that things were being run on somewhat unorthodox accounting principles. For one thing, an awful lot of cash was left in his safe; for another, an awful lot of people had the right to come and demand it without particularising what it was for. Indeed, it was considered somewhat impertinent for him to enquire. He once asked Bart Porter, who made cash withdrawals of up to $100,000, what was being funded, but Porter could not say (he later admitted that it went towards "Dick Tuck–type pranks and dirty tricks"). And when Sloan questioned Liddy's $250,000 budget in April, he found Maurice Stans's guidance puzzling: "I don't want to know and you don't want to know." For the three weeks after the break-in, Sloan's life was a nightmare; he actually wanted someone to investigate what Liddy had done with the money advanced to him out of the CREEP war chest.

It all started on June 21 when Magruder asked to see him. He told him they would have to agree on the figure Sloan had given Liddy and suggested it might be around $75,000 or $80,000. Sloan said that that was far too low. Magruder persisted. Sloan said, "I have no intention of perjuring myself." "You may have to," Magruder replied.

The next day the FBI came to see Sloan while LaRue was soliciting his cooperation on the money problem. LaRue took him in to see Mitchell for guidance. Mitchell's advice was crisp but not exactly what Sloan was looking for. "When the going gets tough, the tough get going," said the CREEP director. Sloan was relieved to find that the FBI men only wanted to ask about Alfred Baldwin, the monitoring man on the Watergate taps, of whom Sloan had never heard.

On the next day, despairing of the atmosphere in CREEP, Sloan took his concerns to people who might be able to take an objective outside view. At a river party for a departing White House aide, Sloan buttonholed his old friend Dwight Chapin. The next day he expressed his concerns. Sloan remembers that Chapin's reaction essentially was "(1) you are overwrought and (2) the important thing is to protect the President and (3) you ought to take a vacation." Sloan went higher—to John Ehrlichman, the man who was supposed to be in overall charge of the President's attempt to "get out the facts" of Watergate. Sloan laid out his view that "somebody external to the campaign has to look at this because it raised in my mind the possibility of the entire campaign being involved." Ehrlichman said he would be happy to get Sloan a personal lawyer. But when Sloan seemed inclined to go into his specific worries for the campaign, Ehrlichman stopped him: "Don't tell me any details. I don't want to know."

Sloan kept a cash book reflecting all his receipts and the cash payments he had made. From time to time Stans would ask him to type up a summary for him from this record, and Sloan would keep a copy for himself. On June 23 Stans asked him for such a summary of all receipts and payments of funds received before April 7. It included records of the Mexican checks and the Dahlberg checks and the Liddy payments. He told Sloan to make no copies this time. He said also to destroy his cash book and the copies of all previous summary sheets he had made. Stans himself later destroyed the original Sloan had given him. Stans insisted that this was done to protect the anonymity of the donors: the fact that he had made this decision just six days after the break-in was, he said later, purely coincidental.

Finally on June 24 Sloan thought he was getting somewhere. He told his story to Robert Mardian, whom he understood to be investigating Watergate for Mitchell. Mardian, he says, seemed overwhelmed and shocked: "That goddam Magruder just lied. He told John Mitchell that he authorised $40,000 to Liddy." Sloan told Mardian he didn't want any further dealings with Magruder. He then went on holiday, returning to CREEP only on July 3, two days after John Mitchell resigned.

On July 5 he reluctantly agreed to meet Magruder again. Once more Magruder brought up the question of the payments to Liddy and suggested that Sloan should go see the U.S. Attorney, Harold Titus, and tell him that he had given Liddy only $40,000. Sloan said he'd sleep on it. The next morning he agreed to compromise: if asked whether Liddy had received $40,000 he would say yes, but, if asked whether he had had more, he would also say yes. At that, Magruder seemed to lose interest.

Sloan then went to see Paul O'Brien and Kenneth Parkinson, CREEP's attorneys; they seemed as surprised by his story as Mardian had been, but their reaction was puzzling. They asked him if he couldn't leave town; he flew west to join Maury Stans. He had one final attempt at a discussion with his boss, but found it heavy going. Stans felt that they need not talk about it as it was the political people's problem, not the Finance Committee's. Sloan then told Fred LaRue and Stans that he wanted to resign. On July 14 Stans told him that he had already informed the FBI of his resignation, so Sloan completed the formality by writing a letter. He was off the team.

John Dean, meanwhile, was achieving prodigies of concealment as the linkman between CREEP, the White House, the FBI, the CIA and the Justice Department. At Justice he did not find his old friend Kleindienst keenly cooperative. He had apparently been angered by Liddy's approach at his country club. Dean recalls Kleindienst grumbling that he was always being asked by the White House to take care of things, as if he could by magic make something go away. But Justice did help the cover-up along by agreeing to Dean's request that certain dignified figures in CREEP and the White House— among them Maurice Stans, Charles Colson, and David Young—should not be obliged to appear before the grand jury in person. In an unusual breach of procedure, their sworn statements were taken in private and then read to the jurors. This was done, according to Kleindienst, to avoid the damaging publicity which might result to possibly innocent public officials if they were called formally to the grand jury. It also meant that the grand jurors had no opportunity to cross-examine them. Since the general CREEP policy was, as Mitchell said later, "not to volunteer any information," this did not help the process of judicial discovery. The result was that Sloan's lone voice suggesting that the criminality might go higher than Liddy went uncorroborated. The grand jury accepted the perjured testimony of both Bart Porter and Magruder. Dean says that Henry Petersen, the Assistant Attorney General, told him that Magruder only "got through by the skin of his teeth." It was enough.

On August 29 the President paid public tribute to the work

of his young legal counsel, and tried to reassure the nation. In addition to cooperating fully with the official investigators, he said, "Within our own staff, under my direction, Counsel to the President, Mr. Dean, has conducted a complete investigation of all leads which might involve any present members of the White House or anybody in the government. I can say categorically that his investigation indicates that no one in the White House staff, no one in this administration, presently employed, was involved in this very bizarre incident." (It was not till summer, 1973, that the White House admitted that the President and Dean had had no contact and that the President's confidence was based on "assurances" from Ehrlichman.) On August 29 Nixon added, "What really hurts in matters of this sort is not the fact that they occur, because over-zealous people in campaigns do things that are wrong. What really hurts is if you try to cover it up."

The cover-up was by now in exceptionally good shape. On September 15 the Justice Department handed down its indictments: Barker, Gonzalez, Martinez, Sturgis, McCord, Hunt, Liddy. And there it stopped. Magruder had, thanks to his well-oiled perjury, escaped, and had blocked the avenue of suspicion leading to higher involvement. Late that afternoon Dean received an unusual summons—to the Oval Office. There he found Nixon and Haldeman. According to Dean's recollection Nixon told him that Bob (Haldeman) had kept him posted on his handling of the Watergate case, and he appreciated what a difficult task it had been. Nixon was glad it had stopped with Liddy. Dean replied that others had done far more difficult things and that all he had done was to "contain" the case and keep it out of the White House. He did not know if he could do this indefinitely. He remembers Nixon saying that he hoped the trial would not be before the election.

They then talked about the problems posed by a possible Congressional enquiry and about stories appearing in the press. Dean remembers Nixon telling him to keep a good list of all the reporters giving trouble "because we will make life difficult for them after the election." The discussion then ranged over the need to make the Federal departments, especially the IRS, more responsive to the White House. Dean recalls Haldeman began to take notes on who should be fired. Haldeman agrees that this was roughly the list of topics discussed, but disagrees with Dean's construction on their meaning. For Dean the meeting clearly indicated that the President knew about and was happy with the cover-up; for Haldeman, it did not.

On October 3, the last major obstacle to the cover-up was surmounted when the House Banking and Currency Committee overruled Wright Patman, the incurably nosey chairman, and decided against holding hearings on CREEP's funny money activities. From then on the Nixon administration had a relatively easy gallop to the election. There were only two small barriers along the way—the press and George McGovern.

CHAPTER 18

A Dignified Response

ON OCTOBER 10, 1972, the Washington *Post* reported that the break-in at the DNC headquarters was linked to an extensive campaign of political sabotage, conducted by officials in the White House and the Committee to Re-Elect the President. The story named Donald Segretti as a leading activist in the sabotage campaign. Some days later the *Post* connected Segretti with Dwight Chapin, the President's appointments secretary. Herbert Kalmbach and H. R. Haldeman were also mentioned in connection with the espionage.

So great an upwelling of the truth, coming within a month of the election date, required an appropriate response. The White House had already had occasion to chastise the Washington *Post*, the only newspaper that effectively hung in on the story after the initial burst of coverage on the actual break-in. But the October revelations, suggesting involvement at the highest level of the White House, were of quite a different order from anything that had been printed before. It was time to wheel up the Big Lie.

From CREEP, the official message was loftily dismissive. The articles in the Washington *Post* were "a collection of absurdities." The finance chairman, Maurice Stans, looked down and saw "a senseless pack of lies." The political director, Clark MacGregor, deemed the *Post*'s work "vicious and contemptible." John Mitchell, who stayed on in Washington after his resignation to practice law and to watch over the cover-up, handled the situation with characteristic cruel vulgarity. He told a *Post* reporter that the newspaper's proprietor, Mrs. Katherine Graham, had better watch out. Because, said Mitchell, "Katie Graham is going to get her tit caught in a big fat wringer."

Ronald Ziegler, whose initial talent in communications techniques had been honed while working as a Disneyland barker on college vacations, had his finest hour. In those days he used to say, "Welcome aboard, folks. My name's Ron. I'm your skipper and guide down the River of Adventure. . . . Note the alligators. Please keep your hands inside the boat. They're always looking for a handout. Look back at the dock, it may be the last time you ever see it. Note the natives on the bank; they're always trying to get a head."

Now, speaking on behalf of the President of the United States, he would "not dignify with comment stories based on hearsay, character assassination, innuendo, and guilt by association." The charges against Haldeman were "a blatant attempt at character assassination." He wanted the White House press corps to know: "We respect the free press. I respect the free press. I don't respect the type of journalism, the shabby journalism, that is being practised by the *Washington Post*."

Ziegler had not achieved these flights of indignation entirely unaided. It later emerged in the Watergate hearings that one of the highest-level operations in the White House was the task of coaching Ziegler for his sessions with the media when there seemed any possibility of Watergate or related matters surfacing on the agenda. Amazingly, the record of one such session was preserved to become Witness Exhibit 22, attached to John Dean's testimony before the Senate committee. The scene was the Roosevelt Room in the White House on October 15. Those present were Ron Ziegler; John Ehrlichman; Patrick Buchanan, a White House speechwriter; Richard Moore, an aide who advised on public relations; Dwight Chapin, the injured party; John Dean, who had just remarried and been recalled from his honeymoon in Florida; and Dean's assistant, Fred Fielding. The subject: how Ron should handle the *Post*'s story on the Segretti connection with Chapin.

The basic idea of the practice was to anticipate the nastiest questions that might crop up at Ziegler's next conference and to suggest the most suitable form of reproof. Members of the group would oscillate between being devil's advocates and at other times a Ziegler surrogate. On the record of the transcript, which was taken by Dwight Chapin's secretary, Ziegler himself did not say very much. It was, for him, primarily an input session. But first, it seems, Ehrlichman, who had not been involved in the Segretti side of the operation, wanted some clarification about the individual under discussion. Ehrlichman asked, "What kind of guy is this fellow? What kind of appearance?" Someone said Segretti was short and baby-faced. "Well, if he's so short, how did he get into the army?" asked Ehrlichman.

"Maybe he lied about his height," suggested Fielding.

The serious business of the meeting began when Ziegler ran the following thought up the flagpole: "Now I can tell you. I have nothing more to say on this subject beyond what Dwight Chapin said in his statement. But I can tell you this. At no time has anyone in the White House or this administration condoned such activities as spying on individuals, surveillance of individuals, or sabotaging campaigns in an illegal way." Ehrlichman offered a more personalised thought: "Dwight Chapin is terribly offended at the treatment he got over the weekend. I approached him [on] the possibility of coming here [i.e., to the press briefing]. He said he would never again speak to any member of the press and he would like your apologies. . . ." Richard Moore seemed more attracted to the Olympian approach. His key contribution was: "What is the right of anyone to expect an answer from this podium on a story based on sources you will not reveal? Good citizens are being vilified based on irresponsible unidentified stories and stories which drew broad-sweeping conclusions."

At times, it must be conceded, the White House rehearsal group posed rather more penetrating questions to themselves than came up at the real press conference. For example, one member of the group breaks in: "Ron, that was a self-righteous, self-serving statement. Did Dwight Chapin, the President's appointments secretary, a man who meets with the President regularly, hire Segretti and instruct him to engage in espionage?" Ziegler, the real one, then says, "Gentlemen, I have nothing to add to what Mr. Chapin has already said on this, and that the story is fundamentally inaccurate and based on hearsay." Someone suggests that maybe the President himself should issue a statement. According to the transcript, Ehrlichman, speaking as Ehrlichman not the surrogate Ziegler, is not keen on the idea: "Chapin is the White House, and the separation—you bridge the separation when you get the President in."

On the next morning, Ziegler told the White House press corps that surveillance activities were "not condoned by anyone in this administration. . . ." and so on. Perhaps the most depressing thing about propaganda is that it works, for a while at least. And it did on Watergate. The White House staked its reputation against that of the *Washington Post* and won. It had "the Dean report" (which later turned out to be nonexistent) as evidence of White House noninvolvement in Watergate; and it had the FBI investigation—so thorough, said Nixon, that it made the 1948 Alger Hiss case look like a Sunday School exercise—as evidence that the level of culpability ended with Hunt and Liddy; and it had Ziegler programed for contemptuous denial.

The *Post* was outgunned, and as its story sources, primarily disenchanted FBI agents and disillusioned CREEP subordinates, had to be protected, it was in no position to detail the evidence for the truth of its allegations. Moreover, the *Post* investigative team, built round Bob Woodward and Carl Bernstein, the two diligent young reporters who had first covered the break-in, was practically alone. The *New York Times* routinely followed up the *Post*'s stories but never mobilised an independent investigation of its own. (The *NYT* had initially been misled by "the Cuban Connection" and never caught up.) And the Los Angeles *Times*, the only other paper with the necessary investigative resources, did not show strongly until well after the election. For the *Post* it was a period that required strong nerves and a lot of faith in two young reporters. Looking back on it, the *Post*'s owner, Katherine Graham, said, "I've lived with White House anger before, but I've never seen anything that achieved this kind of fury and heat." At times the *Post* was so alone that "we asked ourselves if there was some enormous Kafka plot, if we were being led down a road to discredit the paper. The reputation of the *Post* was totally at stake." Privately, Ben Bradlee, her executive editor, apparently put it more bluntly: "The *Post* really had its dick on the table."

Six months later, in the afterglow of justification, the "American Press" took credit for the exposure of Watergate, but only a very narrow segment deserved it. It was essentially a story on which there was no substitute for shoeleather, knocking on doors, and getting half a dozen discouraging "No comments" for every whispered "Come in." But there were so many loose ends dangling from the day of the break-in that there had to be a bigger story there for those willing to expend the energy in dragging it out. Few other than Bernstein and Woodward were prepared to do so. There are 2,200 reporters stationed in Washington. According to a census carried out by press critic Ben H. Bagdikian in May, 1973, only 14 had done substantial work on the Watergate scandal.

But there was a more fundamental reason why the *Washington Post*'s stories made so little impact at the time they were first printed. By the fall of 1972 it was the press, not the administration, that lacked credibility. It was a situation that the White House had been fostering for a very long time. Indeed, one of the most successful enterprises undertaken by the Nixon administration was its undermining of public confidence in the press. There was nothing accidental about the fact that the media should constitute the largest single group on the White House "enemies list." Nor was it an accident that the journalists on it should be among the best in the country.

The tone of the White House's approach to the press was set by Nixon himself. Over the years the President's White House press conference had come to have almost a constitutional function—it was the only forum in which the head of state could be seen to be accountable on a wide range of issues facing the nation. Every President since Roosevelt had given an average of between twenty-four and thirty-six press conferences a year. In his first term Nixon averaged seven a year. His aides made little secret of the fact that he found even these rare occasions a boring chore. Ehrlichman once explained that the President was tired of hearing all those "flabby" and "dumb" questions.

Within the White House, the campaign against the press was seen as a quest for "balance." Their assault on the networks and the big Eastern media chains was compared to populist crusades of the past—against the national banks, the railroads, and the utilities. The thrust of the campaign worked at two levels: one at the level of public opinion and the other at the traditional privileges of the American press. The leader of the public campaign had always been Vice-President Agnew, whose frequent and colourful blasts against "the elite corps of impudent snobs" who wrote for the richer newspapers, were regularly, and dutifully, reported in the press that was being lambasted. Most of Agnew's rhetoric was, to be fair, complete rubbish. But he was doing an effective job. Asked if it was that easy to change public opinion, Patrick Buchanan, Nixon's speechwriter who occasionally helped out Agnew with a few choice phrases, said, "Yes. Drip by drip. It really wears them down." And that is precisely what happened. In 1971, the American Civil Liberties Union issued a report in which it stated, "In a relatively short time the press in the United States has moved and has been moved from what many considered a position of extreme security to one of extreme vulnerability. There are some who say freedom of the press is now in the greatest danger of being lost in America; there are others who say it is all but lost already."

The judgment was premature, but it was an indication of a changing climate of opinion. On the less public level the increasingly widespread practice of subpoenaing reporters' notes and tapes and the networks' unused film jeopardised the working journalist's ability to preserve confidentiality for his sources, or even to obtain them in the first place. In the summer of 1972 the Supreme Court decided by 5 to 4 (with all the Nixon appointees voting in favor) that journalists had no First Amendment rights to refuse to appear before grand juries or to withhold sources of information. The effect inevitably was one that dried up newsmen's sources still further.

One of the oddities of the whole media debate was how many people who should know better fell for the argument that it was about an unrepresentative "liberal" press establishment versus a conservative majority opinion which the President perceived was unrepresented. The argument later found its most elegant expression in Theodore White's book *The Making of the President, 1972.* In it, White depicts the "baronial" press establishment as immensely powerful and dedicated to a fight against Richard Nixon and his view of the country. But this is to mistake the whole nature of what the press is about. Its most important public service is not to reflect opinion, nor even lead it for or against the President. The function that justifies a free press is its ability to find out and reveal. Sometimes it has to reveal matters that people would rather not know, but if it ceases to have that function it risks becoming no more than an instrument of propaganda.

In pursuit of "the Silent Majority," there were a lot of things that the Nixon administration felt people would be better off not knowing about. The crux of the press debate was not "conservatism" versus "liberalism" but a conflict between those who wanted a tidily organised "reality" and those who have the ability to find out and present the tedious complexity of the real thing. It often, though not invariably, was the case that rich and powerful newspapers were better equipped to ascertain the truth. In dealing with a White House which was increasingly prey to the view that "truth" is something that the majority of people believe, or can be persuaded to believe, any powerful newspaper worth its salt was bound to find areas of conflict. Indeed, the real press problem of Nixon's first term was the tendency among pressmen themselves to take the White House propaganda machine seriously.

Thus, by the time Watergate "broke" as a story, much of the press was intensely defensive at the time when it should have displayed its most aggressive instincts. And in the rare instances where aggression was displayed, it was not hard for the White House to dismiss Watergate as a "caper" which the "Eastern Establishment Press" was exploiting, not for the sake of the truth but for its own political ends.

In the final stages of the presidential election campaign, George McGovern tried hard to push the Watergate issue and bring it out as the central focus of the campaign. To no avail. A Gallup poll taken in October showed that barely half the voters had even heard or read about the Watergate incident. And eight of ten of those who had, did not see it as a reason to vote for McGovern. McGovern's chief political adviser, Frank Mankiewicz, later lamented: "The Senator responded correctly and responsibly to the Watergate revelations, but the public didn't react. The cover-up was working."

McGovern, in fact, had little going for him. His campaign had proved even more disastrous than the CREEP strategists, in their wildest dreams, could have hoped. McGovern's credentials as the White House's favourite opposition candidate were essentially those that had made the Democrats so grateful to have Goldwater in opposition back in 1964. Like Goldwater, McGovern aroused passionate loyalty in an activist section of his party and intense nervousness among those who were trying to keep a workable coalition of interests on the road. But whereas Goldwater's radicalism was founded on a return to the individualist values of an illusory golden age in the past (the right-wing dream), McGovern's was based on progress towards an era of community and brotherhood in the future (the left-wing dream). After winning the nomination in July against the wishes of the solid traditionalist core of the party, McGovern had to prove himself as a practical man, capable of healing the wounds caused by his controversial nomination. He did the reverse.

Till now his main strength had been in the largely middle-class peace constituency. Now he had to build a bridge back to the solid labour base of the party. It was a difficult but not impossible task; only a few months earlier, Al Barkan, chief of the AFL-CIO's Committee on Political Education, had stated that labour's primary objective in 1972 must be "the defeat of Richard Nixon's bid for re-election." It turned out that the bridge McGovern chose was of rather flimsy construction. The hurried choice of Missouri Senator Tom Eagleton as his running-mate was prompted by the idea that he could bring in the labour vote. In the event, it repelled votes wholesale. Throughout the crucial first month of McGovern's candidacy, the press was dominated first by stories of Eagleton's previously undisclosed medical history (he had been hospitalised three times with nervous exhaustion and had twice been given electric shock therapy); then by stories of McGovern's agonies over whether to drop his running-mate (which he finally did after first pledging "1000 percent support" for Eagleton); and finally by his desperate quest for someone to share the Democratic ticket with him (winding up with Edward Kennedy's brother-in-law, Sargent Shriver, the seventh man to be offered the job). There have been many worse scandals in American politics, but few have been so embarrassing. In the end, the AFL–CIO leadership refused to endorse the Democratic candidate for the first time in twenty years.

Even Vietnam turned out to be a counterproductive issue. Unlike the Nixon campaign, the McGovern entourage had little capacity for keeping a secret. One of the worst kept was the Senator's own efforts at arms-length diplomacy with Hanoi. The process had begun on the day after his nomination with a call to Pierre Salinger, who had been the late President Kennedy's press secretary. According to Salinger, McGovern asked him to undertake "a delicate mission." The North Vietnamese had asked the McGovern organisation to send a representative to Hanoi, and it seemed worth exploring. As Salinger was going to Paris, the candidate asked him to make some soundings with the North Vietnamese negotiators at the peace talks. Salinger went to Paris and explained to the North Vietnamese that a Hanoi visit would be difficult politically, but despite this, he, Salinger, would be willing to go if the trip would result in the release of thirty or forty prisoners. He emphasised that "Senator McGovern would prefer peace in Vietnam today to being President, if that is the choice." But it was not. On August 9, the North Vietnamese told Salinger that no prisoners would be released. On the next day, Henry Kissinger renewed his secret talks in Paris with Le Duc Tho of Hanoi's politburo. The North Vietnamese had evidently decided that there was no longer much point in doing McGovern any favours—it was already painfully apparent that he was not going to be President. Just to make matters worse, the sad little story "leaked," and McGovern and Salinger surfaced with different versions. On the one hand, it gave an appearance that McGovern was flirting with the enemy in time of war (though officially no war had ever been declared in Vietnam); on the other, it appeared that the enemy was not ready to do business with him. Neither appearance was very helpful to his campaign.

To compound the problems, somebody was planning dirty tricks on McGovern. Only two days after the Watergate break-in, the secretary to George Meany, president of the AFL–CIO, received a telephone call. The caller said he was Gary Hart, McGovern's campaign director, speaking from New York. He said that Senator McGovern wanted him to come there immediately for a meeting. The secretary explained that Meany had just arrived back that day from a visit to Europe and had already left New York for Washington. "All right, tomorrow then," the caller said impatiently. Annoyed by the caller's brusqueness, the secretary explained that Meany had a full schedule of appointments for the following day. "You don't seem to understand," rasped the caller, "Senator McGovern wants him to come to New York. . . . It will be to Meany's benefit."

Gary Hart maintains he was not in New York that day, but had gone out to the Midwest because of a family illness. When, two weeks later, he heard about the outrage "his" call to Meany had caused, he tried to reach the union leader to explain, "but I could never get through to him." To this day many of those on the McGovern staff believe that the hoax call was an important element in the AFL–CIO decision not to back McGovern.

After his nomination the tricksters stayed in business. Frequently, people representing themselves as spokesmen for homosexual groups handed out leaflets announcing "Gays for McGovern." In fact McGovern had given his support to the gay movement: now it seemed the trick was to embarrass him with it; one leaflet distributed in California carried an obscene picture of President Nixon. Frank Mankiewicz remembers at least a dozen occasions when inexplicable and disruptive things affected the campaign organisation.

"We would visit a town and McGovern would put in an appearance. We would say to the people who organised the meeting: 'Gee, that's a good crowd.' And they would say: 'You bet it is, considering the fact that you called this off a few days ago.' At times I wondered and worried about this, and then another problem would come up and I'd forget it."

In two major rallies, held in San Francisco and Los Angeles in October, McGovern aides found that calls had been placed to practically every radio and television station in the area to say that events had been canceled at the last minute. "After a while," says Mankiewicz, "we began to think we were as incompetent as we seemed to be. It evolved into a real defeatist psychology."

It has not yet been established how far CREEP was responsible for this mood; according to one Senate Watergate witness, there were still three spy sources in the McGovern staff as the autumn campaign got under way. Their reports were coded "Ruby 1," "Ruby 2," and "Crystal." In April, 1973, *Time* magazine credited Charles Colson with misrepresenting McGovern's "gay" support but Colson promptly denied the allegation. Certainly, Donald Segretti was not too active in the late stages. After the *Washington Post*'s initial revelation, Segretti was instructed by John Dean to keep moving out of range of the press. In fact, he deliberately went to ground surfacing only occasionally in some obscure town to ring Dean and ask what the newspapers were saying about him now. He spent the last week before the election in the desert near Palm Springs, California.

For a strong candidate, with a dynamic campaign the *Washington Post*'s revelations could have been turned into a potent Democratic vote-winner. But McGovern was effectively defeated before the revelations were made, and his attempt to make it the issue smacked of desperation politics. His moral outrage seemed to verge on the hysterical. With hindsight, it is possible to see that the situation was indeed desperate. But his apocalyptic rhetoric was off-putting at the time. The White House, with its alert appreciation of the smear technique, used McGovern's diminishing credibility to take the edge off the *Post*'s enquiry; the newspaper was labeled "McGovern's partner in mud-slinging."

Twelve days before the election, Henry Kissinger felt that he was able to announce that as a result of his secret negotiations, peace in Vietnam was "at hand." Only one more negotiation session with Hanoi was needed, he said. The final reason for McGovern's candidacy appeared to have been stripped away. Kissinger, it later transpired, had been over-optimistic. After the election, negotiations were broken off and over Christmas Nixon ordered the bombing of areas of Hanoi and Haiphong. Over 5,000 North Vietnamese were killed or wounded; 98 U.S. pilots were killed, wounded or captured. On January 27, 1973, an agreement was signed in Paris. Nixon said it brought "peace with honour" to Southeast Asia. The bombing continued in Cambodia. By then the election was over and done with. McGovern's campaign had been a shambles; the President's "image" had been cool and statesmanlike. Nixon promised a structure of peace abroad and a "New Federalism" designed to decentralise power and return it to the people at home. The nation voted accordingly.

On November 7, election day, 47,167,319 Americans voted to have Richard Nixon as their thirty-seventh President. George McGovern was the choice of 29,168,509. Nixon's numerical margin was larger than any President's had ever been. His 60.7 percent of the entire vote was second only to Lyndon Johnson's 61.1 percent landslide in 1964. Nixon was the victor in forty-nine states of the Union. Massachusetts, the country's most doggedly liberal state, was the only one to go for McGovern. (This was a phenomenon that gave rise to a popular bumper sticker after the Watergate revelations really began to roll in spring, 1973—"Don't Blame Me, I'm from Massachusetts.")

It was truly an overwhelming victory and one that immediately produced talk of "a new majority." Nixon himself felt that he had changed old allegiances in the country. There was, however, virtually no sign of the Emerging Republican Major-

ity which had been the original impetus for Nixon's strategy
back in 1968. Indeed, Nixon very carefully neglected the customary chore of extending his coattails to Republican candidates. They could only pull him back. In some cases, according
to evidence subsequently laid before the Senate Watergate
Committee, the White House actively, though covertly, supported Democrats who were more ideologically attuned to
Nixon's outlook than their Republican opponents. In the other
election—for Congress—the Democrats remained very much
in charge. No fundamental allegiances had been changed.
Nixon had outwitted an honourable but unsophisticated opponent in a bad year for the Democratic nomination process. And
even that might not have proved possible had it not been for
the deafening silence of the men who conducted the Watergate
burglary. By the time of the election this had already cost
something like $250,000—but, given the stakes involved, it was
cheap at the price.

CHAPTER 19

Two-Way Street

IN THE gloom of an early December afternoon a Boeing 737, United Airlines flight 553, was approaching Chicago's Midway Airport. The weather was bad; fog and drizzle had cut visibility down to a few yards. As the plane came in, the tower told the pilot to turn and try a second approach. He never made it. At 2:27 P.M. on December 8, while still a mile and a half from runway 31L, the plane took a sudden nose dive and crashed into a row of single-story bungalows. Only fifteen of the plane's fifty-five passengers survived.

Among the dead was Dorothy Hunt, wife of E. Howard Hunt. Just what was the purpose of her fatal trip is still unclear. What is known is that the following day, investigators searching through the wreckage discovered Mrs. Hunt's sodden handbag. Inside they found $10,000 in $100 bills, and on one of them was penciled the message "Good luck, F.S." At the time they were puzzled: why should Mrs. Hunt be carrying such a large sum of money in cash? According to a relative, questioned later, she was going to Chicago to make an initial down-payment on a Holiday Inn franchise. Even more intriguing than the destination of the money was its origin; the meaning of those mysterious initials has never been explained. The best guess is that "F.S." stood for Frank Sturgis, one of the Watergate defendants.

The discovery of the money was the first indication anybody had that for the past five months a river of cash had been flowing secretly into the pockets of the Watergate Seven and their attorneys. By the time of Mrs. Hunt's death around $300,000 had changed hands. The sum would later approach the half-million mark.

That somebody would have to offer the Watergate Seven an incentive to remain silent was clear to the President's legal counsel from the beginning. Within days of the break-in, Hunt had passed on an ominous message to Dean saying, "The writer has a manuscript of a play to sell." The question was: who was to put up the money? The answer was somebody who had as little as possible to do with the White House and CREEP. As we have seen, John Dean's initial suggestion was that the CIA should provide the wherewithal. But when that idea was rejected the White House and CREEP were driven back on their own not inconsiderable resources.

On June 28, eleven days after the break-in, Dean, LaRue, and Mardian met with Mitchell in his office at CREEP to discuss the problem. According to Dean, all were agreed that it was imperative to raise "support money in exchange for the silence of the men in jail." The others later described it as "a defense fund." Mitchell wanted the White House, not CREEP, to make the first move, so as the meeting ended he quietly drew John Dean to one side. Speaking in a low voice that no one else could hear, he suggested, so Dean says, that "the White House, and in particular John Ehrlichman, would be very interested to accommodate the needs of these men." Ehrlichman of course had supervised the plumbers' previous operations—what Mitchell called "the White House horrors."

Later that day Dean contacted both Ehrlichman and Haldeman, and it was agreed that Herb Kalmbach, the President's peripatetic personal counsel, was just the man for such a humanitarian mission. But first Herb would have to do a bit of extracurricular fund-raising.

Ever ready to oblige, Kalmbach took the night flight from Los Angeles. The following morning, he booked into the Statler Hilton Hotel. From there he rang John Dean at the Executive Office Building, suggesting that they should meet in the coffee shop of the Hay Adams, just down the road. This rendezvous was a bit too public for the conversation Dean had in mind, so he steered Kalmbach out to a more secure venue—a bench in Lafayette Park.

Dean surprised Kalmbach by waving his arms vigorously in the park. The idea, apparently, was to distract attention. Though Dean came straight to the point, he was less than frank. "We are thinking of raising funds for the legal defense of the Watergate defendants and their families," he said. "And we would like you to do the job." He said he had talked to Haldeman, Ehrlichman, and Mitchell, and they all agreed it was very important that Kalmbach take it on. Between $50,000 and $100,000 was needed. Fred LaRue would tell Kalmbach the individual amounts and when they were to be distributed. Kalmbach was impressed with the need for urgency but thought that there were more straightforward ways of accomplishing such an evidently humane task. "Why don't you set up a public committee, or alternatively get the defendants to mortgage their homes?" he suggested. Dean murmured something about there not being enough time and anyway, he added, a public committee might be misinterpreted. Secrecy and speed, he urged, were of the essence.

Reluctantly, Kalmbach agreed to help, and said that if discretion was what the White House wanted then there was only one man he would trust to deliver the money: Tony Ulasewicz. Since the previous year, Ulasewicz had been distinctly underemployed. And so when Kalmbach, later that afternoon, called him at his home in upstate New York to say that he had a job for him, Ulasewicz hurried down to Washington. He arrived the following day.

By that time Kalmbach had already collected some money for him to deliver. After leaving Dean in Lafayette Park, Kalmbach went back to his hotel and called the Republicans' other great fund-raiser, Maurice Stans. He explained that he had just been given a "special assignment" by John Dean, that he needed $50,000 to $100,000 immediately and could Maury help? As it happened, he could. A couple of hours later Stans arrived with a bundle of $100 bills. Not all of them were new, but together they totaled $75,100. Just where this money came from remains a mystery. Stans has admitted handing the money over, but beyond saying that it was not CREEP money, he has declined to identify the source.

Kalmbach was much relieved; it seemed that within a matter of hours he had already done all, if not more, than he had been requested. John Dean had asked for "at least" $50,000, and here he was with $75,000. LaRue had come to the Statler to tell him how the money was to be distributed, and now all that remained was that delivery. The next day, in Kalmbach's hotel room, the respectable lawyer and pillar of Orange

County's Lincoln Club and the ex-policeman from New York's Lower East Side got down to an earnest discussion of how best to preserve secrecy.

It was agreed that nobody should use his real name and that all communications should be from public phone booths (earlier Kalmbach and LaRue had agreed to call each other "Mr. Bradford"). When Kalmbach rang Ulasewicz it was arranged that he should describe himself as "Mr. Novak," and Ulasewicz should answer to "Mr. Rivers." Just to be on the safe side a few more pseudonyms were invented: among them, Tom Kane, John Ferguson, and Tommy Smith. This seemed sensible at the time, but later it was to cause some confusion. A cloak of secrecy also shrouded the identity of the defendants. Hunt was to be known as "the writer," the name he had given himself; his wife, reasonably enough, was "the writer's wife." Ulasewicz had arrived without a briefcase, so when the time came to hand over the money, he had nothing in which to put it. A search of Kalmbach's hotel room revealed an empty laundry bag, which Ulasewicz appropriated. From that time onwards the money was always referred to as "the laundry."

The job of delivering "the laundry" proved to be more difficult than anticipated. During their talk the previous day, Kalmbach and LaRue had agreed that the money should be passed to the defendants via their lawyers. The only difficulty was that the lawyers themselves had not been consulted about this plan. Shortly after receiving the $75,000, Kalmbach told Ulasewicz to contact Douglas Caddy, the friend Howard Hunt had visited for legal advice in the small hours of June 17. Ulasewicz carried out his instructions to the letter. He rang Caddy and, introducing himself as "John Rivers," he inquired about "the cost of the script, of the play, and of the players." Caddy, it became evident, did not much like the sound of this drama. Paul O'Brien, CREEP's attorney, was the next member of the legal profession to be approached. The result was equally discouraging. "He showed no interest in any script, players, or any type of message that I would give," Ulasewicz later ruefully complained.

Ulasewicz began to despair that he would ever get rid of what he called "his cookies." The money had been transferred from the laundry bag to a brown paper bag, tied with string but Ulasewicz was deeply conscious of the fact that, either way, it was he who was holding it. He was making so many calls to Kalmbach—("I began to call them Kalmbach come-back calls")—that he took to wearing a bus conductor's change dispenser at his waist to carry all the dimes and quarters he needed. The anti-hijacking security checks at the airports were another problem. On one occasion Ulasewicz was standing in line at Washington's National Airport waiting to board the Eastern Airlines shuttle for New York when a fellow passenger two or three places in front of him set off the automatic metal detector. The resulting search was a thorough one. Ulasewicz, who does not look like the kind of man who normally carries $50,000 in ready cash, developed an acute coughing fit and took the train home.

Relief, however, was at hand. In the first week of July, Ulasewicz called Hunt's attorney, William O. Bittman, and gave him the now standard message about scripts and players. "Yes," said Bittman, "I was expecting a call. But you realise this is very unusual. I do now know if you are an attorney, but an attorney does not anticipate fees and costs in this manner." "Well," said Ulasewicz, "I am instructed not to negotiate in any manner. I understand that you would have a figure and I am prepared to settle now." After a flurry of phone calls Bittman eventually came up with a figure: his initial fee, he said, would be $25,000. From the manner of its delivery it was plain that this fee was no ordinary payment. The hand-over was orderly but decidedly unconventional.

Sealing the $25,000 in a plain brown envelope which he had bought in a nearby drugstore, Ulasewicz hurried into the lobby of Bittman's office building. From there he called Bittman's office, told him that the money had arrived, and that if he cared to come down he would find it on a ledge by the telephone directories. Just to make sure that there would be no mistake he asked Bittman the colour of his suit. He was told that it was brown. Shortly afterwards a man wearing a brown suit emerged from the elevator, picked up the envelope, and disappeared upstairs. Ulasewicz had completed his first mission.

It was not to be the last. Soon afterwards, Ulasewicz made his first contact with Mrs. Hunt, "the writer's wife." As the Bittman "drop" had worked so well, Ulasewicz saw no reason to change his methods. He called Mrs. Hunt and asked her to come at exactly midday to National Airport and to go to the last telephone booth in the row opposite the Northwest Orient Airlines counter. Shortly before she was due Ulasewicz placed the money—$40,000—in a luggage locker and then Scotch-taped the key underneath the coin box in the phone booth. Mrs. Hunt's instructions were specific: go straight to the phone booth, remove the key, and go to the locker—don't hesitate. At twelve o'clock precisely she appeared and did exactly what she had been told. The plan had worked perfectly. But Mrs. Hunt was less than satisfied. "It's not enough," she told Ulasewicz later. "There will be problems."

Mrs. Hunt soon explained that she was acting on behalf of all the defendants and made it clear that there were no cheap rates. For a start she wanted a total of $130,000 for legal fees ($25,000 apiece for Hunt, Liddy, McCord, and Barker and $10,000 each for Sturgis, Gonzalez and Martinez). On top of that there were living expenses over the next five months. These came to $59,000 ($15,000 for the three leaders and sums ranging from $6,000 to $2,000 for the lesser fry). Poor Ulasewicz; he had been told that he must in no circumstances negotiate, yet every time he picked up the phone Mrs. Hunt's demands became more insistent and more wide-ranging. By mid-July she was asked to be compensated for the loss of her job and its accompanying fringe benefits; she required a special payment for Mrs. Liddy, who was, she said, suffering from "psychiatric problems," and an "under-the-table" payment to Barker to extract him from some unspecified difficulty in Miami. She was, said Ulasewicz, onto a good thing and her attitude was "to milk it." Ulasewicz tried hard to keep a running check on these demands. By the time the "negotiations" ended in mid-September, she was asking, so Ulasewicz calculated, for between $400,000 and $450,000. Ulasewicz and Kalmbach found all this rather alarming. It was also somewhat inconvenient: the first Hunt and Bittman payments had all but exhausted the original $75,000; by mid-July, more fund-raising was obviously necessary. And this time it was CREEP that came to the rescue.

Early in June—well after the April 7 deadline—the finance committee of CREEP had received a further $63,000 in cash from anonymous contributors who were so shy that they neglected to reveal their identities even to CREEP. Duke Sloan, CREEP's treasurer, has since told the General Accounting Office that he put it aside until the identities of the donors could be established. But in the meantime a use was found for it elsewhere. At the beginning of July it was passed, together with another small parcel of unreported CREEP funds, to Fred LaRue, who later gave it, in two installments, to Herb Kalmbach to help him with his little difficulty with the Hunts. Ulasewicz took delivery and set off again for another round of airport meetings with Mrs. Hunt and, on one occasion, G. Gordon Liddy.

Kalmbach was worried. The operation was turning out to be far bigger and more elaborate than he had been led to believe: he had never found his turns with Ulasewicz to be very comic, and the payments, which had been supposed to be "nonnegotiable," were now quite out of hand. "It was like a James Bond scenario," he later told the Senate Committee. So on July 26 he went to see his old friend John Ehrlichman at the White House to seek reassurance. "John," he said, "I am looking right into your eyes. I know Jeanne and your family, you know Barbara and my family. You know my family and my reputation mean everything to me, and it's just absolutely necessary, John, that you tell me, first, that John Dean has the authority to direct me in this assignment, that it is a proper assignment, and I am to go forward in it." Ehrlichman, Kalmbach felt, recognised that this was indeed a solemn occasion. Kalmbach still remembers Ehrlichman's reply vividly. "Herb," he said, "John Dean does have the authority, it is proper, and you are to go forward." With that seemingly cast-iron assurance, Kalmbach set off for California to raise yet more money.

On July 31, five days after his heart-to-heart with Ehrlichman, Kalmbach called on another old friend, Thomas V. Jones, chairman of the Northrop Corporation in California, and picked up another $50,000—which Jones says he gave as a political contribution to President Nixon's re-election campaign and which he assumed would be duly reported. It didn't turn out that way. The sole beneficiaries were the Watergate defendants.

But raising the Jones money was Kalmbach's final contribution to the cause. While out in California with Ulasewicz for the pick-up—the hand-over took place in Kalmbach's car —the President's personal attorney asked the ex-cop for advice: "Tony, what's your opinion of all this?"

Ulasewicz, who somehow manages to combine a kindly nature with a talent for tawdry work, decided to give it to him straight. "Well, Mr. Kalmbach," he replied, "I will tell you, something here is not kosher. It's definitely not your ball game, Mr. Kalmbach. Whatever has happened, we started with no negotiations, we are into negotiations; we started with $75,000, and we have now got something like $220,000 coming in and we are only approaching half. I know that the next conversation I have that figure has got to go up, from all the inferences and all."

Kalmbach, very sensibly, took Ulasewicz's warning more seriously than John Ehrlichman's reassurance. (Ehrlichman, it later transpired before the Senate Watergate Committee, had forgotten giving any such assurance.)

At the end of August, Kalmbach told Dean and LaRue that he was off the team. All that remained was to tot up the amounts, check the totals with LaRue, balance the books—and destroy the records. On September 21, at a meeting in Dean's office two days after Ulasewicz had made his fourth and final payment to Mrs. Hunt, this was duly done. Kalmbach had raised $220,000, of which $154,000 had been channeled to Mrs. Hunt. From now on Fred LaRue was to be both fund-raiser and paymaster-general. Ulasewicz left $29,900 for him on a ledge in the Howard Johnson's Motel, across the street from LaRue's apartment building—the Watergate.

Untraceable funds were becoming hard to find. CREEP's reserves of unreported cash had now been exhausted, and with Kalmbach out of the action there was little hope of prising further wads from loyal but unsuspecting Republicans. Meantime, the pressure from the Hunts was unrelenting. Shortly after the election, Chuck Colson received a call from his old friend and protégé, E. Howard Hunt. According to a tape transcript of the conversation which later surfaced in the columns of the redoubtable Jack Anderson, Hunt was deeply concerned. After discussing his plight, Hunt got down to essentials. "One of the initial inputs I've read about," he said, "is that while this is done by a bunch of wild-assed guys . . . well that's fine, for we're protecting the guys who are really responsible . . . and, of course, that's a continuing requirement.

"But at the same time," Hunt continued, "this is a two-way street. As I say, and as I said before, we think now is the time when the money should be made, and surely the cheapest commodity available is money."

According to John Dean, the tape of this conversation later found its way to Camp David, where on November 15 the White House high command was in retreat, planning the construction of Nixon's second administration. In the President's empty office, Dean played Ehrlichman and Haldeman the tape. It was fast becoming clear that any further money for the "defense fund" would have to be supplied by the White House itself.

As it happened, Haldeman had $350,000 of what appeared to be virtually untraceable funds in his charge. Back in the spring, as the April 7 deadline of the new campaign fund law approached, CREEP had discovered that it had more cash than it knew what to do with. The new law, however, laid down that any unspent money had to be reported and its source identified. Shortly before this inconvenient requirement came into effect, $350,000 from previous campaign funds was hastily sent to the White House; it ended up in Bob Haldeman's safe. Although he had dipped into it to finance occasional polls, most of it was still there.

In the first week of December, Haldeman's assistant, Gordon Strachan, was sent to deliver the first bundle—$50,000— to Fred LaRue. It was not enough. Before the Watergate Seven trial opened at the beginning of January, Hunt's demands, says Dean, "reached a crescendo." LaRue needed more money fast. "Give them the whole damn bundle," Haldeman told Strachan, "but make sure you get a receipt." Strachan did what he was told. He arrived at LaRue's apartment to offer him $280,000 in cash. Before picking up the money LaRue donned a pair of gloves and said, "I never saw you." Nonplussed but determined, Strachan asked for his receipt. LaRue refused and said, "You'll have to talk to John Dean about that."

Strachan later told the Senate Watergate Committee: "At that point I became more than a little suspicious. Frankly, after Mr. LaRue put on the gloves, I did not know what to say so I said nothing. Nor did I know what to do—so I left."

With Haldeman's help, money had ceased for the time being to be a problem. But cash was not the only relief the defendants wanted. As the year turned and the Watergate trial began, word wafted up to the highest level in the White

House that some of the Seven felt they had suffered enough in a good cause. If not freedom now, they wanted at least the prospect of early release. As they faced charges which could carry penalties of up to fifty-five years in jail and $50,000 in fines, this was, in terms of the normal processes of justice, an absurd wish. Nonetheless it was in the President's power to make it come true. But if he indicated that the power would be exercised, before the trial was over, he would be guilty of a perversion of justice. It was an intriguing problem.

CHAPTER 20

Scorched Earth

THERE IS only one person in the United States who can offer pardons and reprieves to convicted criminals, and that is the President himself. Article II Section 2 of the Constitution not only appoints the President Commander in Chief of the Army and Navy, it also gives him the power "to grant reprieves and pardons for offences against the United States, except in cases of impeachment." It is generally known as "executive clemenecy" and is the one Presidential prerogative about which there has been no argument. In the 197 years of the history of the Republic it has been an established fact that if the President says that a felon should go free, then his word is final: not even the Supreme Court has the power to gainsay him.

All claims are normally processed through one of the more obscure parts of the bureaucracy: the office of the Pardon Attorney in the Justice Department, which reviews the petitions and passes on its recommendation to the President. But these are for guidance only; the power itself cannot be delegated.

Over the last forty years the practice of individual Presidents has varied considerably: the official statistics show that some have been a good deal more clement than others. While Franklin Delano Roosevelt leads the field with an average of 313.6 pardons per year, Richard Milhous Nixon comes near the bottom of the list with 146.2 per year. Only Eisenhower, at 145.2 per year, was marginally less forgiving.

In his first year as President, Nixon set a record: he granted no reprieves and no pardons. But he has since relented. In 1972, for example, he awarded 235 pardons and 20 reprieves. That reprieves should be harder to obtain than pardons is easily explained. Under the ground rules established by Robert Kennedy when he was Attorney General, pardons are normally offered only to petitioners who have already completed their sentence. The conditions governing reprieves are, in theory, more stringent. According to the Kennedy rules they should only be given to prisoners who are critically ill, or who have rendered some "meritorious service."

The President, as we have seen, is not obliged to follow these rules: exceptions can always be made. And on December 23, 1971, Nixon made a sizable one. Among the sixteen people whose sentences were commuted by presidential fiat that year was James Hoffa, the former president of the Teamsters' Union who, in 1964, had been sentenced to thirteen years in prison on charges of fraud and bribery. Nixon commuted his sentence from thirteen to six and one-half years, thus effecting his immediate release. "It is a bit difficult," said the *New York Times,* "to avoid the suspicion that imminence of the 1972 election was a factor in Mr. Nixon's decision to release him." (It is possible that the *Times* would have been even more censorious had it known that Harold J. Gibbons, the Teamsters' liberal vice-president and Hoffa's leading opponent within the union, was listed as a high-priority "enemy" in Chuck Colson's book.)

The idea that the President might be inclined to offer the Watergate burglars a reprieve occurred to Hunt soon after his arrest. According to McCord, Hunt first floated it in the fall of 1972. "Subsequently," he says, "Hunt mentioned it in almost every telephone call." But in this pretrial stage, Hunt's main objective was to extract as much cash as possible from the White House; it was not until the beginning of January, on the eve of the trial itself, that he began to push really hard on the clemency issue.

It was Hunt's patron, Charles Colson, who first got the message. Distressed by his wife's death, Hunt wrote him an impassioned letter in which he indicated that he was willing to plead guilty but only if the White House would promise that he would receive executive clemency. On January 2 CREEP's attorney, Paul O'Brien, telephoned John Dean in California, where he was preparing to leave for Washington in the President's new plane, Air Force One. Over the phone O'Brien merely said that there were "serious problems" and that "Hunt was off the reservation." On Dean's return to Washington that evening, the nature of the problem was explained in detail. Colson was the only man, O'Brien explained, who could quiet Hunt down. Next morning, Colson sent Hunt's letter to John Dean with a seven-word memorandum. "What the hell do I do now?" it asked.

After a talk with Hunt's lawyer Bittman, Colson, so Dean says, was "extremely shaken," and shortly afterwards he arrived in Ehrlichman's office saying it was "imperative" that Hunt be given some assurances of executive clemency. According to Dean, Ehrlichman agreed, but said that nothing should be done until he had had a word with the President himself; on no account was Colson to approach the President direct.

Both Nixon and Ehrlichman have emphatically denied that executive clemency for the Watergate defendants was ever authorised, either then or subsequently. Dean, on the other hand, claims that not only did Ehrlichman later tell him he had given Colson an "affirmative" on the executive-clemency question, but that Colson confided to him that he had disregarded Ehrlichman's order and had in fact raised the matter with the President himself. As a result William Bittman, Hunt's lawyer, had received from Colson "a general assurance" that his client would get what he was asking for. Within a matter of days some impression that executive clemency was on offer was filtering down—among others, to James McCord.

The White House had good reason to include McCord, for by the first week in January he was, as John Dean put it with appropriate delicacy, "becoming an increasing problem." The first indication that McCord, like Hunt, had a foot outside the reservation had come during Christmas week when Jack Caulfield, who had originally recommended McCord for his security job with CREEP, received an anonymous letter. The metaphors were triumphantly mixed but the meaning was plain enough. "Dear Jack," it read, "I am sorry to have to tell you this but the White House is bent on having the CIA take the blame for the Watergate. If they continue to pursue this course, every tree in the forest will fall and it will be scorched earth. The whole matter is at the precipice right now. Pass the message that if they want it to blow, they are on exactly the right course. I am sorry that you will get hurt in the fallout." There was no signature but it did not take Caulfield very long to

work out the author's identity. A glance at the envelope revealed that the letter had been posted in Rockville, Maryland.
Caulfield knew only one person there who had reason for concern about the CIA's reputation—the CIA's former agent,
James McCord.

Soon after his arrest, McCord realised that the White House
might be tempted to offload the responsibility for Watergate.
He had no doubt where his loyalties lay: the CIA's interests
came first. He and his family were a close second, and CREEP
and the White House were, by now, a very poor third. So he
opened up a secret correspondence with his old employers. On
July 30 he sent his first message to Richard Helms himself. It
was marked "personal" and promised, "From time to time I
will send along things you may be interested in from an info
standpoint." It was unsigned.

Meanwhile McCord had hatched an ingenious plot to engineer his own freedom with minimum stress on his loyalties.
He was sure that the phones of the Chilean and Israeli embassies were tapped by the administration, and in the fall he
made *pro forma* calls to both embassies, in the hope that he
would be overheard. He would then raise the issue at his trial,
and the government would be faced with a dilemma: either to
drop the case against him or to admit the existence of taps on
the embassies. One flaw in the plan was that he had no proof
that his conversations actually were recorded. Another was
that even if they had been, the government might well choose
to deny it. Even so, it was not as nutty an idea as it might
sound: a very similar revelation proved to be the straw that
broke the back of the case against Daniel Ellsberg for "stealing" the Pentagon Papers.

Throughout the fall McCord grew increasingly resentful of
the White House. He was especially disgusted by seeing a picture of Jeb Magruder surrounded by his children. Magruder's
perjury seemed to have assured his future, and after the election he was given the high-visibility job of stage-managing the
Inaugural. McCord's own future looked less rosy.

It was not until the week before Christmas that his fears for
the CIA were confirmed to him. On December 21 his attorney
—a young man named Gerald Alch, a junior partner of F. Lee
Bailey, the Boston whiz-lawyer who specialised in extracting
clients from the juicier and more sensational situations—invited McCord to an expensive lunch at the Monocle Restaurant

in Washington. Over the entree Alch suggested, according to McCord, that in his defense he should claim that Watergate was a CIA operation. When McCord protested that he no longer worked for the CIA, Alch countered by saying that McCord could testify that he had been recalled: the records of the agency, which would shortly be under new management, could be appropriately doctored. Alch denies this story. However, it was now clear that the CIA was in for a transformation. Earlier in December, the Washington newspapers ran unattributed but obviously authoritative stories indicating that a shake-up in the CIA power structure was imminent. The obdurate Helms was going. He would be replaced by an outsider, James Schlesinger, architect of the 1971 secret study to streamline and give "effective leadership" to the intelligence services. James McCord was deeply unenthusiastic about this development.

On the day after his lunch with Alch, McCord resumed his correspondence with the CIA. This time his letters were signed and were addressed not to Helms but to Paul F. Gaynor, an old friend who worked in the CIA's office of security. "Dear Paul," McCord wrote. "There is tremendous pressure to put the operation off on the company [a euphemism for the agency used by old CIA hands]. Don't worry about me, no matter what you hear. The way to head this off is to flood the newspapers with leaks and anonymous letters that the plan is to place the blame on the company for the operation. This is of immediate importance because the plans are in the formative stage now and can be pre-empted now if the story is leaked so that the press is alerted. It may not be headed off later when it is too late. The fix is on . . . I will do all I can to keep you informed. Keep the faith." On December 29 he wrote to Gaynor again, outlining his wiretapping defense plan. And on January 5 he sent his final letter. "Yesterday they tried to get all the defendants to plead guilty, thus protecting those higher up of involvement and that failed. Barker and Hunt were allegedly to plead [guilty], so it is said. McCord and Liddy refused." Three days later the trial began, and James McCord began to get some unusual feedback from the White House.

Late in the afternoon after the first day's hearing, McCord and one of his co-defendants, Bernard Barker, were taken by Alch to see Hunt's lawyer, William O. Bittman. McCord understood from Alch that the purpose of the visit was to decide whose word they would accept "regarding a White House offer of executive clemency." Alch says this is untrue. In any case, it was all rather messy. "I became angered," McCord told the Senate Watergate Committee, "at what seemed to be the arrogance and audacity of another man's lawyer calling in two other lawyers' clients and pitching them for the White House." After being kept waiting outside Bittman's office he stormed off in a huff. Alch later told McCord that he would be called the same night "by a friend I had known in the White House."

Dean says that Mitchell had heard of McCord's "disagreement" with Alch and asked him to send Jack Caulfield, the former White House "investigator," to find out from McCord what he planned to do. Mitchell denies this. In any case, that afternoon Dean had called Jack Caulfield in California, where he was attending a drug conference, and asked him to deliver a message to McCord. Caulfield demurred. He was, as he later explained to the Senators, not anxious to become overly involved in an operation that he clearly recognised as very dangerous. It might help if Tony Ulasewicz was also used to share the load.

Ulasewicz already had some idea of McCord's plight. In the fall Caulfield, who was fond of and felt partly responsible for McCord, had had Ulasewicz make a series of anonymous phone calls to offer McCord and his family help. This time Ulasewicz called him at home at half past midnight and told him he had a message from Caulfield: McCord should go down Route 355 to the pay phone near the Blue Fountain Inn.

There Ulasewicz called again and read out the message John Dean had transmitted through Caulfield: "Plead guilty. One year is a long time. You will get executive clemency. Your family will be taken care of and when you get out you will be rehabilitated and a job will be found for you." McCord's reply was cool: "I can't discuss such matters over the phone," he said. But he did not seem altogether disinterested. When Ulasewicz called the following evening to arrange a meeting with Caulfield, McCord accepted the invitation.

McCord, however, says he had no intention of accepting clemency; he was simply milking the situation for all the evidence of White House involvement he could get. Later, in defense of his beloved CIA and of himself, it would be turned to explosive use. In the meantime he kept a very detailed personal diary.

His meeting with Caulfield took place at one of Washington's more romantic venues: a vantage point off the George Washington Parkway overlooking the Potomac. In summer it is a favourite place for courting couples, but on the evening of January 12 it was deserted save for two men discussing a proposition for the perversion of justice which both thought had the blessing of the President of the United States. They sat in Caulfield's car, and there in the darkness Caulfield explained to his friend that the offer of executive clemency came "from the highest levels" of the White House.

McCord was unimpressed. He wanted his freedom, but he wanted it on his terms which, he explained, could be met only if the White House went along with his bizarre wiretapping defense plan. Caulfield said that he would see what he could do, and on this unsatisfactory note the meeting ended.

Two days later Caulfield and McCord met again on the parkway. In the interim Caulfield had reported back to Dean, and Dean said he would check on the wiretapping scheme (he later told Caulfield it was no good). He then, says Caulfield, told him to go back to McCord and "impress upon him as fully as you can that this offer is a sincere offer which comes from the very highest levels of the White House." Caulfield replied: "I have not used anybody's name with him. Do you want me to?" "No," answered Dean, "I don't want you to do that, but tell him that this message comes from the very highest levels." "Do you want me to tell him that it comes from the President?" persisted Caulfield. "No, don't do that. Say that it comes from way up at the top."

On the Parkway, Caulfield did his best to impress upon his friend the urgency of the situation. Caulfield's pitch, later summarised by McCord before the Senate Committee, was as follows: "The President's ability to govern is at stake. Another Teapot Dome scandal is possible, and the government may fall. Everybody is on track but you. You are not following the game plan. Get closer to your attorney. You seem to be pursuing your own course of action." McCord's response was to say that he was inclined to be independent. Caulfield made one final effort. Would McCord, he asked, give a commitment that he would remain silent? "No," said McCord.

After that there was really nothing more to be said. One last meeting ten days later served no useful purpose. As the two men drove through the Virginia countryside, Caulfield offered his friend a small piece of advice. "Jim," he said, "I have worked with these people and I know them to be as tough-minded as you or I. When you make your statement don't underestimate them. You know that if the administration gets its back to the wall, it will have to take steps to defend itself." "I have already thought through the risks," McCord replied, "and will take them when I'm ready. I have had a good life and my will is made out."

But McCord did not immediately carry out his threat to go public, and the trial went ahead, according to "the game plan" —much to the chagrin of Chief Judge John J. Sirica of the United States District Court, Washington, D.C. Sirica, a right-wing Republican from immigrant Italian stock, is the senior judge on the Washington circuit and without question the most formidable. His nickname "Maximum John" is earned from his habit of handing out unusually severe sentences to those who have the misfortune to appear before him. His other foible is that he does not really enjoy being lied to in his court. As the evidence indicating that the entire operation began and ended with Liddy unrolled, Sirica made no attempt to conceal either his incredulity or his impatience at what he regarded as the prosecution's ineptitude. Whenever he felt the prosecutors were not asking the right questions, he cast aside judicial impartiality and put them himself. Was it not true, he asked of the defendants, "that you have been under great pressure to plead guilty?" To Barker he said: "I want to know where the money comes from. There were $100 bills floating around like coupons." And when Barker replied that he had got the money "in the mail in a blank envelope," Sirica snapped back, "I'm sorry, I don't believe you." These tactics upset the defense lawyers, who complained that Sirica was usurping the role of the prosecution, but the judge was not to be deterred by any such footling objections. "I don't think we should sit up here like nincompoops," he replied. "The function of a trial is to search for the truth."

But Sirica's efforts were vain; the cover-up was not moved. The key evidence for the prosecution was provided by Al Baldwin, the ex-FBI man hired by McCord to monitor the wiretaps (Baldwin, because of his evidence, escaped prosecution himself—and, like McCord, became a candidate for "double agent" theories). Only Liddy and McCord pleaded not guilty, and neither made more than a token defense or suggested that any superiors were involved. Both were found guilty on January 30. Sentencing was deferred till March. But whereas Liddy's reticence was apparently unconditional—dictated by his concept of a soldier's duty to protect his commanders—McCord's game plan was altogether more ambitious. He was not about to throw away his invaluable chips in the limited world of a court of law.

McCord wanted the maximum exposure for his revelations (many of which, being based on hearsay, were not admissible in a court). Even before the trial opened, he had a good idea of where the exposure might best be made. Although McGovern had failed to ignite the Watergate issue during the campaign, the Democratic leadership, encouraged by the Washington *Post* revelations, became increasingly anxious to pursue the story after the election. On November 17 Mike Mansfield, the courtly and sometimes rather slow-moving Senate Majority Leader, wrote to both Senator Eastland, the Chairman of the Judiciary Committee, and Senator Ervin, the Chairman of the Government Operations Committee, requesting that they make a joint recommendation to the leadership on how to proceed with an investigation.

On January 3, Mansfield made his concern public. "The so-called Watergate affair," he told the caucus of Democratic Senators, "appears to have been nothing less than a callous attempt to subvert the political process of the nation in blatant disregard of the law." He thought that Watergate, and the false letters distributed in Florida about Muskie, Jackson, and Humphrey, "warranted attention."

Realising that some sort of Congressional investigation was inevitable, the White House Congressional liaison office now worked overtime to try and see that it was chaired by Eastland rather than Ervin. Eastland had been very kind to Kleindienst during his confirmation–ITT hearings, whilst Ervin, a crusty old Constitutionalist from North Carolina, had long been distinguished for his hatred of bugging, no-knock entry, and all the other favours which John Mitchell had extended to help the police perform their duties. On January 11, however, the Democrats selected Ervin as the chairman. The White House, says Dean, was not pleased. McCord, on the other hand, must have been delighted.

On February 7, 1973, the Senate passed Resolution Number 60. By a vote of 77 to 0 it established "a select committee of the Senate to conduct an investigation and study of the extent, if any, to which illegal, improper, or unethical activities were engaged in by any persons, acting individually or in combination with others, in the presidential election of 1972, or any campaign, canvass, or other activity related to it." Specifically the committee was charged with an investigation of the planning and circumstances of the Watergate break-in and with determining whether there was any evidence of a subsequent cover-up. The committee was also empowered to look into any other dirty tricks that may have been played during the course of the 1972 presidential campaign. The Senate gave the committee half a million dollars to finance this inquiry. There was good reason to expect that its hearings would be televised. Nixon's top aides then gathered for two days of meetings to discuss how to defuse the threat posed by the committee. They were at something of a loss. Haldeman suggested, for example, that a story be put out linking McGovern to 1972 anti-Nixon demonstrations and indicating that the finance came from foreign and communist sources. Another of his recommendations was leaking a story that George McGovern had fathered an illegitimate child in Texas back in the 1940s. Haldeman felt this could be done tastefully by ensuring that, when the White House was asked for official comment, the line would be that it had known all along but the President had instructed that the story not be used "under any circumstances." (Later, Haldeman was to admit that there was no evidence for either of these smear stories.) But before any diversionary tactics could be properly developed, the White House found itself faced with yet another Watergate-related problem—the Senate hearings for Pat Gray's nomination as permanent director of the FBI.

CHAPTER 21

Slowly in the Wind

AT THE end of the first week in March, L. Patrick Gray III sent an SOS to John Ehrlichman at the White House. He was having a hard time. The Senate hearings into his nomination as director of the FBI had opened a week before, and the Democrats on the Judiciary Committee had immediately zeroed in on the FBI's handling of the Watergate enquiry. The unfortunate Gray had been forced to reveal that John Dean had sat in on all FBI interviews with White House personnel and had been given access to FBI reports. The Senators were anxious to know whether Gray had extended any other favours to the White House.

"I'm being pushed awfully hard in some areas," Gray told Ehrlichman. And he begged him to tell John Dean to keep absolutely mum about the fact he had personally taken delivery of the "sensitive" material found in Howard Hunt's White House safe. "You have got to tell John Wesley to stand very tight in the saddle," Gray implored. Ehrlichman said he would and offered words of encouragement. "Keep up the good work, my boy. Let me know if I can help."

Ehrlichman's real feelings about Gray's predicament are best gauged from the transcript of a phone call he made to Dean immediately after he had soothed the FBI's unhappy acting director.

> EHRLICHMAN: Hi. Just had a call from your favourite witness.
> DEAN: Which is?
> EHRLICHMAN: Patrick J. Gray.
> DEAN: Oh really?
> EHRLICHMAN: And he says to make sure that old John Dean stays very, very firm on his story that he delivered every docu-

ment to the FBI, and that he doesn't start making nice distinctions between agents and directors.

DEAN: Yes, he's really hanging tough. You ought to read the transcript. He makes me gag.

EHRLICHMAN: Let him hang there. . . . Let him twist slowly, slowly in the wind.

Ehrlichman's graphic image derives from the last paragraph of *Brave New World*, Aldous Huxley's vision of totalitarianism. The Savage, the last remaining unprogramed human being, has hanged himself; the people come to stare.

While Gray was thus suspended, clamour arose from the Judiciary Committee for John Dean's appearance. From what Gray had said so far, it was obvious Dean was in a position to throw a good deal of light on the subject of whether there had been a White House cover-up of Watergate. From being one of the least-known White House aides, Dean became famous overnight.

His sudden arrival in the public eye had been preceded only a fortnight before by an equally dramatic change of status inside the White House itself. In the last week of February his title suddenly became meaningful, and he began personally to counsel the President for the first time. He had last met Nixon on September 15, five months before. But between February 27 and April 16 he had some twenty-one meetings (mostly private) and fourteen phone conversations with Nixon. It was an elevating but somewhat nerve-wracking experience.

Exactly what was said about Watergate at these meetings has been the focus of intense debate ever since Dean disclosed their contents, first in a series of tantalising and incomplete leaks to the newspapers and later in a full account to the Senate Watergate Committee. As nearly all the conversations were private, the only practical way of corroborating the truth of Dean's assertions is for the President to produce the secret tape recordings that were, unknown to Dean, made at the time. Although the President and Bob Haldeman, who was the only other witness present during some but not all of these talks, have categorically denied Dean's charges that they were party to a cover-up, remarkably few of Dean's facts have been disputed. The main conflict is over differences of interpretation. The President and Haldeman have listened to some of the tapes and both admit the meaning of certain key passages is ambiguous. In mounting their defense they have chosen, understandably, to interpret the tapes in such a way as to support their case. As the contents of the tapes were not available at the time of writing, we have thought it reasonable to base our account on this period largely on Dean's version, but to indicate major points of disagreement where they occur.

To a man who had not previously enjoyed his most intimate confidence, the President was remarkably forthcoming. Their conversations ranged over Pat Gray's problems in obtaining confirmation of his nomination as FBI Director (the President thought his performance so stupid that he was probably incapable of running the FBI) through executive privilege to frank estimates of the mood of individual Senators. There was also a good deal of talk about the President's conviction that the most effective way to counter all these allegations about wiretapping would be to put pressure on the FBI to disclose that Nixon himself had been wiretapped during his 1968 campaign. But Watergate was the main topic.

Though Dean had been convinced since the previous September that the President had been aware of the cover-up, he must have been faced with a problem. He probably realised that the cover-up could not be continued indefinitely, but to have blurted out all the details might present him with distinctly personal problems. Dean knew that "deniability" was the name of the game. If the President knew about the cover-up, then he also knew that Haldeman and Ehrlichman had a strategic role in it. For a young man who had not only a healthy respect for his superiors but also a strong survival instinct, it was a tricky situation.

The first meeting on February 27 went fairly easily. The President explained that he had called Dean in because Watergate was taking up too much of Haldeman's and Ehrlichman's valuable time, and as they were "principals in the matter," Dean could perhaps be "more objective." Dean says he was puzzled by this reference. If the President thought of his two top aides as Watergate "principals," it seemed odd that he should have faith in their subordinate's objectivity. (Ehrlichman later claimed that Dean misunderstood the reference; the President was simply concerned at the amount of time he and Haldeman were spending on the pressing Watergate-related problem of executive privilege, and wanted Dean to take over.) Just as the meeting was ending, Dean remembers Nixon congratulating him on his Watergate work during the campaign; it was McGovern's only issue and the White House had defused it. Dean replied that he was not sure it could be contained indefinitely.

Next day the two men met again, and this time Dean remembers being more direct. He told Nixon that he had been involved in the cover-up. "I briefly described to him why I thought I had legal problems, in that I had been a conduit for many of the decisions that were made and therefore could be involved in an obstruction of justice." By Dean's account Nixon was not very interested. "He would not accept my analysis and refused to listen to further details."

Over the next week the spotlight at the Gray hearings began to move in Dean's direction. It was a development the White House did not welcome. On March 12, after discussions with Dean himself, the President invoked the doctrine of executive privilege in an unusually comprehensive form. Nixon stated: "The manner in which the President personally exercises his assigned executive powers is not subject to questioning by another branch of government. If the President is not subject to such questioning, it is equally appropriate that members of the staff not be so questioned, for their roles are an extension of the Presidency." The Senate Judiciary Committee was unimpressed. The following day it voted unanimously to demand Dean's immediate appearance.

That day Dean had his longest meeting with the President so far. The main topic was the problems Gray and Dean were having with the Judiciary Committee. But towards the end, the conversation turned towards Watergate. Until now Dean had spoken only in general terms about the cover-up: he had mentioned his own role and had discussed the difficulty in maintaining it. But this time he was much more specific. He told Nixon that the Watergate Seven were still clamouring for money but that the funds had run out. At this point Haldeman came in. Nixon then enquired how much was needed, and Dean replied that it would probably take at least $1 million. "That," Nixon reportedly said, "would be no problem." Looking over at Haldeman he repeated the remark. After asking Dean who was asking for the money and on being told it was Hunt, the President then remarked that he had discussed giving executive clemency to Hunt with both Ehrlichman and Colson.

Both Nixon and Haldeman have emphatically denied this

account. Haldeman says that he cannot remember being present at this meeting (the White House logs confirm that he was), but says that the tapes reveal that this discussion about money and clemency was at a later meeting on March 21. For his part, the President says he only mentioned money and clemency in order to lead Dean on and "smoke him out," and that after saying the $1 million was "no problem," he had added, "John, it's wrong, it won't work, we can't give clemency and we have got to get this story out." All parties agree that there was no discussion of these explosive issues during the following week in which Dean met Nixon almost daily.

The external pressures on Dean continued to mount. On March 15 Nixon held his first press conference since January to announce the appointment of the veteran diplomat, David Bruce, as America's first de facto ambassador to China (his official title was head of the U.S. liaison mission). The President was first astonished and then angered that this "historic announcement" elicited not a single question: the only subject in which the press showed any interest was John Dean's continued nonappearance before the Judiciary Committee. There was also pressure from another direction.

Dean had received yet another in the seemingly endless series of monetary demands from Howard Hunt. On the afternoon of March 20 Dean told Richard Moore (who besides advising the President on public relations acted as a father-confessor to his younger colleagues) that he had just had a message from Hunt (whose receipts were by this time in excess of $400,000) for a further $72,000 for living expenses and $50,000 for attorney's fees. Hunt reportedly said that if he did not receive the money within a week he would "reconsider his options and would have a lot to say about the seamy things he had done for Ehrlichman at the White House."

Dean decided that there was no longer any point in equivocation. And at his meeting with the President the next morning he did not, according to his account, mince any words. "Mr. President," he began, "there is a cancer growing on the Presidency," and if that cancer were not removed "then the President himself would be killed by it." He then proceeded to do what he had up to now avoided: he named names. He described Magruder's grand-jury perjury, Hunt's prodigious monetary demands, Kalmbach's fund-raising; he also implicated Haldeman, Ehrlichman, Mitchell and, of course Dean.

Dean then sat back and waited for the explosion. But it never came. "After I had finished," Dean says, "I realised that I had not really made the President understand, because after he asked a few questions, he suggested it would be an excellent idea if I gave some sort of briefing to the Cabinet and that he was very impressed with my knowledge of the circumstances, but he did not seem particularly concerned with their implications." Later that afternoon and on the following day, Dean says, there was a series of meetings with Haldeman and Ehrlichman at which it was suggested that maybe Mitchell could take the blame for the Watergate break-in.

The White House version of the event of March 21/22 differs from Dean's. It alleges that Dean's recital was nothing like as comprehensive as he says. Even so Nixon claims that it was sufficiently startling for him to order "intensive new enquiries," of which he took personal charge. Just how intensive these new enquiries were is open to some doubt. Though Nixon says that he "personally ordered those conducting the investigations to . . . report . . . directly to me," he made no such request to Richard Kleindienst or Henry Petersen at the Justice Department or to Pat Gray at the FBI. On March 22, Day One of the new White House investigation, Nixon had a lunchtime meeting with John Mitchell. Although Mitchell had been portrayed by Dean as a key figure in the conspiracy only the previous day, the President, according to Mitchell, never even mentioned the subject. If the White House was serious in its intent, there was by this time no shortage of material to investigate: Washington was awash with revelations. That day, Gray had cracked further: he confessed that Dean had "probably lied" to FBI agents working on the Watergate enquiry.

On the twenty-third, Gray received a call from the President. He remembers Nixon telling him: "There will be another day to get back at our enemies and there will always be a place for you in the Nixon administration." Nixon then made a curious reference to Gray's call of the previous July in which he had tried to warn Nixon that some of his top aides were trying to "mortally wound" him. The President reminded Gray that he had urged him to make a "thorough and aggressive" investigation. Gray was puzzled by this reference. "I had an eerie feeling," Gray later told the Senate Watergate

Committee, "that the President was trying to put something on the record."

A few hours before this call, the McCord threat, latent since early January, was finally carried out. It was the day the sentences on the Watergate burglars were due. But before delivering them, Judge John Sirica read in court a letter from McCord alleging that there had been "political pressures" on the Watergate defendants to plead guilty, that perjury had been committed, that figures more exalted than Liddy were involved, and that "several members of my family have expressed fear for my life if I disclose knowledge of the facts of this matter." The burglars, with the notable exception of McCord, then received their punishment.

Strictly speaking, it was more than they deserved: Liddy got "not less than 6 years 8 months and not more than 20 years," Barker and the Cubans were sentenced "provisionally" to 40 years apiece, and Hunt got a similarly "provisional" 35 years. McCord's sentence, however, was postponed, and he was released on $100,000 surety bond. Judge Sirica then explained the reasons for his harshness; they sounded uncomfortably like judicial blackmail: "You must understand that I hold out no promises or hopes of any kind. But I do say that should you decide to speak freely I would have to weigh that factor in appraising what sentence will be finally imposed in each case." Later that afternoon John Dean escaped from his house, where he had been besieged by TV reporters, and at Nixon's suggestion drove to Camp David. The White House maintains the President still trusted Dean because his March 21 account had been less than complete, and sent him there to write a report. Dean says it was only on his arrival at Camp David that he learned that a report was expected, and the instructions came not from Nixon, but Haldeman.

The McCord letter had blown the cover-up sky high. The weekend after its publication, he was interviewed by Sam Dash, the Senate Watergate Committee's chief counsel. The conversation was supposed to be private, but its substance quickly leaked. On Monday morning the *Los Angeles Times* tied Dean and Magruder to the break-in. Team spirit had had its day. It was now everyone for himself. With varying degrees of speed, the more junior members of the team scurried around, found themselves lawyers, sought advice, went to the prosecutors, testified before the grand jury, talked to the staff of the Senate Watergate Committee and, perhaps most important of all, leaked to the press. Almost every day seemed to bring more and more fantastic revelations in the *Washington Post* and the *New York Times*. And each day's revelations encouraged someone else to take the icy plunge into the truth. As everyone was anxious for his own version to be out front, suddenly White House staffers were remarkably accessible to newsmen.

Up on the mountain, Dean developed a writing block. The problem was, which version of the "truth" was really required: complete or bowdlerized? Neither Haldeman nor Ehrlichman could offer any useful guidance, Mitchell was "hanging tough" in New York, and Magruder was developing an acute state of the jitters. It was obvious, at least to Magruder, that the fact that he had lied to the Watergate grand jury earlier in the year would have to come out—probably sooner rather than later.

At this stage, says Dean, the White House plan was to pass the blame off on Mitchell; a stratagem that the ever-watchful Martha quickly perceived. On March 27 she called the *New York Times* to say that "someone" was trying to make a "goat" of her husband. "I'm really scared," she said. "I have a definite reason. I can't tell you why. But they are not going to pin anything on him. I won't let them, and I don't give a damn who gets hurt. I can name names." But Mitchell was not the only available "goat." John Dean too felt he was being measured for the necessary horns and tail. In that morning's papers, Ron Ziegler, the President's spokesman, was quoted as saying that the President had just called Dean to express confidence in him—this was despite the *Los Angeles Times* story. The news came as a surprise to Dean. He had received no such call. "I began to feel that I was in some obscure way being set up," he later said.

On his return to Washington with his report still unwritten, Dean's suspicions hardened. "By now," he says, "Ehrlichman and Haldeman fully realised I was not playing ball and would in fact present a serious problem to them. It was also evident to me that they were doing everything they could to protect themselves against my knowledge." On March 30, two days after leaving Camp David, Dean was relieved of his Watergate responsibilities. According to the White House, the reason for this move was Dean's failure to produce his report. Further White House investigation of the matter was to be handled by the ubiquitous John Ehrlichman. By the weekend of March 31/April 1 Dean had decided that the White House, so long a haven from the storms outside, had become altogether too unnerving a place. After spending the weekend closeted with his lawyers, he sought a new sanctuary in the welcoming arms of the government prosecutors and began to deliver a verbal report, in the hope of gaining at least partial immunity from prosecution.

A fortnight later, the prosecutors had another visitor— the by now thoroughly demoralised and frightened Jeb Magruder. The meeting took place on April 14, and afterwards Magruder went to tell Ehrlichman what he had done. On leaving Ehrlichman he bumped into Bart Porter in the street. "It's all over," he told Porter, and passed on the apparently remarkable instruction, "I just came from the White House. The President has directed everybody to tell the truth."

In his dealings with the prosecutors, Magruder was considerably less subtle than Dean. The Dean tactic could be likened to a strip-tease; as each item was removed, the promise of what remained became ever more alluring. Magruder, on the other hand, took all his clothes off at once. The prosecutors were surprised and shocked at the spectacle, and went rushing round to Henry Petersen, the Assistant Attorney General, to tell him that they had, for the first time, hard evidence that Mitchell, Mardian, Magruder, Ehrlichman, Haldeman, and Dean were all possible candidates for a criminal prosecution. Petersen in turn passed this on to his boss, Attorney General Richard Kleindienst.

It was not a complete surprise. Immediately after his interesting conversation with Magruder that afternoon, Ehrlichman had phoned Kleindienst and had told him that "Mr. Magruder has been over here at the White House and has been telling us that he has been meeting with the United States Attorney's office and giving them testimony and evidence that would implicate people high and low in the White House and the campaign committee." Before Kleindienst could make any reply, Ehrlichman put down the phone. The details came later, after Kleindienst returned from a dinner. At 1 A.M. on April 15, U.S. Attorney Harold Titus, chief prosecutor Earl Silbert, and Petersen arrived at Kleindienst's home to tell him what they had learned from Magruder and Dean. Kleindienst is not normally over-emotional, but as he sat taking notes on his wife's stationery of the involvement of some of his closest friends, he could not contain his sorrow. Kleindienst wept. Not since his mother died, he said later, had he been so upset.

Kleindienst did not get much sleep that night. The meeting ended at 5 A.M., and at 8:30 he was on the phone to the President, who said he would meet him after morning prayers. When the service was over the two men went over to the Executive Office Building, where the President attempted to console his distraught Attorney General. According to Kleindienst, the President seemed "dumbfounded" and "very upset," but Henry Petersen, who joined them for a second meeting, clad in T-shirt and sneakers—he had just been summoned from his boat—was impressed by the President's calm. "In his situation I would have been cussing and fuming," Petersen said later.

There was no doubt in Petersen's mind as to how the President should deal with Haldeman and Ehrlichman. "I can't guarantee you that we have a criminal case at this point," he told Nixon, "but I can guarantee you that these people are going to be a vast source of embarrassment to the Presidency, and for that reason I think the best thing you could do would be to get rid of them immediately." Nixon thanked him for his candour and concern but said that it was only fair that the charges should be investigated first.

The President then turned to the question of Dean. He said that he supposed that Dean had been unable to write his report because of his "involvement" and speculated that "perhaps Dean was trying to lighten the load on himself by impeaching Haldeman and Ehrlichman." Dean had, the President said, virtually admitted his guilt. He asked whether he should request Dean's resignation. "My goodness, no," Petersen replied. "He is the first man who came in to cooperate with us and we certainly don't want to give the impression that he is being subjected to reprisal because of his cooperation." Petersen then suggested that the President should do nothing about Dean until he had heard from him, Petersen.

The President did not take the advice. At nine that evening he had an interview with John Dean. "Almost from the outset," Dean told the Senate Committee, "the President began to ask me a number of leading questions which made me think that the conversation was being taped, and that a record was being made to protect himself." Dean did not know that every conversation the President had in his office was taped.

Towards the end of the interview Nixon, Dean says, recalled that they had discussed the difficulty of raising money for the Watergate defendants and that he had mentioned that raising $1 million was "no problem." According to Dean, the President then added that in saying that he had, of course, been joking. Throughout the interview Nixon remained sitting in his chair. But then, just as Dean was preparing to leave, "a most interesting thing happened." Dean describes the President rising from his chair and retreating to a far corner of the office where he said "in a barely audible tone" that he "was probably foolish to have discussed Hunt's clemency with Colson."

The next morning the President summoned Dean again. He presented him with two letters, one asking for his resignation, the other offering him "immediate and indefinite leave of absence." As both linked Dean's departure to his "involvement" with Watergate, and as neither contained any reference to Haldeman or Ehrlichman, Dean refused to comply. Instead he drafted a letter which read, "Dear Mr. President, you have informed me that Bob Haldeman and John Ehrlichman have verbally tendered their requests to be given an immediate and indefinite leave of absence from your staff. By this letter I also wish to confirm my request that I be given such a leave of absence from your staff." Nixon said, "It wasn't what he wanted." Later Nixon rang Dean to say that he would be making a statement but that there would be no mention of any resignations.

In view of what had been going on, the statement, when it came, was surprisingly brief and unspecific. On April 17 Nixon announced that on March 21 "serious charges" had come to his attention and that he had personally assumed charge of "intensive new enquiries." He also mentioned that Kleindienst and Petersen had met him the previous Sunday "to review the facts which had come to me in my investigation." He then went on to soften his position on executive privilege. White House aides could now testify under oath and "answer all proper questions," but none should be given immunity. Ron Ziegler then informed the White House press corps that all previous White House Watergate statements were, as he put it, "inoperative."

Soon afterwards he tendered a personal apology to the *Washington Post* in front of the assembled press. As he finished, a mitigating thought seemed to strike him, and he began, "But . . ." The qualification was cut off by a cry from the rear: "Now don't take it back, Ron."

The White House was now in a state of siege, and outside the walls some of its friends were beginning to show some signs of personal distress. On April 19 Herb Kalmbach called his good friend John Ehrlichman for guidance and reassurance. Ehrlichman recorded the call. ("I feel like I've been kicked in the stomach," Kalmbach said when he learned of this later.) Ehrlichman told him that Dean was telling all. "The whole enchilada?" inquired Kalmbach, who has some command of the Mexican vernacular. He was very unhappy. He reminded Ehrlichman of his eye-to-eye assurances that his payments to the Watergate burglars were proper. Kalmbach was about to go to the grand jury to give evidence. "God," he said, "if I can just make it plain it was humanitarian and nothing else."

By this time the legality of Kalmbach's fund-raising activities was among the least of the White House's problems. There was every sign that the lid on the plumbers' operation was about to blow. On April 15 John Dean offered the prosecutors another tidbit. He told them about the Ellsberg burglary. It did not take them long to realise, just how important this information was: the case against Daniel Ellsberg for "stealing" the Pentagon Papers was then being heard in Los Angeles, and they knew that if the details were not disclosed to the judge they, as officials of the Department of Justice, could be placed in the unhappy position of being parties to a conspiracy to obstruct justice. On April 18 Petersen went to see the President to explain the difficulty. But he had not gone very far when Nixon cut him short, saying: "I know about that. This is a national security matter. You stay out of that. Your mandate is to investigate Watergate."

This troubled Petersen. After a week's debate, he and Kleindienst decided that the legal issues must take priority over alleged "national security" interests. On April 25 Kleindienst told Nixon. The President backed down, and two days later

America learned of the plumbers' existence through the Ellsberg trial judge. On the 26th the New York *Daily News* revealed that Gray had destroyed documents belonging to Howard Hunt. 24 hours later Gray resigned as acting Director of the F.B.I.

On the evening before his resignation, he had had a quiet talk with Henry Petersen in which the two men exchanged confidences. "Pat, I'm scared," Petersen confided. "I'm scared because it seems that you and I are expendable and Haldeman and Ehrlichman are not." In fact, Petersen was mistaken. On the evening of April 27 the President left for Camp David, taking his private secretary, Rose Mary Woods, his speechwriter, Ray Price, and his red setter, King Timahoe. For once Haldeman and Ehrlichman had been left behind. And over the weekend it was learned that the President was going to make another statement, live, on national television. It would have to be a good one.

CHAPTER 22

Hitting the Fan

AT NINE o'clock in the evening of April 30 the cameras in the White House zoomed in on the President. He was sitting at his desk flanked by a photograph of his family and a bust of Abraham Lincoln. He looked tired, and his voice trembled as he began to speak.

He announced that Haldeman and Ehrlichman—"two of the finest public servants it has been my privilege to know"—had resigned. They had done so because it was necessary to restore the public's confidence in the democratic process. John Dean had "also resigned." Richard Kleindienst had felt his close friendship with many of those tarred by Watergate made it impossible for him to continue as Attorney General. His resignation had been reluctantly accepted. The President boldly assumed "responsibility" for the excesses of the campaign, but went on to describe why, nonetheless, they were not his fault. He had been absorbed in the construction of peace and had left his re-election in the hands of others. He promised that there would be no whitewash in the White House and no immunity for the guilty. He asked the people to pray for him, and he asked God to "bless America and . . . each and every one of you."

As the television lights faded, Nixon blinked back his tears. "It wasn't easy," he muttered. Perhaps even harder was his next self-imposed task. He walked out of the Oval Office and down the passage to the White House press room, where he encountered a group of reporters and photographers. "Gentlemen," said the President, "we have had our disagreements in the past, and I hope you give me hell every time I'm wrong."

Most of those who had responsibility for analysing his speech thought he was wrong now. It had been an extraordinarily illogical performance. If Haldeman and Ehrlichman were such fine public servants, then why did they have to go? If the President was responsible, why was he so anxious to have the guilty punished? If there was to be no concealment, then why was he cutting off immunity, the option most likely to produce revelation? And if disclosure was to be cherished, why was John Dean dismissed without a word of thanks? Although the telecast was intended to restore confidence in the Presidency, its effect was almost exactly the reverse.

A Gallup poll published the following week revealed that the number of people who approved Nixon's work as President had sagged still lower—down to 45 percent from the 68-percent approval rating only three months earlier. The number of people who believed "Nixon knew" had actually increased. Of those who had an opinion, four out of seven did not believe Nixon's account was the whole truth; fully 40 percent thought he had advance knowledge of the Watergate bugging (something that neither McCord nor Dean had alleged); 50 percent believed he played an active part in the cover-up; and 30 percent thought he should be impeached if that were proved.

Under the impetus of a new skepticism, the revelations became a stampede. Stories that would once have taken an investigative reporter months to develop were coming out into newspaper offices for no more than the cost of the AP wire service. On the day of Nixon's telecast, the Ellsberg trial judge, Matt Byrne, revealed from the bench that he had been offered the directorship of the FBI since Pat Gray's resignation. The circumstances were not conducive to a restoration of confidence in the administration. John Ehrlichman, who had a very personal interest in the Ellsberg case, had made the offer on two occasions. Nixon had been present at one of their meetings. On the day after Judge Byrne's disclosure, the FBI informed his court that it had recently established that Ehrlichman had known about a burglary of Ellsberg's psychiatrist's office as long ago as September, 1971. Judge Byrne ordered further enquiry.

By now there were at least six separate investigations into various aspects of Watergate. In Washington, Sam Ervin's

Senate committee had nearly completed its preparations for public hearings, and an increasingly aggressive grand jury, established by Judge Sirica, was fast accumulating evidence of the White House cover-up. On May 2, the *New York Times* reported that the grand jury had amassed sufficient evidence to indict Haldeman, Ehrlichman, Mitchell, Dean, Magruder, and LaRue for their Watergate roles. In New York another grand jury had been quietly gathering evidence on the Mitchell-Vesco-Stans connection and was on the point of indicting the former Attorney General and former Secretary of Commerce for, among other things, "defrauding the United States." Their indictment was closely followed by the resignation of G. Bradford Cook, head of the Securities and Exchange Commission, after only nine weeks in the post. (Cook admitted altering an SEC complaint against Vesco at Stans's request.) In Orlando, Florida, yet another Federal grand jury indicted Donald Segretti for his activities during the 1972 Florida presidential primary.

On May 3, the *Washington Post* disclosed the existence of the Cambodia "leak" wiretaps and the fact that one of the victims was Morton Halperin, who had been both a friend of Ellsberg and a Kissinger aide. (Kissinger had previously advised the country against the inward-looking danger of indulging in an "orgy of recriminations" over Watergate.) While at Halperin's house, Ellsberg had used his phone and had been overheard by the FBI. This disclosure sent the Ellsberg trial spiraling into chaos. Judge Byrne demanded the offending tapes; the FBI could not find them. On May 11, the judge decided he had had enough. "The conduct of the government," said Byrne, ". . . precludes the fair and dispassionate consideration of the issues by the jury." Ellsberg was free to go; soon afterwards the relevant tapes were discovered—in John Ehrlichman's safe at the White House.

The humiliating collapse of the Pentagon Papers case was merely the prelude to further embarrassments. During his testimony before the grand jury in Washington, Howard Hunt remarked, almost in passing, that the CIA had supplied the equipment and disguises he and Liddy had used in the Ellsberg burglary. Matt Byrne made the information public. Within days yet more investigations were under way; the Senate Armed Services Committee and the Appropriations Committee both set out to probe White House–CIA relations. Helms was called back from Iran. Cushman cut short a trip to Europe, and the seamy origins of the plumbers came tumbling out.

Watergate, like Topsy, just grew and grew. More and more White House deceptions and counterdeceptions were being brandished daily, and the judgment of the President seemed ever more strange. It was not surprise when the Senate insisted that Elliot Richardson, Nixon's nominee for Attorney General, appoint a Special Watergate Prosecutor if he was to be confirmed; there just was not too much confidence in the integrity of the administration to be had in Washington at the time. Very reluctantly, the President agreed. He was said to be displeased when Richardson chose Archibald Cox, a somewhat patriarchal Democrat from Boston.

On April 30 Nixon had tried to shake hands with the hearts of the American people. It was a gesture that had served him well in the past but this time his overture had been rejected. On May 22 he made another attempt to explain just what had happened to his administration. Instead of an emotional appeal direct to the people, he now issued a four-thousand-word statement. In it he acknowledged that he had approved the Cambodia "leak" wiretaps, the 1970 intelligence plan with its proposals for illegal bugging, espionage, and burglary, and the setting up of the plumbers unit. He admitted that after the Watergate break-in he had ordered that the FBI uncover no plumbers' activities, and that with hindsight he should have been more aware of the warnings of a cover-up that he had received. It was a tantalizing document, and the Washington press corps pounced upon its obscurer passages in the press briefing provided by Nixon's spokesmen. On this occasion two of Nixon's legal counsels, Len Garment and Fred Buzhardt, were wheeled out to help Ronald Ziegler. By any standards it was a rough session.

It was Garment who took the brunt of the questioning. How did he explain the differences between the April 30 statement and the present one? Mr. Nixon now has a "clearer recollection" of the events surrounding the burglary, Garment replied. Well, what about this 1970 plan? Does it authorise breaking and entering in domestic-security cases? "I really don't know," said Garment. At this point Buzhardt came to Garment's rescue. "I would not address it further," he warned. "It's a classified document." "Do you realise you are leaving unanswered the question of whether the President of the United States approved felonies?" another reporter shouted. In the general hubbub Buzhardt's reply went unheard. "If the President can justify breaking the laws, doesn't that lead on to Watergate?" one newsman asked. "I'll leave that to historians," Garment replied.

The Senate Watergate Committee, which had just started its public hearings, did not feel it could wait that long.

CHAPTER 23

At This Point in Time

ROOM 318 in the Old Senate Office Building—better known as the Senate Caucus Room—is one of the more imposing of Washington's public halls. The walls are faced with marble and flanked by gigantic Corinthian columns that rise fifty feet to a coffered ceiling from which hang four crystal chandeliers. The windows are draped with curtains of heavy red velvet. By 10 A.M. on Thursday, May 17, there was standing room only in the Caucus Room, as a crowd of about 550 people—275 of them reporters and other professional observers—milled about waiting for the public hearings of the Senate Select Committee on Presidential Campaign Activities to begin. The members of the public had been queuing all night to get in, and even the reporters, not normally early risers, had been there since eight in the morning. All the major networks were there; the *New York Times* had sent five men. *Women's Wear Daily* was also represented. There was also a generous assortment of celebrities. Dan Ellsberg and his wife Patricia sat in the fourth row, just behind Lee Remick. To judge from the chatter in the VIP seats, many of the occupants were only there by dint of much arm-twisting and string-pulling. In short it was, like the opening night of the Kennedy Center, one of Washington's see-and-be-seen scenes.

The seven Senators who filed into the Caucus Room shortly after ten o'clock that morning were virtually unknown outside their own electoral bailiwicks. Three—the vice-chairman, Howard Baker of Tennessee, Edward Gurney of Florida, and Lowell Weicker of Connecticut—were Republicans and four —the chairman, Sam Ervin of North Carolina, Daniel Inouye of Hawaii, Joseph Montoya of New Mexico, and Herman

Talmadge of Georgia—were Democrats. One acquired instant celebrity: the boyish good looks of Senator Baker soon had him soaring into *Women's Wear Daily*'s "stud" list (along with actor Robert Redford and pop star Mick Jagger).

Like every other member of the committee, Baker is a lawyer, amply endowed with that profession's gift for lucid exposition. A highly effective trial lawyer from Huntsville, Tennessee, where he earned the nickname "Ole Two-to-Ten" (his clients rarely got more, even for murder), he entered the Senate in 1966, where for a time he was overshadowed by his father-in-law, the late Everett Dirksen of Illinois. On Capitol Hill Baker was regarded as bright, highly ambitious and, despite his hawkish stand on Vietnam, essentially middle-of-the-road; Baker describes himself as "sort of medium to medium-rare." As the hearings commenced, nobody could be sure whether that made him a Nixon supporter.

About Edward Gurney there were no such reservations. The White House thought of him as a friend, who as a beneficiary of Nixon's "Southern strategy" in 1968—he became the first Republican Senator from Florida since Reconstruction—could be relied on to keep the President's interests firmly in mind. The same could not be said of Lowell Weicker, the third and most junior Republican on the committee, and the most wealthy. His fortune comes from the Bigelow carpet business—but the money is old enough for the Weickers to be classed as East Coast patricians, never the most conspicuous members of Nixon's constituency. That Weicker was no friend to the White House was obvious even before the hearings began; he was one of the few Republicans publicly on record with a denunciation of Bob Haldeman.

Of the Democrats on the committee, Joseph Montoya was the least known, though the little that was known suggested that he would be the committee's most liberal member. Herman Talmadge was regarded as a typical Southern "heavy," while Daniel Inouye was seen as a conscientious but unassuming party man. Inouye was the most conspicuous of the Seven: a much-decorated war veteran, he is of Japanese extraction and he had lost his right arm while fighting in the European war. (Inouye's most-told story is of the time when he first arrived on Capitol Hill and nervously approached Sam Rayburn, the Speaker of the House, Inouye murmuring that he might not know who he was. "Of course I do," said

Rayburn, "how many other one-armed Japs do you think we have here?")

The White House did not expect much joy out of Inouye. "His name is pronounced 'ain't no way,'" Ehrlichman pointedly joked before the hearings, "because there 'ain't no way' he is going to give us anything but problems."

That the rank-and-file members of the committee were not men of national reputation was no accident; it was the result of a deliberate piece of political calculation by the Senate Majority and Minority leaders, Mike Mansfield and Hugh Scott. Ostensibly the Senate was setting out on an objective fact-finding mission. But as the exercise necessarily involved politicians sitting in judgment on other politicians, including the President himself, the dangers of the enquiry developing into a messy partisan brawl were obvious. This was the one occasion on which the Senate's star performers, a Muskie or a Fulbright or a Proxmire, were not needed. What nobody quite perceived was the latent star quality of the committee's seventy-six-year-old chairman.

Sam Ervin has so dominated the hearings and become such a cult figure, that it is difficult to remember how little-known he was, outside the senate, at the beginning of 1973. His press conference on the eve of the hearings was only his third in his nineteen years in the Senate. When he first stepped into the limelight, he was frequently compared to Charles Laughton's Senator in Otto Preminger's classic Washington drama, *Advise and Consent.* The physical resemblance is indeed remarkable: the same slow Southern drawl, the white hair, the jowls and eyebrows almost permanently atwitch. But Laughton's Senator was a wheeler-dealer, an operator in the time-honoured Washington manner; Ervin is not a cloakroom politician. He is of Scots-Presbyterian stock and, like his father, spent most of his life practicing law in the little town of Morganton, a textile-mill and furniture-making community in the Blue Ridge foothills of the Appalachian mountains. It is Bible-belt country, where religion and politics are unclouded by doubt and uncertainty. But he is not quite the simple country lawyer he likes to pretend. He graduated with honours from the Harvard Law School and became a member of North Carolina's Supreme Court. But throughout his career, which now spans more than fifty years, he has clung fast to two guiding principles: a belief in the sanctity of individual rights and an abiding love of the Constitution of the United States, which he describes as "the most precious possession of the American people."

He also has a rare eloquence derived from much reading and rereading of his three basic texts, the Constitution, the Authorized Version of the Bible, and the works of William Shakespeare. "Sam is the only man I know," says Howard Baker, "who can read a transcript of a telephone conversation and make it sound like the King James version of the New Testament."

The Constitution is, of course, open to many interpretations, but Ervin's is essentially that of a Jeffersonian liberal. For him the Constitution is above all the protector and guarantor of individual liberties. It is this conviction that helps to explain the aspect of the man that most puzzles liberals: how someone who passionately defends civil liberties can almost in the same breath with equal vehemence oppose civil rights. Ervin was, for example, one of the leading opponents in the Senate of the Supreme Court's historic Brown decision which opened the way to the desegregation of America's schools. Throughout the fifties and sixties he filibustered civil-rights legislation like any other Dixiecrat. Yet he violently opposed a crime bill John Mitchell had proposed for the District of Columbia, whose population is over 70 percent black. "It is," said Ervin, "an affront to the Constitution . . . unjust and unwise . . . as a mangy hound is full of fleas . . . a garbage pail of some of the most repressive, nearsighted, intolerant, unfair, and vindictive legislation that the Senate has ever been presented."

Ervin sees no contradiction. In both instances he is, in his view, defending the Constitution against encroachment. "When freedom for one citizen is diminished," Ervin argues, "it is in the end diminished for all. Nor can we preserve liberty by making one branch of government its protector, for though defense of liberty be the purpose, the perversion of it will be the effect. The whole fabric of the Constitution—the Federal system and the separation of powers doctrine—is designed to protect us against such centralization: but even the language and the lessons of the Constitution cannot stop a people who are hell-bent on twisting the document to the will of a temporary majority."

In Washington, Ervin became the Senate's leading constitutional expert, a role that led to his chairmanship of numerous committees on executive privilege and the separation of powers. This expertise was one of the main factors in his selection for the Watergate job. It was evident even before the hearings opened that Ervin did not share the White House view of these fundamental topics. And as the White House framed ever more complex "guidelines" on executive privilege for aides who would be giving testimony, Ervin became increasingly impatient. He is a man for old verities rather than "new guidelines."

When the White House suggested that perhaps its aides should testify to the committee on a private and informal basis, and not under oath, Ervin exploded: "Divine right went out with the American Revolution and doesn't belong to White House aides. 'What meat do they eat that makes them grow so great?' I am not willing to elevate them to a position above the great mass of the American people. I don't think we have any such thing as royalty or nobility that exempts them. I'm not going to let anybody come down at night like Nicodemus and whisper something in my ear that no one else can hear. That is not executive privilege. It is executive poppycock." Ervin was giving the White House notice that the committee would spare no one "whatever his station in life may be." Ervin had his way: the White House aides testified publicly and under oath.

The direction the enquiry would take was not immediately apparent. The formal task of the committee was to produce a report leading to legislative reform if abuses were revealed. But it was the process of discovery that was more important than any hypothetical legislation. For that process might lead to incrimination of the President himself.

Long before the public hearings opened, Ervin and Samuel Dash, his chief counsel, had decided that the only logical way for the committee to operate was to start with the bit players: the secretaries, the ex-policemen, and the diligent but lowly members of the CREEP and White House hierarchies. Only when the groundwork had been established and the inner workings of the White House and CREEP had been laid bare would the enquiry move on to the principal actors in the drama. The virtue of this approach was that when the "big" witnesses appeared, their room for manoeuvre would be substantially reduced; unless, of course, they wished to be caught in the mesh of conflicting testimony. Despite the complaints of Senators Talmadge and Gurney, who wanted to get the major figures on as soon as possible, this procedure was followed. After eleven days and eighteen witnesses, the committee reached Jeb Stuart Magruder.

Magruder made only one rather odd attempt to justify what he had done. While at college, he told the Senators, he had taken a course of ethics under the Reverend William Sloane Coffin, a passionate opponent of the Vietnam war, who had urged the students to burn their draft cards. "I respect Mr. Coffin tremendously," Magruder said. "He was a very close friend of mine." Yet what Coffin had done was, Magruder argued, just as illegal as any of the acts he had committed. (Coffin promptly wrote an article for the *New York Times* pointing out that while he had openly broken laws, "Jeb operated behind closed doors." During his time at college, Coffin recalled, "I worried about Jeb. I used to say to him, 'You're a nice guy, Jeb, but not yet a good man. You have lots of charm but little inner strength. And if you don't stand for something you're apt to fall for anything.' ")

Magruder was on the stand for over five hours, and in that time he implicated Haldeman, Ehrlichman, Mitchell, Dean, Colson, Strachan, Stans, Sloan, Kalmbach, Mardian, LaRue, Parkinson, Porter, and himself. About the only senior person on the White House and CREEP staffs at whom he had not pointed a finger was the President himself. That was the role of the next key witness, John Dean.

Dean had originally been scheduled to appear at the Caucus Room on Monday, June 18, the very day on which Chairman Brezhnev of the U.S.S.R. was due to meet President Nixon in Washington. The visit, the first by a Russian leader since the Johnson-Kosygin meeting in 1967, was designed to set the seal on Nixon's global achievements and affirm the beginning of a new era of East-West relations. At this juncture it was thought that the sight of so vigorous and so public a scrubbing of dirty linen would be embarrassing. And so the committee, with only Senator Weicker dissenting, voted to suspend the hearings for a week. "I don't know why the two can't move along together," Weicker protested. "They might give an idea to Brezhnev of the strength of our kind of government."

The White House, while publicly celebrating the new entente, used this respite to mount a two-pronged anti-Dean offensive. It went into the leaking business on its own account in an attempt to defuse the more explosive parts of Dean's forthcoming testimony. Abandoning an earlier claim that the White House logs of the Nixon-Dean meetings were "presidential papers" whose contents could never be revealed, even under subpoena, the White House said that the logs showed that on March 21 the President had told Dean that payment of hush-money was wrong and that "it would not work." It was also disclosed that Dean had "borrowed" $4,000 from a campaign cash fund to pay for his Florida honeymoon. Horror-stricken attitudes were struck. "Nothing is so incredible," said Hugh Scott, the Senate Minority leader, the day after the honeymoon story appeared, "that this turncoat will not be willing to testify to it in exchange for a reward. . . . A man who can embezzle can easily tell lies." The columnist Joseph Alsop was moved to describe Dean as a "bottom-dwelling slug."

On the morning of Monday, June 25, Dean finally appeared. In the flesh he looked older and more careworn than the man in the stock newspaper photographs, which showed Dean flashing a brilliant smile. In the course of the next four days it rarely appeared. The voice, too, was deeper and more evenly pitched than one might have expected from such a young man. Unlike Magruder, Dean made no attempt to apologise for what he had done.

It took him the whole of the first day to read the 245-page statement on which he had been working since mid-April. "The Watergate matter," he began, "was an inevitable outgrowth of a climate of excessive concern over the political impact of demonstrators, excessive concern over leaks, an insatiable appetite for political intelligence, all coupled with a do-it-yourself White House staff, regardless of the law." Dean then offered some chilling vignettes. Like the story of the man with the sign. As Dean told it, in the winter of 1971 the President was gazing out of a White House window when he saw a solitary demonstrator with a large sign standing in Lafayette Park. The President flipped, and the White House staff started running in all directions. The word went down from Haldeman to Larry Higby, his assistant, who rushed into Dean's office to tell him to tackle the job of sign removal. Dean ran out and bumped into Dwight Chapin who said he was going to get "some thugs" to remove both man and sign. Dean advised caution and called the Secret Service. At this point, sanity crept in. The SS man called the Park police, who gently persuaded the man to go take his sign someplace else.

The drama was if anything heightened by Dean's manner. He sat hunched at the witness table, his mouth only inches from the microphone, pausing only occasionally to take small, birdlike sips of water from the glass on the table. As the day wore on it was at times difficult, just looking at him, to grasp that he was accusing the President of the United States of some of the gravest crimes in the statute book.

The toughest questions came on Dean's third day—not from a Republican but a Democrat. "In order," as he put it, "to give the President his day in court," Daniel Inouye had volunteered to present the White House account of the Dean-Nixon meetings to the witness. This had been written by Nixon's special counsel, Fred Buzhardt. And from the opening paragraph it was clear what lines the White House counterattack would follow. "There is no reason to doubt," Inouye read, "that John Dean was the principal actor in the Watergate cover-up, and that while other motivations may have played a part, he had a great interest in covering up for himself." There then followed a list of thirty-nine questions, challenging the accuracy of his testimony and designed to portray him as the chief villain. Dean was unshaken. The White House also attacked John Mitchell, whom it described as Dean's patron.

That the White House should have chosen this moment to attack Mitchell was a clear indication of the panic Dean had caused. Mitchell had not yet testified, and no one, including the White House, knew exactly which way he would go. This would hardly encourage him to speak well of the White House. The following day Gerald Warren, the deputy White House press secretary, made an attempt to repair the damage by giving the impression that the memo was Fred Buzhardt's own. "It is not the President's position and it is not the White House position," Warren said. The inference was that the work of the President's special counsel had become inoperative.

When he did appear on July 10, Mitchell made it clear that he had come to defend both himself and the President against all charges. Though his hands trembled, he performed this task with iron-clad determination. Faced with evidence from at least six previous witnesses that he had participated in both the planning and the cover-up of Watergate, Mitchell toughed it out. Some allegations he flatly denied; others overstrained his recollection. Previous witnesses had been, on the whole, polite and anxious to please; Mitchell was his normal self. He treated Sam Dash like a high-powered New York lawyer giving a country cousin a lesson in cross-examination. He had told the President nothing, he said, and the President had not once ever asked him anything—an observation that caused Sam Ervin to recall that it was curiosity that had killed the cat.

The only relief—and it was not light—from the tedium of Mitchell's testimony was his gallows humour. Maybe, he said, he should have thrown Gordon Liddy "out of the window" when he came to talk to him about the Watergate break-in; asked if it wasn't hard to get all involved to coordinate their cover-up story, he suggested that, "It would have been simpler to take them out on the White House lawn and shoot them all." Mitchell strove to convey the impression that the whole hearing was an exercise in futility. The "performing" Senators were irrelevant, he told a reporter. "All that matters is the idiot-tube."

He only became flustered in the closing minutes of his second day when Weicker mounted a full-scale attack. Having established that Mitchell knew about the Ellsberg burglary, he pressed him on his failure, as Attorney General, to discharge his duty by passing on the information to the Ellsberg case judge. Mitchell did not enjoy this line of questioning one bit. As he rose from his chair, his face flushed and his eyes watering, his angry mutter was caught by the still-live microphone. "It's a great trial being conducted here, isn't it!"

Mitchell's display of sullen obduracy cast a pall over the hearings. Dean had incriminated the President but, although his first wife Karla said he never told lies, who was now to corroborate his story? Not Mitchell, not Haldeman, not Ehrlichman, certainly not the President himself. For the committee, there seemed no alternative but to slog it out through a maze of conflicting testimony from which no clear conclusion might ever emerge.

It was on Friday the thirteenth that the miracle occurred. At 2:15 that afternoon a junior member of the committee staff, Donald Sanders, was conducting a routine interview with Alexander Butterfield, a little-known Haldeman aide. Sanders had been told that Butterfield was in charge of the White House's "internal security." Asked if Dean could be right that his April 15 conversation with Nixon had been taped, Butterfield reluctantly told Sanders about the President's secret tape-recording system, which had existed for over two years. The following Monday Butterfield came to the Caucus Room to tell his story, the implication of which was that there need never have been any conflict over the true nature of Dean's contacts with the President. It was all there in the White House, firmly and infallibly on record. The news was greeted in total silence; it took several seconds for the audience to grasp the significance of what Butterfield was saying. Then somebody spoke. "Wow," he said.

The committee was overjoyed. At last, it seemed, what Baker had described as "the central question" of presidential guilt or innocence could be resolved. Although Ervin's earlier requests that the President produce his papers had been turned down, the committee clearly could not afford to pass up this opportunity. Correspondence with the White House was resumed. The day after the Butterfield revelation, Ervin wrote a carefully worded letter to the President, who was lying in Bethesda Military Hospital recovering from a bout of viral pneumonia—his first illness in fifty-six months as President—respectfully asking for the papers and tapes. Ervin wished the President a speedy recovery and asked to hear from him "at your earliest convenience."

Ervin was not alone in his anxiety to scrutinise the papers and tapes; Special Watergate Prosecutor Archibald Cox wanted them too. The day after the Ervin letter Cox made a similar, though more toughly worded, request. Of the two, Cox had the better claim. In refusing to give up his papers, Nixon had told Ervin that as part of the legislature he had, under the constitutional doctrine of the separation of powers, no right to probe into the inner workings of the executive. But these arguments did not apply to Cox. As a government appointee, he was a member of the executive branch, so on the face of it there were no constitutional obstacles in his way.

The committee had to wait five days for Nixon's answer, for it was not until the weekend that the President was pronounced fit and allowed to make the seventy-mile drive to Camp David to ponder his reply. When it came the following Monday it was, as expected, an uncompromising no. What was unexpected, however, was Nixon's admission that the tapes were ambiguous. "As in any verbatim recording of informal conversations," the President said, "they contain comments that persons with different perspectives and motivations would inevitably interpret in different ways."

It was, as Ervin quickly pointed out, "a rather remarkable letter. . . . You will notice," he said, "the President says he has heard the tapes or some of them and they sustain his position. But he says he is not going to let anybody else hear them for fear they might draw a different conclusion. In other words, the President says they are susceptible of, as I construe it, two different interpretations, one favourable to his aides and one not favourable to his aides."

Nixon's refusal left the committee with no alternative but to seek a resolution in the courts. On the afternoon of July 23, immediately after receiving Nixon's letter, the committee voted unanimously to serve a subpoena on the President. The word "historic" has been much overworked, not least by Nixon himself. But it does apply here. When later that afternoon Rufus Edmisten and Terry Lenzner, two of the committee's young lawyers, delivered the subpoena to Citizen Richard Nixon at the White House, it was the first time in American history that Congress had so challenged a President.

It was inevitably an issue that the Supreme Court would have to decide. The matter was out of the committee's hands; in the meantime, all it could do was to press on with the investigation. The next crucial witnesses on the list were John Ehrlichman and Bob Haldeman.

The image of Haldeman and Ehrlichman that had emerged from much of the previous testimony, was not engaging, though Ehrlichman, who would sometimes talk politics in a discursive fashion, was depicted as the less ferocious of the two. Haldeman was strictly an orders man who terrified the young men who worked for him. Gordon Strachan testified that on one occasion he was awakened at four in the morning. It was Haldeman, calling from the Presidential plane, Air Force One, to bawl him out for making a mess of some routine task. The unhappy and still-sleepy Strachan thought it was a nightmare —until he called the White House switchboard and discovered that Haldeman himself had indeed been on the line.

This was the image; the testimonial appearance turned out to be rather different. The reflective Ehrlichman became the tough guy, and the hard-nosed Haldeman appeared to be distinctly soft round the edges.

Nobody liked John Ehrlichman. That he should attack John

Dean and defend himself and the President was only to be expected. But few people were prepared for his tone. The joviality he effected was not very warming. As he read his prepared statement, through heavy half-glasses, he thrust his chin aggressively forward and waved his arms about when he felt emphasis was needed. The words, uttered in cadences remarkably like Nixon's own, matched the manner. He began by treating the Senators to an eighth-grade civics lecture on the responsibilities of the Presidency.

The first clash came early in the cross-examination when the normally mild-mannered Sam Dash was asking Ehrlichman about the creation of the plumbers unit.

> DASH: . . . were you assigned a role to create in the White House a capability for intelligence-gathering at any time?
> EHRLICHMAN: I do not know quite what you are getting at . . .
> DASH: I do not know why you have to find out what I am getting at. If you just answer my question as I asked it.
> EHRLICHMAN: It is an obscure question.
> DASH: It is a simple question. If the answer is no, say no. If the answer is yes, say yes.

Senator Weicker was anxious to know how Ehrlichman could justify the White House's private investigations of the sexual and drinking habits of its political opponents. Ehrlichman launched into a diatribe on the Congress's lack of sobriety and the absence of respect in Washington for "family values. . . . You can go over here in the gallery and watch a member totter onto the floor in a condition of at least partial inebriation which would preclude him from making any sort of sober judgment on the issues which confront this country," he said. For once Weicker was lost for words. "You definitely have two concepts of politics in this country meeting head on," he spluttered. "You stick to your version. I am going to stick to mine."

During another argument with Sam Ervin, Ehrlichman, smiling very broadly but not very sweetly, interjected; "Mr. Chairman, you interrupted me. You have a delightful trial-room practice of interrupting something you do not want to hear." What the committee did hear was an extraordinary catalogue of denials.

At no point did Ehrlichman even contemplate the possibility

that he might have done anything wrong. No, he said, neither he nor the President had specifically authorised the Ellsberg burglary, but even if they had such an act was "well within both the constitutional duty and obligation of the President." (The Los Angeles grand jury investigating the burglary did not agree: on September 7th he was arraigned on counts of burglary, conspiracy and perjury. He pleaded not guilty.) Yes, he had approached Judge Matt Byrne during the Pentagon Papers trial but as the judge seemed willing to talk about it where was the harm in that? "I have scoured the canon of ethics to find if I had in any way infringed upon them," he explained. The search proved to be negative. No, he said, he had not told Herbert Kalmbach secretly to deliver hush-money to the Watergate defendants. No, he did not recall that Kalmbach had invoked his wife and family and asked for a solemn pledge that he was being asked to do nothing wrong: "I am sure that if . . . I had looked into his eyes and we had invoked the names of our wives [as Kalmbach had testified] . . . I would remember that solemn occasion. I am pretty sure that kind of request was not made of me," Ehrlichman said. No, he had never promised Chuck Colson that executive clemency could be arranged for Hunt. The President had decided back in July that it was a "closed subject" and "it was not discussed at any time." No, he and Haldeman had never attempted to use the CIA in an attempt to limit the FBI's enquiries into Watergate. No, he had "no recollection" of telephoning the CIA's General Cushman with a request that the agency kit Hunt out for the Ellsberg break-in.

The Senators' credulity had been strained before. But never to quite this extent. They tried hard to conceal their disbelief but without total success. As Daniel Inouye finished one session with Ehrlichman, he leaned back in his chair and muttered under his breath "What a liar!" By the time Ehrlichman was through, he had contradicted at various points the sworn testimony of eighteen previous witnesses.

Ehrlichman's worst moment did not come while he was in the witness chair. The Senators were much too polite to suggest to Ehrlichman that there was at least the possibility he might end up behind bars. In breaks between sessions Ehrlichman was in the habit of bantering jovially with reporters. On one such occasion, Nicholas Von Hoffman, the iconoclastic columnist for the *Washington Post* and an Ehrlichman critic of long standing, joined the circle.

"Ah, Dr. Von Hoffman," said Ehrlichman with a large smile. "What are you writing about these days?"

"About you," said Von Hoffman pleasantly enough.

"You can see I don't read you," said Ehrlichman, still smiling.

"It is just as well," replied Von Hoffman, and politely inquired if Ehrlichman was planning to write a book.

"A column," said Ehrlichman. "Have you talked to your editors lately? I hear there's a space opening up at the *Post*."

"Yeah," said Von Hoffman, laughing. "But where you're going you won't be able to get your copy out."

Harry Robbins Haldeman was not in the least cocksure or arrogant. As he walked into the Caucus Room moments after Ehrlichman had left it, the contrast was striking. His clothes were a reminder of the fifties: the buttoned-down shirt, the suit with its narrow lapels, the Windsor-knotted tie. And, of course, there was the famous crew-cut, its severity much diminished by encroaching baldness.

Like Ehrlichman, Haldeman had brought a statement to read. The voice was pleasantly modulated and there was an occasional turn of phrase that caught the attention. By concentrating exclusively on Watergate, Haldeman said, the committee and others had vastly exaggerated its importance. "The harmless eye of the fly viewed under the microscope can become a terrifying object in spite of its actual insignificance." But where Ehrlichman had been pugnacious, Haldeman was bland and deferential. It made his astonishing disclosure that he had, at the President's own request, listened to two of the tapes of his conversations with John Dean all the more effective. (At the time, the President's position was that the tapes were totally "confidential"; yet Haldeman had been allowed to take away several of them after he left the White House.)

Most of what Haldeman had to say did not differ in any important respect from the Ehrlichman account. Like his former colleague, he pleaded complete ignorance of the Watergate break-in. But Haldeman's manner was such that these denials, though as comprehensive as Ehrlichman's, did not generate the same tension. Only once when Weicker, reciting the long list of departed White House aides and their many apparent errors, suggested that the White House was a place "where everything that was touched was corroded," did Haldeman"'s back stiffen and his eyes grow cold. "No sir, I will not in any way, shape, or form accept that. . . ."

But the effective deflation of Haldeman came near the end of his testimony—and once again it was the indefatigable Weicker who inserted the pin. One reason why Weicker had become so effective as the hearings progressed was that he possessed a dedicated research team that had worked tirelessly combing their way through the mountains of documents the committee had accumulated in search of papers that others had overlooked. One of the documents they had unearthed was a 1971 memo to Haldeman written by a White House advance man in Charlotte, North Carolina, where Nixon was scheduled to make a visit. The White House man had been sent with instructions to look out for demonstrators, and to report back.

This he did, and Haldeman was pleased with what he learned. The demonstrators, he was told, "will be violent; they will have extremely obscene signs." The words "violent" and "obscene" had been underlined in pencil and in the margin, in Haldeman's hand, was written the word "good." The demonstrations, the memo continued, will be directed not only against the President but also towards Billy Graham. Haldeman underlined Billy Graham too. His marginal comment was "great." "The Charlotte police force is extremely tough," the White House man noted, "and will probably use force to prevent any possible disruption of the motorcade or the President's movements." "Good," wrote Haldeman. Weicker read the entire memorandum out, with Haldeman's comments, with dramatic relish. At that point the image of the "new" Haldeman crumbled. He and Ehrlichman were not so different after all.

When the committee adjourned for the summer recess on August 7, it had been sitting for thirty-seven days spread out over nearly three months. The public had been spared 181 hours of television soap operas and quiz shows. The committee had heard evidence from thirty-five witnesses. The official transcript of the proceedings has 7,573 pages which contain over two million words—roughly three times the

length of the Bible. At the beginning of the session Senator
Baker suggested that, "The central question is what did the
President know?" By the end so many rather bizarre interpretations of democracy had been revealed that this was no longer
such a vital issue. The President's desire for knowledge about
Watergate seemed to have been so lukewarm that it was unsurprising that a "Senator" in a *National Lampoon* show Off
Broadway should declare that the real question was, "What
did the President know and when did he stop knowing it?"

Of the great names in the drama of Nixon's re-election,
only that of Charles "Chuck" Colson was absent from the
Senate's roll-call of witnesses. (He was to be the first witness
after the summer recess.) Even so, he had hovered like a bad
fairy over the first stage of the hearings; many of the testimonial areas led back to Colson. And on one occasion, he
played a central role in one of the hearing's more lively
subplots.

On June 28, Weicker accused Colson of trying to plant a
false story in which it was suggested that Weicker had failed
to disclose a White House contribution to his 1970 election
campaign. The Senator gave expression to his indignation in
the committee meetings. At eight the following morning,
Colson arrived in Weicker's office to smooth things over. The
meeting lasted precisely twelve minutes. Colson disclaimed all
responsibility for the smear and enquired if Weicker had some
sort of "grudge" against him.

"I don't have any grudge against you," Weicker said. "I
don't know you . . . but I do know what you stand for, Mr.
Colson, and we live in two different worlds. I deal in hard-
nosed politics . . . you deal in crap." Weicker then asked
Colson if he was the author of a memorandum that had just
been entered into the Senate record, indicating that the President's special counsel requested an IRS audit on an "enemy."
Colson confirmed that he had.

"Well, that's just great, Mr. Colson," said Weicker. "Let
me tell you something . . . you make me sick. That's just
disgusting—the kind of things you suggest in that memo. You
can just get your ass out of my office." Colson was, according
to one witness of the scene, "led from the room like a punch-
drunk fighter."

It was not perhaps the most elegant reassertion of Congressional power, but it was symbolic of a profound change

of mood. Six months earlier, George McGovern made a deeply unpopular but uncannily accurate diagnosis of the state of the Union after Nixon's re-election. On a brief visit to Britain in January, 1973, he gave a lecture at the Oxford Union in which he declared that the United States was "closer to one-man rule than at any time in our history. . . . Fundamentally," said McGovern, "we have experienced an exhaustion of important institutions in America. Today, only the Presidency is activist and strong, while other traditional centres of power are depleted." Congress was impotent, the Republican Party was in "utter vassalage" to the President, the Democratic Party was in disarray and the press was ineffective.

The Watergate summer seemed to change all that. By September Mr. Nixon's popularity had been literally halved and the Presidency was no longer the monolithic, irresistible force it had seemed at the chill beginning of the year; most of the country's once exhausted institutions were showing confused but vital signs of life.

The press had regained both its public support and its self-confidence and Congress had summoned the will—nonexistent in January—to challenge many of the President's policies. Legislation restricting his right to make war had been passed by both Houses and his plans for the dismemberment of the country's major social programs were at least held up. Most important of all, ten years after the Vietnam war was begun without Congressional approval, five years after Richard Nixon had pledged to end it, six months after he declared "peace with honour," Congress finally asserted its right to end U.S. military involvement in Southeast Asia. On August 15, 1973, America stopped bombing Cambodia.

At the beginning of September the trial of two of Mr. Nixon's former Cabinet members, one of them his Attorney General, began. Several more of his closest aides were indicted. The President's own right to place himself above the law was about to be challenged in the highest court in the land. Over twenty Watergate-related investigations were examining the way in which Nixon chose to run his administration and more, it was clear, was to come. The process of revelation might at times seem painful—on September 6 the *New York Post* ran the banner headline "NIXON BUGGED HIS BROTHER"— but it was altogether quite a good year for the Constitution.

Appendix A

In May, 1969, after news of the secret bombing of Cambodia "leaked," the President, in consultation with Attorney General John Mitchell and National Security Affairs Adviser Henry Kissinger, ordered the FBI to place wiretaps on the telephones of thirteen government officials and four newspapermen. The complete list is as follows:

National Security Council: Daniel I. Davidson; Morton Halperin; Anthony Lake; Winston Lord; Richard Moose; Helmut Sonnenfeldt.

Department of Defense: Lieut. Gen. Robert E. Pursley, former senior military assistant to Secretary of Defense Melvin Laird.

Department of State: Richard F. Pedersen, former State Department counselor; Richard L. Sneider, Deputy Assistant Secretary of State for East Asia and Pacific Affairs; William H. Sullivan, former Deputy Assistant Secretary of State for East Asia and Pacific Affairs.

White House: James W. McLane, former staff member, White House Domestic Council; William Safire, former Presidential speechwriter; John P. Sears, former deputy presidential counsel.

Newsmen: William Beecher, former military affairs correspondent for the *New York Times;* Henry Brandon, Washington correspondent of the *London Sunday Times;* Marvin Kalb, C.B.S. diplomatic correspondent; Hedrick Smith, former *New York Times* diplomatic correspondent in Washington.

Appendix B

From the summer of 1971, White House staffers worked on the compilations of lists of "opponents" under the general heading of "Political Enemies Project." The fullest list, entered in evidence before the Senate Watergate Committee on June 27, 1973, reads as follows:

Senators: Birch Bayh, J. W. Fulbright, Fred R. Harris, Harold Hughes, Edward M. Kennedy, George McGovern, Walter Mondale, Edmund Muskie, Gaylord Nelson, William Proxmire.

Members of the House: Bella Abzug, William R. Anderson, John Brademas, Father Robert F. Drinan, Robert Kastenmeier, Wright Patman.

Black Congressmen: Shirley Chisholm, William Clay, George Collins, John Conyers, Ronald Dollums, Charles Diggs, Augustus Hawkins, Ralph Metcalf, Robert N. C. Nix, Parren Mitchell, Charles Rangel, Louis Stokes.

Miscellaneous Politicos: John V. Lindsay, Mayor, New York City;

Eugene McCarthy, former U.S. Senator; George Wallace, Governor, Alabama.

Organizations

Black Panthers, Hughie Newton [Huey Newton]
Brookings Institution, Lesley Gelb and others
Business Executives Move for VN Peace, Henry Niles, Nat. Chmn.; Vincent McGee, Exec. Director
Committee for an Effective Congress, Russell D. Hemenway
Common Cause, John Gardner, Morton Halperin, Charles Goodell, Walter Hickel
COPE, Alexander E. Barkan
Council for a Livable World, Bernard T. Feld, President; Prof. Physics, MIT
Farmers Union, NFO
Institute of Policy Study, Richard Barnet, Marcus Raskin
National Economic Council, Inc.
National Education Association, Sam M. Lambert, President
National Student Association, Charles Palmer, President
National Welfare Rights Organization, George Wiley
Potomac Associates, William Watts
SANE, Sanford Gottlieb
Southern Christian Leadership [Council], Ralph Abernathy
Third National Convocation on The Challenge of Building Peace, Robert V. Roosa, Chairman
Businessmen's Educational Fund

Labor

Karl Feller, Pres., Internat. Union of United Brewery, Flour, Cereal, Soft Drink and Distillery Workers, Cincinnati
Harold J. Gibbons, International Vice Pres., Teamsters
A. F. Grospiron, Pres., Oil, Chemical & Atomic Workers International Union, Denver
Matthew Guinan, Pres., Transport Workers Union of America, New York City
Paul Jennings, Pres., International Union of Electrical, Radio & Machine Workers, D. C.
Herman D. Kenin, Vice Pres., AFL–CIO, D.C.
Lane Kirland, Secretary-Treasurer, AFL–CIO (but we must deal with him)
Frederick O'Neal, Pres., Actors and Artists of America, New York City
William Pollock, Pres., Textile Workers Union of America, New York City
Jacob Potofsky, General Pres., Amalgamated Clothing Workers of America, New York City
Leonard Woodcock, President, United Auto Workers, Detroit
Jerry Wurf, International President, American Federal, State,

County and Municipal Employees, Washington, D.C.
Nathaniel Goldfinger, AFL–CIO
I. W. Abel, Steelworkers

Media

Jack Anderson, columnist, "Washington Merry-Go-Round"
Jim Bishop, author, columnist, King Features Syndicate
Thomas Braden, columnist, Los Angeles *Times* Syndicate
D. J. R. Bruckner, Los Angeles *Times* Syndicate
Marquis Childs, chief Washington correspondent, St. Louis *Post-Dispatch*
James Deaken, White House correspondent, St. Louis *Post-Dispatch*
James Doyle, Washington *Star*
Richard Dudman, St. Louis *Post-Dispatch*
William Eaton, Chicago *Daily News*
Rowland Evans, Jr., syndicated columnist, Publishers Hall
Saul Friedmann, Knight Newspapers, syndicated columnist
Clayton Fritchey, syndicated columnist, Washington correspondent, *Harpers*
George Frazier, Boston *Globe*
Pete Hamill, *New York Post*
Michael Harrington, author and journalist; Member, Executive Committee Socialist Party
Sydney Harris, columnist, drama critic and writer of "Strictly Personal," syndicated Publishers Hall
Robert Healy, Boston *Globe*
William Hines, Jr., journalist; science and education, Chicago *Sun-Times*
Stanley Karnow, foreign correspondent, *Washington Post*
Ted Knap, syndicated columnist, New York *Daily News*
Edwin Knoll, Progressive
Morton Kondracke, Chicago *Sun-Times*
Joseph Kraft, syndicated columnist, Publishers Hall
James Laird, Philadelphia *Inquirer*
Mex Lerner, syndicated columnist, *New York Post;* author, lecturer, professor
Stanley Levey, Scripps-Howard
Flora Lewis, syndicated columnist on economics
Stuart Loory, Los Angeles *Times*
Mary McGrory, syndicated columnist on New Left
Frank Mankiewicz, syndicated columnist, Los Angeles *Times*
James Millstone, St. Louis *Post-Dispatch*
Martin Nolan, Boston *Globe*
Ed Guthman, Los Angeles *Times*
Thomas O'Neill, Baltimore *Sun*
John Pierson, *Wall Street Journal*
William Prochnau, Seattle *Times*
James Reston, *New York Times*

Carl Rowan, syndicated columnist, Publishers Hall
Warren Unna, *Washington Post*, NET
Harriet Van Horne, columnist, *New York Post*
Milton Viorst, reporter, author, writer
James Wechsler, *New York Post*
Tom Wicker, *New York Times*
Gary Wills, syndicated columnist, author of "Nixon-Agonistes"
The *New York Times*
Washington Post
St. Louis *Post-Dispatch*
Jules Duscha, *Washingtonian*
Robert Manning, Editor, *Atlantic*
John Osborne, *New Republic*
Richard Rovere, *New Yorker*
Robert Sherrill, *Nation*
Paul Samuelson, *Newsweek*
Julian Goodman, Chief Executive Officer, NBC
John Macy, Jr., Pres., Public Broadcasting Corporation; former Civil Service Comm.
Marvin Kalb, CBS
Daniel Schorr, CBS
Lem Tucker, NBC
Sander Vanocur, NBC

Celebrities

Carol Channing, actress
Bill Cosby, actor
Jane Fonda, actress
Steve McQueen, actor
Joe Namath, New York Giants [Jets]; businessman; actor
Paul Newman, actor
Gregory Peck, actor
Tony Randall, actor
Barbra Streisand, actress
Dick Gregory, comedian

Businessmen

Charles B. Beneson, President, Beneson Realty Co.
Nelson Bengston, President, Bengston & Co.
Holmes Brown, Vice President, Public Relations, Continental Can Co.
Benjamin Buttenweiser, Limited Partner, Kuhn, Loeb & Co.
Lawrence G. Chait, Chairman, Lawrence G. Chait & Co., Inc.
Ernest R. Chanes, President, Consolidated Water Conditioning Co.
Maxwell Dane, Chairman, Exec. Committee, Doyle, Dane & Bernbach, Inc.
Charles H. Dyson, Chairman, The Dyson-Kissner Corp.
Norman Eisner, President, Lincoln Graphic Arts

Charles B. Finch, Vice President, Allegheny Power System Inc.
Frank Heineman, President, Men's Wear International
George Hillman, President, Ellery Products Manufacturing Co.
Bertram Lichtenstein, President, Delton Ltd.
William Mancaloff, President, Concord Steel Corp.
Gerald McKee, President, McKee, Berger, Mansueto
Paul Milstein, President, Circle Industries Corp.
Stewart R. Mott, Stewart R. Mott Associates
Lawrence S. Phillips, President, Phillips–Van Heusen Corp.
David Rose, Chairman, Rose Associates
Julian Roth, Senior Partner, Emery Roth & Sons
William Ruder, President, Ruder & Finn, Inc.
Si Scharer, President, Scharer Associates, Inc.
Alfred P. Slaner, President, Kayser-Roth Corp.
Roger Sonnabend, Chairman, Sonesta International Hotels

Business Additions

Business Executives Move for Vietnam Peace and New National
    Priorities:
Morton Sweig, President, National Cleaning Contractors
Alan V. Tishman, Exec. VP, Tishman Realty & Construction Co.,
    Inc.
Ira D. Wallach, President, Gottesman & Co., Inc.
George Weissman, President, Philip Morris Corp.
Ralph Weller, President, Otis Elevator Company

Business

Clifford Alexander, Jr., Member, Equal Opportunity Comm., LBJ's
    Spec. Assistant
Hugh Calkins, Cleveland lawyer, member, Harvard Corporation
Ramsey Clark, partner, Weiss, Goldberg, Rifkind, Wharton &
    Garrison; former Attorney General
Lloyd Cutler, lawyer, Wilmer, Cutler & Pickering, Washington, D.C.
Henry L. Kimelman, chief fund raiser for McGovern; Pres., Over-
    view Group
Raymond Lapin, former Pres., FNMA: corporation executive
Hans F. Loeser, Chairman, Boston Lawyers' Vietnam Committee
Robert McNamara, President, World Bank; former Secretary of
    Defense
Hans Morgenthau [Robert Morgenthau], former U.S. Attorney in
    New York City
Victor Palmieri, lawyer, business consultant, real estate exec., Los
    Angeles
Arnold Picker, Muskie's chief fund-raiser; Chmn. Exec. Comm.,
    United Artists
Robert S. Pirie, Harold Hughes' chief fund-raiser; Bost lawyer
Joseph Rosenfield, Harold Hughes' money man; retired Des Moines
    lawyer

Henry Rowen, Pres., Rand Corp., former Asst. Director of Budget (LBJ)

R. Sargent Shriver, Jr., former U.S. Ambassador to France; lawyer, Strasser, Spiegelberg, Fried, Frank & Kempelman, Washington, D.C.

Theodore Sorensen, lawyer, Weiss, Goldberg, Rifkind, Wharton & Garrison, New York

Ray Stark, Broadway producer

Howard Stein, President and Director, Dreyfus Corporation

Milton Semer, Chairman, Muskie Election Committee; lawyer, Semer and Jacobsen

George H. Talbot, Pres., Charlotte Liberty Mutual Insurance Co., headed anti-VN ad

Arthur Taylor, Vice President, International Paper Company

Jack Valenti, President, Motion Picture Association

Paul Warnke, Muskie financial supporter, former Asst. Secy. of Defense

Thomas J. Watson, Jr., Muskie financial supporter; Chmn., IBM

Academics

Michael Ellis De Bakey, Chmn., Dept. Surgery, Baylor University; Surgeon-in-chief, Ben Taub General Hospital, Texas

Derek Curtis Bok, Dean, Harvard Law School

Kingman Brewster, Jr., President, Yale University

McGeorge Bundy, President, Ford Foundation

Avram Noam Chomsky, Professor of Modern Languages, MIT

Daniel Ellsberg, Professor, MIT

George Drennen Fischer, Member, Executive Committee, National Education Assn

J. Kenneth Galbraith, Professor of Economics, Harvard

Patricia Harris, educator, lawyer, former U.S. Ambassador; Chmn., Welfare Committee Urban League

Walter Heller, Regents Professor of Economics

Edwin Land, Professor of Physics, MIT

Herbert Ley, Jr., former FDA Commissioner; Professor of Epidemiology, Harvard

Matthew Stanley Meselson, Professor of Biology, Harvard

Lloyd N. Morrisett, Professor and Associate Dir., Education Program, U. of Calif.

Joseph Rhodes, Jr., Fellow, Harvard; Member, Scranton Comm. on Campus Unrest

Bayard Rustin, civil rights activist; Dir., A. Phillip Randolph Institute, New York

David Selden, President, American Federation of Teachers

Arthur Schlesinger, Jr., Professor of Humanities, City University of New York

Jeremy Stone, Director, Federation of American Scientists

Jerome Wiesner, President, MIT

Samuel M. Lambert, Pres., National Education Assn.

Index